Microsoft® Office Specialist
Exam Reference
for

MICROSOFT®
OFFICE 2010

COURSE TECHNOLOGY
CENGAGE Learning™

Australia • Brazil • Japan • Korea • Mexico • Singapore • Spain • United Kingdom • United States

COURSE TECHNOLOGY
CENGAGE Learning

Microsoft® Office Specialist Exam Reference for Microsoft® Office 2010 is published by Course Technology, Cengage Learning.

Vice President, Publisher: Nicole Jones Pinard

Executive Editor: Marjorie Hunt

Associate Acquisitions Editor: Amanda Lyons

Senior Product Manager: Christina Kling Garrett

Associate Product Manager: Kimberly Klasner

Editorial Assistant: Brandelynn Perry

Content Project Manager: Lisa Weidenfeld

Director of Marketing: Elisa Roberts

Senior Marketing Manager: Ryan DeGrote

Print Buyer: Fola Orekoya

Contributing Authors: Rachel Biheller Bunin, Pam Conrad, Lisa Ruffolo, Barbara Waxer, Lynn Wermers

Developmental Editors: Pam Conrad, Lisa Ruffolo, Barbara Waxer

Proofreader: Suzanne Huizenga

Indexer: Elizabeth Cunningham

Cover Image: Tiplyashin Anatoly/ Shutterstock.com

Composition House: GEX Publishing Services

Book Designer: GEX Publishing Services

The Microsoft Office Specialist Exams, the Exam Objectives, logos, the Microsoft Office Specialist Program, the Microsoft Technology Associate Certification Paths and the VAC Program are the sole property of Microsoft Corporation.

For product information and technology assistance, contact us at
Cengage Learning Customer & Sales Support, 1-800-354-9706

For permission to use material from this text or product, submit all requests online at
cengage.com/permissions
Further permissions questions can be emailed to **permissionrequest@cengage.com**

Library of Congress Control Number: 2011927626

ISBN 13: 978-1-111-96977-6

ISBN 10: 1-111-96977-9

Course Technology
20 Channel Center Street
Boston, Massachusetts 02210
USA

Cengage Learning is a leading provider of customized learning solutions with office locations around the globe, including Singapore, the United Kingdom, Australia, Mexico, Brazil, and Japan. Locate your local office at:
www.cengage.com/global

Cengage Learning products are represented in Canada by Nelson Education, Ltd.

To learn more about Course Technology, visit
www.cengage.com/coursetechnology

To learn more about Cengage Learning, visit
www.cengage.com

Purchase any of our products at your local college store or at our preferred online store
www.cengagebrain.com

Printed in the United States of America
1 2 3 4 5 6 16 15 14 13 12 11

BRIEF TABLE OF CONTENTS

About this Book   xi

Exam Tips   1

Microsoft Word 2010 Exam Reference   15

Microsoft Excel 2010 Exam Reference   139

Microsoft Access 2010 Exam Reference   211

Microsoft PowerPoint 2010 Exam Reference   249

Index   325

TABLE OF CONTENTS

About this Book   xi

Exam Tips

What Is Microsoft Office Specialist Certification?   1
Certification Benefits   2
The Microsoft Office Specialist Certification Process   3
1. Choose an Exam   5
2. Find a Testing Center   5
3. Prepare for the Exam   6
4. Take a Pretest   9
5. Purchase an Exam Voucher   9
6. Take the Exam and Receive the Results   10
Specifics about the Exam   11
Exam Tips   13

Microsoft Word 2010 Exam Reference

Getting Started with Word 2010   **15**
Start and Exit Word   15
View the Word Window   16
Use the Ribbon   16
Open, Save, and Close Documents   17
Navigate in the Document Window   19
Use Views   20
Use Keyboard KeyTips   21
Get Help   21

Word Objective 1: Sharing and Maintaining Documents   **23**
Apply Different Views to a Document   23
Apply Protection to a Document   26
Manage Document Versions   29
Share Documents   30
Save a Document   34
Apply a Template to a Document   35

Word Objective 2: Formatting Content   **36**
Apply Font and Paragraph Attributes   36
Navigate and Search Through a Document   42
Apply Indentation and Tab Settings to Paragraphs   47
Apply Spacing Settings to Text and Paragraphs   53
Create Tables   55
Manipulate Tables in a Document   56
Apply Bullets to a Document   60

Word Objective 3: Applying Page Layout and Reusable Content   **62**
Apply and Manipulate Page Setup Settings   62
Apply Themes   65
Construct Content in a Document by Using the Quick Parts Tools   66

Create and Manipulate Page Backgrounds   68
Create and Modify Headers and Footers   69

Word Objective 4: Including Illustrations and Graphics in a Document   **71**
Insert and Format Pictures in a Document   71
Insert and Format Shapes, WordArt, and SmartArt   76
Insert and Format Clip Art   82
Rotate a Graphic   85
Apply and Manipulate Text Boxes   85

Word Objective 5: Proofreading Documents   **88**
Validate Content by Using Spelling and Grammar Checking Options   88
Configure AutoCorrect Settings   90
Insert and Modify Comments in a Document   91

Word Objective 6: Applying References and Hyperlinks   **93**
Apply a Hyperlink   93
Create Endnotes and Footnotes in a Document   94
Create a Table of Contents in a Document   96

Word Objective 7: Performing Mail Merge Operations   **99**
Set Up Mail Merge   99

Word 2010 Expert Objectives

Word Expert Objective 1: Sharing and Maintaining Documents   **102**
Configure Word Options   102
Apply Protection to a Document   103
Apply a Template to a Document   104

Word Expert Objective 2: Formatting Content   **106**
Apply Advanced Font and Paragraph Attributes   106
Create Tables and Charts   107
Construct Reusable Content in a Document   108
Link Sections   111

Word Expert Objective 3: Tracking and Referencing Documents   **112**
Review, Compare, and Combine Documents   112
Create a Reference Page   114
Create a Table of Authorities in a Document   115
Create an Index in a Document   118

Word Expert Objective 4: Performing Mail Merge Operations   **121**
Execute Mail Merge   121
Create a Mail Merge by Using Other Data Sources   123
Create Labels and Forms   126

Word Expert Objective 5: Manage Macros and Forms   **129**
Apply and Manipulate Macros   129
Apply and Manipulate Macros Options   130
Create Forms   133
Manipulate Forms   137

Microsoft Excel 2010 Exam Reference

Getting Started with Excel 2010   **139**
    Start and Exit Excel   139
    View the Excel Window   140
    Use the Ribbon   140
    Open, Save, and Close Workbooks   141
    Navigate in the Worksheet Window   142
    Use Keyboard KeyTips   143
    Get Help   144

Excel Objective 1: Managing the Worksheet Environment   **145**
    Navigate Through a Worksheet   145
    Print a Worksheet or Workbook   146
    Personalize the Environment by Using Backstage   149

Excel Objective 2: Creating Cell Data   **151**
    Construct Cell Data   151
    Apply AutoFill   156
    Apply and Manipulate Hyperlinks   158

Excel Objective 3: Formatting Cells and Worksheets   **160**
    Apply and Modify Cell Formats   160
    Merge or Split Cells   162
    Create Row and Column Titles   162
    Hide or Unhide Rows and Columns   165
    Manipulate Page Setup Options for Worksheets   166
    Create and Apply Cell Styles   167

Excel Objective 4: Managing Worksheets and Workbooks   **168**
    Create and Format Worksheets   168
    Manipulate Window Views   172
    Manipulate Workbook Views   173

Excel Objective 5: Applying Formulas and Functions   **175**
    Create Formulas   175
    Enforce Precedence   175
    Apply Cell References in Formulas   176
    Apply Conditional Logic in a Formula   177
    Apply Named Ranges in Formulas   179
    Apply Cell Ranges in Formulas   180

Excel Objective 6: Presenting Data Visually   **181**
    Create Charts Based on Worksheet Data   181
    Apply and Manipulate Illustrations   181
    Create and Modify Images by Using the Image Editor   183
    Apply Sparklines   184

Excel Objective 7: Sharing Worksheet Data with Other Users   **186**
    Share Spreadsheets by Using Backstage   186
    Manage Comments   187

Excel Objective 8: Analyzing and Organizing Data   **188**
Filter Data   188
Sort Data   190
Apply Conditional Formatting   190

Excel 2010 Expert Objectives

Excel Expert Objective 1: Sharing and Maintaining Workbooks   **193**
Apply Workbook Settings, Properties, and Data Options   193
Apply Protection and Sharing Properties to Workbooks
    and Worksheets   194
Maintain Shared Workbooks   195

Excel Expert Objective 2: Applying Formulas and Functions   **196**
Audit Formulas   196
Manipulate Formula Options   198
Perform Data Summary Tasks   199
Apply Functions in Formulas   200

Excel Expert Objective 3: Presenting Data Visually   **202**
Apply Advanced Chart Features   202
Apply Data Analysis   203
Apply and Manipulate PivotTables   204
Apply and Manipulate PivotCharts   205
Demonstrate How to Use the Slicer   206

Excel Expert Objective 4: Working with Macros and Forms   **207**
Create and Manipulate Macros   207
Insert and Manipulate Form Controls   209

Microsoft Access 2010 Exam Reference

Getting Started with Access 2010   **211**
Start and Exit Access   211
Use Backstage View   212
Open a Database   212
View the Database Window   213
Use the Navigation Pane   213
Use the Ribbon   214
Save and Close Objects and Databases   215
Use Keyboard KeyTips   216
Get Help   216

Access Objective 1: Managing the Access Environment   **217**
Create and Manage a Database   217
Configure the Navigation Pane   219
Apply Application Parts   219

Access Objective 2: Building Tables   **220**
Create Tables   220
Create and Modify Fields   222
Sort and Filter Records   224
Set Relationships   225
Import Data from a Single Data File   227

Access Objective 3: Building Forms   **228**
  Create Forms   228
  Apply Form Design Options   229
  Apply Form Arrange Options   231
  Apply Form Format Options   233

Access Objective 4: Creating and Managing Queries   **235**
  Construct Queries   235
  Manage Source Tables and Relationships   237
  Manipulate Fields   238
  Calculate Totals   239
  Generate Calculated Fields   239

Access Objective 5: Designing Reports   **240**
  Create Reports   240
  Apply Report Design Options   241
  Apply Report Arrange Options   243
  Apply Report Format Options   245
  Apply Report Page Setup Options   246
  Sort and Filter Records for Reporting   246

Microsoft PowerPoint 2010 Exam Reference

Getting Started with PowerPoint 2010   **249**
  Start and Exit PowerPoint   249
  View the PowerPoint Window   250
  Use the Ribbon   250
  Change Views   251
  Use Task Panes   252
  Use Keyboard KeyTips   253
  Use Backstage View   254
  Create, Open, and Close Presentations   254
  Navigate in the PowerPoint Window   255
  Save Presentations   256
  Get Help   256

PowerPoint Objective 1: Managing the PowerPoint Environment   **258**
  Adjust Views   258
  Manipulate the PowerPoint Window   259
  Configure the Quick Access Toolbar   259
  Configure PowerPoint File Options   259

PowerPoint Objective 2: Creating a Slide Presentation   **261**
  Construct and Edit Photo Albums   261
  Apply Slide Size and Orientation Settings   263
  Add and Remove Slides   264
  Format Slides   266
  Enter and Format Text   269
  Format Text Boxes   274

PowerPoint Objective 3: Working With Graphical and Multimedia Elements   **281**
Manipulate Graphical Elements   281
Manipulate Images   286
Modify WordArt and Shapes   291
Manipulate SmartArt   292
Edit Video and Audio Content   295

PowerPoint Objective 4: Creating Charts and Tables   **297**
Construct and Modify Tables   297
Insert and Modify Charts   301
Apply Chart Elements   303
Manipulate Chart Layouts   304
Manipulate Chart Elements   305

PowerPoint Objective 5: Applying Transitions and Animations   **306**
Apply Built-In and Custom Animations   306
Apply Effect and Path Options   307
Manipulate Animations   308
Apply and Modify Transitions Between Slides   310

PowerPoint Objective 6: Collaborating on Presentations   **311**
Manage Comments in Presentations   311
Apply Proofing Tools   312

PowerPoint Objective 7: Preparing Presentations for Delivery   **313**
Save Presentations   313
Share Presentations   316
Print Presentations   318
Protect Presentations   318

PowerPoint Objective 8: Delivering Presentations   **319**
Apply Presentation Tools   319
Set Up Slide Shows   320
Set Presentation Timing   322
Record Presentations   323

Index   **325**

ABOUT THIS BOOK

HOW TO USE THIS BOOK

Microsoft® Office Specialist Exam Reference for Microsoft® Office 2010 is a reference tool designed to prepare you for the Microsoft Office Specialist exams for Word 2010, Excel 2010, Access 2010 and PowerPoint 2010. This book assumes that you already understand the concepts that are the basis for the skills covered in this book, and, therefore, the book can be used as a study companion to brush up on skills before taking the exam, or as a desk reference when using the core Microsoft Office programs.

The Structure of this Book

There are five chapters in this book. The first chapter, Exam Tips, provides some background information on the Microsoft Office Specialist program, the general process for taking an exam, and some helpful hints for preparing for and successfully passing the exams.

The remaining four chapters each cover a different core Microsoft Office 2010 program: Word, Excel, Access, and PowerPoint. Each program-specific chapter begins by covering program basics in a brief Getting Started section. This section covers the basic skills that are not specifically covered in the Microsoft Office Specialist exams, but that are essential to being able to work in the program. Each Getting Started section is followed by the complete set of objectives tested by the Microsoft Office Specialist exams. These sections are labeled and ordered to exactly match the Objectives tested in the Microsoft Office Specialist Exams. Bulleted steps containing clear instructions are provided for each objective.

Because there are often different ways to complete a task, the book provides multiple methods where appropriate, including Ribbon, Shortcut, Menu, Button, Keyboard, Mouse, Toolbar, and Task Pane methods. The Microsoft Office Specialist exams allow you to use any one of these methods, so you can choose the one with which you are most comfortable to complete the task.

Computer Setup Assumptions

This book assumes the following regarding your computer's setup:
- ▶ You have installed Office 2010 using the Typical installation.
- ▶ You have a document open and ready to use when required to work within a specific application. Also, if the steps instruct you to format an Excel worksheet or a Word document, you can format the open document or worksheet in any way you want, choosing options that are appropriate for your needs.
- ▶ You have an Internet connection to complete certain steps, and you are familiar with how to connect to the Internet.
- ▶ Your screen may look different from some of the figures in the book depending on your computer's screen resolution and any additional programs you have installed. These differences will not affect your ability to use the book and complete the steps.

EXAM TIPS

> ▶ What is Microsoft Office Specialist certification?
> ▶ Certification benefits
> ▶ The Microsoft Office Specialist certification process
>   ✓ Choosing an exam
>   ✓ Finding a testing center
>   ✓ Preparing for the exam
>   ✓ Taking a pretest
>   ✓ Purchasing an exam voucher
>   ✓ Taking the exam and receiving exam results

WHAT IS MICROSOFT OFFICE SPECIALIST CERTIFICATION?

Certification is an established trend in the Information Technology industry that helps match skilled people who want jobs with employers who are hiring skilled workers. Typically, a software or hardware company creates and gives exams that test competence on using specific programs or products. People who pass the exam demonstrate their ability to use the software or hardware effectively. By passing an exam, a person becomes "certified" and can prove his or her competence and knowledge of the software or hardware to prospective employers and colleagues. As a potential employee, you may have a better chance at landing a job if you are certified in the skills required for the job. As an employer, certification is another way to screen for qualified employees.

The Microsoft Office Specialist program is the only comprehensive, performance-based certification program approved by Microsoft to validate desktop computer skills using the Microsoft Office 2010 programs. Exams are available for:

▶ Microsoft Word®
▶ Microsoft Excel®
▶ Microsoft Access®
▶ Microsoft PowerPoint®
▶ Microsoft Outlook®
▶ Microsoft SharePoint®

The Microsoft Office Specialist program provides computer program literacy, measures proficiency, and identifies opportunities for skills enhancement. Successful candidates receive a Microsoft Office Specialist certificate that sets them apart from their peers in the competitive job market. The certificate is a valuable credential recognized worldwide as proof that an individual has the desktop computing skills needed to work productively and efficiently.

By encouraging individuals to develop advanced skills with Microsoft business desktop software, the Microsoft Office Specialist program is helping to fill the demand for qualified, knowledgeable people in the workplace. Microsoft Office Specialist certification also helps satisfy an organization's need for a qualitative assessment of employee skills.

The Microsoft Office Specialist exams are developed, marketed, and administered by Certiport, Inc., a company that has an exclusive license from Microsoft. The exams are available in a variety of different languages and are administered in more than 100 countries. Exams must be taken at an authorized Microsoft Office Specialist Certiport Center, which administers exams in a quiet room with the proper hardware and software. Trained personnel manage and proctor the exams.

CERTIFICATION BENEFITS

Achieving Microsoft Office Specialist certification in one or several of the Microsoft Office 2010 programs can be beneficial to you and your current or prospective employer. Earning Microsoft Office Specialist certification acknowledges that you have the expertise to work with Microsoft Office programs. Individuals who are Microsoft Office Specialist certified report increased competence and productivity with Microsoft Office programs. They are also more highly regarded and have increased credibility with their employers, co-workers, and clients. Certification sets you apart in today's competitive job market, bringing employment opportunities, greater earning potential and career advancement, and increased job satisfaction.

For example, if you have passed the Microsoft Word 2010 certification exam, you have an advantage when interviewing for a job that requires knowledge and use of Word to complete business-related tasks. Certification lets your prospective employer know that you not only have the necessary skills to perform that aspect of the job, but that you also have the initiative to prepare for, sign up for, pay for, and take an exam. Certification can help you increase your productivity within your current job and is a great way to enhance your skills without taking courses to obtain a new degree.

The Microsoft Office Specialist Certification Process

As with any process, there are steps. If you are organized, the process can be simple and you will achieve your goals. There are six steps to successfully completing Microsoft Office Specialist certification, as outlined in Table ET-1 and discussed in the remainder of this introductory chapter.

Table ET-1 Microsoft Office Specialist Certification Process

What to do	How to do it
1. Choose an exam.	Choose from one of the following exams, based on your skills and interests: • Microsoft Word 2010 • Microsoft Excel 2010 • Microsoft Access 2010 • Microsoft Outlook 2010 • Microsoft PowerPoint 2010 • Microsoft SharePoint 2010
2. Find a testing center.	Find an authorized testing center near you using the Certiport Center locator at www.certiport.com/Portal/Pages/LocatorView.aspx.
3. Prepare for the exam.	Select the method that is appropriate for you, including taking a class or purchasing self-study materials.
4. Take a pretest.	It is recommended that candidates take a practice test before taking an exam. • Register with Certiport by going to the Certiport Web site at www.certiport.com/portal/ and create an account using the username and password of your choice. • Click the link to view the practice tests available. • Follow the online instructions for purchasing a voucher and taking the practice test. • After completing the pretest, you will receive a recommended study and certification plan customized to your needs.

(continued)

Table ET-1 Microsoft Office Specialist Certification
Process (continued)

What to do	How to do it
5. Purchase an exam voucher.	Contact the Certiport Center and make an appointment for the Microsoft Office Specialist exam you want to take. Check the center's payment and exam policies. To purchase an exam voucher: 1. Go to www.certiport.com/portal/. 2. Create an account using the username and password of your choice—if you have not already done so. 3. At the My Certiport screen, click the Purchase Exam Voucher button and follow the onscreen instructions to purchase a voucher.
6. Take the exam and receive the results.	When you go to the Certiport Center to take the exam, you must bring the following: ✓ A printout of the voucher you purchased online ✓ Your Certiport username and password ✓ A valid picture ID (driver's license or valid passport) To take the exam: 1. Log in to the exam. 2. Read the exam directions. 3. Start the exam. 4. Receive exam results. You will find out your results immediately. If you pass, you will receive your certificate two to three weeks after the exam.

Note: If you have earned a Microsoft Certified Application Specialist certification in Microsoft Office 2007, it is still valid. The name has just been changed to Microsoft Office Specialist. You can request an updated certificate from Microsoft that contains the new name.

1. CHOOSE AN EXAM

The Microsoft Office Specialist certification program offers exams for the main applications of Microsoft Office 2010, including Microsoft Word 2010, Excel 2010, PowerPoint 2010, Access 2010, Outlook 2010, and SharePoint 2010. The Microsoft Office Specialist certification program provides exams in two levels: Core and Expert. There is also a Master level that requires completion of more than one exam. You can also take a Microsoft Office Specialist exam for expert levels of Word 2010 and Excel 2010 that cover more advanced skills. You can earn the highest level of certification, Microsoft Office Specialist Master, by passing three required exams—Word 2010 Expert, Excel 2010 Expert, and PowerPoint 2010—and one elective exam—Access 2010 or Outlook 2010. Choose one or more applications that will help you in your current position or job search, or one that tests skills that match your abilities and interests.

To see the skills required to pass a specific exam:
1. Go to www.microsoft.com/learning/en/us/certification/mos.aspx.
2. Click the Microsoft Office Specialist Certifications tab.
3. Search for an exam in the application you want to explore, and then click the exam number link for the exam you want to take to display more detailed information.

2. FIND A TESTING CENTER

You must take Microsoft Office Specialist certification exams at an authorized testing center, called a Certiport Center. Certiport Centers are located in educational institutions, corporate training centers, and other such locations. Verify that there is a testing center close to you using the Certiport Center locator at www.certiport.com/Portal/Pages/LocatorView.aspx.

Once you locate a Certiport Center near you, you will need to call and schedule a time to take the exam. Some centers may offer walk-in exams, but be sure to call and check the policies of the center you choose. Exams are offered in multiple languages and in several countries, although each site might not offer all languages. If you require a specific language, you should check with the Certiport Center before registering for the exam.

3. Prepare for the Exam

How you prepare for an exam depends on your current skill level, which you can determine by reading through the exam objectives and taking a pretest.

(Review the "To see the skills required to pass a specific exam" information in the Choose an Exam section for information on locating exam objectives. See the Take a Pretest section for more information on pretests.)

If you are new to an Office program, you might want to take an introductory class and learn the program in its entirety. If you are already familiar with the program, you may only need to purchase study materials and learn unfamiliar skills on your own. Reading through the exam objectives and taking a practice test can help you determine where you may need extra practice. If you use the program regularly, you might only need to review the skills on the objectives list for the exam you choose and brush up on those few that are problem areas for you or that you don't use regularly.

Take a Class

Taking a class is a good way to help prepare you for a certification exam, especially if you are a beginner. If you are an experienced user and know the basics, consider taking an advanced class. The benefits of taking a class include having an instructor as a resource, having the support of your classmates, and receiving study materials such as a lab book. Some classes are even geared specifically towards taking and passing a certification exam, and are taught by instructors who have passed the exam themselves. Your local community college, career education center, or community/continuing education programs will most likely offer such courses. You can also check the Certiport Center in your area. Classes range from one day to several weeks in duration. You could also take a distance learning class from an online university or through one of the local options listed above. Distance learning offers the flexibility of learning from home on your own time, while teaching the same skills as a traditional classroom course.

Purchase Materials for Self-Study

You can prepare on your own to take an exam by purchasing materials at your local bookstore or from an online retailer. To ensure that the study materials you are purchasing are well-suited to your goal of passing the Microsoft Office Specialist certification exam, you should consider the following: favorable reviews (reviews are often available when purchasing online); a table of contents that covers the skills you want to master; and the Microsoft Office Specialist Approved Courseware logo. The Microsoft Office Specialist Approved Courseware logo indicates that Certiport has confirmed that the book accurately covers all of the skills for a particular Microsoft Office Specialist exam and that it provides testing material on these skills. The logo certifies that Microsoft recognizes the book as being an adequate tool for certification preparation. Depending on your abilities, you might want to purchase a book that teaches you the skills and concepts step-by-step and then tests your knowledge. If you only require a refresher, this book is all that you need. (Because this book is designed as a reference guide and does not contain material that tests your knowledge of skills, it does not have the Microsoft Office Specialist Approved Courseware logo.)

Here is a list of suggested products published by Course Technology, Cengage Learning that you can use for self-study. You can purchase these books online at www.cengage.com/coursetechnology.

Illustrated Series: For detailed information on this Course Technology book series, visit www.cengage.com/ct/illustrated/

Books:
- ▶ Microsoft Word 2010–Illustrated Complete
  (ISBN: 0-538-74714-5)
- ▶ Microsoft Excel 2010–Illustrated Complete
  (ISBN: 0-538-74713-7)
- ▶ Microsoft Access 2010–Illustrated Complete
  (ISBN: 0-538-74717-X)
- ▶ Microsoft PowerPoint 2010–Illustrated Introductory
  (ISBN: 0-538-74716-1)

Video Companions:
- ▶ Microsoft Office 2010 Illustrated Introductory Video Companion
  (ISBN: 1-111-57756-0)
- ▶ Microsoft Office 2010 Illustrated Second Course Video Companion
  (ISBN: 1-111-97012-2)
- ▶ Microsoft Office 2010 Illustrated Fundamentals Video Companion
  (ISBN: 1-111-57976-8)
- ▶ Microsoft Word 2010 Illustrated Introductory Video Companion
  (ISBN: 1-111-97006-8)
- ▶ Microsoft Word 2010 Illustrated Complete Video Companion
  (ISBN: 1-111-97007-6)
- ▶ Microsoft Excel 2010 Illustrated Complete Video Companion
  (ISBN: 1-111-97008-4)
- ▶ Microsoft Excel 2010 Illustrated Introductory Video Companion
  (ISBN: 1-111-97009-2)

- ▶ Microsoft Access 2010 Illustrated Complete Video Companion (ISBN: 1-111-97010-6)
- ▶ Microsoft Access 2010 Illustrated Introductory Video Companion (ISBN: 1-111-97011-4)
- ▶ Microsoft PowerPoint 2010 Illustrated Introductory Video Companion (ISBN: 1-111-97013-0)

Origins Series: For detailed information on this Course Technology book series, visit www.cengage.com/ct/origins

Books:

- ▶ Microsoft® Office Word 2010 Complete (ISBN: 1-111-52951-5)
- ▶ Microsoft® Office Excel 2010 Complete (ISBN: 1-111-52952-3)
- ▶ Microsoft® Office Access 2010 Complete (ISBN: 1-111-52990-6)
- ▶ Microsoft® Office PowerPoint 2010 Complete (ISBN: 1-111-52953-1)

New Perspectives Series: For detailed information on this Course Technology book series, visit www.cengage.com/ct/newperspectives/

Books:

- ▶ New Perspectives on Microsoft Word 2010, Introductory (0-538-74894-X)
- ▶ New Perspectives on Microsoft Word 2010, Comprehensive (0-538-74892-3)
- ▶ New Perspectives on Microsoft Excel 2010, Introductory (0-538-74239-9)
- ▶ New Perspectives on Microsoft Excel 2010, Comprehensive (0-538-74291-7)
- ▶ New Perspectives on Microsoft Access 2010, Comprehensive (0-538-79847-5)
- ▶ New Perspectives on Microsoft PowerPoint 2010, Comprehensive (0-538-75372-2)

Video Companions:

- ▶ New Perspectives on Microsoft Word 2010, Introductory Video Companion (1-111-96969-8)
- ▶ New Perspectives on Microsoft Word 2010, Comprehensive Video Companion (1-111-57782-X)
- ▶ New Perspectives on Microsoft Excel 2010, Introductory Video Companion (1-111-96968-X)

▶ New Perspectives on Microsoft Excel 2010, Comprehensive Video Companion (1-111-57784-6)
▶ New Perspectives on Microsoft Access 2010, Comprehensive Video Companion (1-111-57781-1)
▶ New Perspectives on Microsoft PowerPoint 2010, Comprehensive Video Companion (1-111-57783-8)

Shelly Cashman Series: For detailed information on this Course Technology book series, visit www.scseries.com

Books:
▶ Microsoft Word 2010: Comprehensive (1-4390-7900-5)
▶ Microsoft Excel 2010: Comprehensive (1-4390-7901-3)
▶ Microsoft PowerPoint 2010: Comprehensive (1-4390-7903-X)
▶ Microsoft Access 2010: Comprehensive (1-4390-7902-1)
▶ Microsoft Outlook 2010: Comprehensive (0-538-47530-7)

Video Companions:
▶ Video DVD for Microsoft Office 2010: Brief (1-111-52783-0)
▶ Video DVD for Microsoft Office 2010: Introductory (0-538-74844-3)

4. TAKE A PRETEST

Consider taking an online pretest. A pretest lets you determine the areas you should brush up on before taking the certification exam. It is a self-assessment that tests you on the exam objectives and indicates your level of proficiency. Go to www.certiport.com/portal/, click the Login link, and then create a user account with a username and password of your choice. After taking a pretest, you will receive a customized learning plan, which is a report that recommends a course of study, including courseware materials appropriate to your needs. You can register and pay for a pretest voucher at www.certiport.com/portal/.

5. PURCHASE AN EXAM VOUCHER

If your Certiport Center verifies that you need a voucher to take the test, you need to purchase a voucher. The voucher is your proof that you registered and paid for the exam in advance. To pay for the exam and obtain a voucher, go to www.certiport.com/portal/ and log in. If you have not registered previously, click the Login link and create a user account with a username and password of your choice. At the My Certiport screen, click the Purchase Exam Voucher button, and then follow the onscreen instructions to purchase a voucher. You can charge the exam fee on any major credit card.

6. TAKE THE EXAM AND RECEIVE THE RESULTS

Make an Appointment

Contact a Certiport Center near you and make an appointment for the Microsoft Office Specialist exam you want to take. The Certiport Center staff can answer any questions you may have about scheduling, vouchers, and exam administration. Check the center's policies about payment and about changed or missed appointments, in case something comes up that prevents you from taking the exam at the appointed time. Verify the materials that you should bring with you when you take the exam. While some centers may accept your voucher as proof of payment, other centers may have other fees and may require that you pay them directly for the test itself.

Take the Exam

The day of the exam, prepare yourself by ensuring you have slept well the previous night, have eaten, and are dressed comfortably. Arrive at the test site a half an hour before the scheduled exam time to ensure you have plenty of time to check in with the center, acquaint yourself with your surroundings, and complete the login information.

You must bring the following to the Certiport Center on the day of the test:

- ✓ Your voucher, which is a printout of the electronic document you received when you paid for the test online. You will need to enter the voucher number when you log in to the test. If necessary, check with the Certiport Center to see if bringing the voucher number, rather than a printout, is acceptable.
- ✓ Your Certiport username and password, which you will also have to enter at test login. You will have created a username and password when you paid for the voucher online.
- ✓ A valid picture ID (driver's license or valid passport).

If you forget any of these required items, you may not be permitted to take the exam, and will need to reschedule your test for another time.

You may not bring any study or reference materials into the exam. You may not bring writing implements, calculators, or other materials into the test room. The Certiport Center administrator may give you a small dry-erase board and marker for taking notes during the exam, but these must be returned to the proctor when you are finished.

Receive the Results

So you have taken the test. What happens next? Exam results appear on the screen as soon as you complete the exam, so you'll know your score right away. You will receive a printout of your score to take with you. If you need additional copies, go to www.certiport.com/portal/, and then log in and go to MyCertiport, where you can always access your exam results. If you pass the exam, you will receive an official certificate in the mail in approximately two to three weeks.

The exam results are confidential.

Retaking the Exam

Depending on the voucher you have purchased, you may be allowed to take the exam one more time without any additional fee if you do not pass the exam the first time. If you purchased a voucher with a free retake, a second chance to take the exam might be all you need to pass. Study your exam results and note areas you need to work on.

There is no waiting period for retaking a failed Microsoft Office Specialist exam. Retake vouchers can only be used to retake the same exam that was failed. Retake vouchers must be used within 30 days of the initial failed exam. You can retake the exam as many times as you want, although you may need to purchase an additional voucher for the retake. All vouchers must be used prior to their expiration dates, without exception. If a retake was purchased, the retake voucher is sent by e-mail after a failed exam. Check your Certiport Center's exam retake policies for more information.

No refunds will be given if you do not pass, and you may also be charged for a missed exam appointment, depending on the Certiport Center's policies.

SPECIFICS ABOUT THE EXAM

Each exam is administered within a functional copy of the Microsoft program corresponding to the exam that you are taking. The exam tests your knowledge of the program by requiring you to complete specific tasks in the program.

▶ **Proctor:** A proctor will take you to the test room containing one or more computers and make sure you complete the login process and that the test is running correctly. He or she will then leave the room, but will remain available nearby in case you run into technical difficulties. Before the proctor leaves, be sure you know where he or she will be located, so you can find him or her quickly if necessary.

▶ **Logging in:** The first step is to log in to the exam. You will need to complete the candidate information section, which includes your Certiport username and password, and the necessary information for completing and mailing your certificate. Then the proctor will assist you in starting the exam.

▶ **Reading the instructions:** The first screens you see after you log in are directions and test-taking tips. You should read all of these, as this information will help you become familiar with the exam environment. The timed portion of the exam does not include your reading of these start-up directional screens, so take your time and make sure you understand the directions before starting the exam.

▶ **Understanding the "live" program environment:** The exam is "live in the program," which means that you will work with an actual document, spreadsheet, presentation, etc. and must perform tasks on that document.

▶ **Completing tasks:** You can use any valid method available in the program to complete a task, including keyboard shortcuts. For example, if asked to center text in a Word document, you can click a button on the Ribbon or press [Ctrl][E] to center the text. If you press [Spacebar] repeatedly to move the text to the center of the document, however, you will lose credit, as this is not an appropriate way to center text.

▶ **Using the Reset button:** If you start a question with incorrect steps and want to correct them, you can use the Reset button to return the document to its original state and redo the question from the beginning. Keep in mind that if you click the Reset button, all of your work on that question will be erased and the clock will not restart.

▶ **Saving questions for later:** If you come upon a difficult question that you can't answer readily, you can click the Skip button so you can come back to it after you complete all the other questions, assuming you have time left. You cannot go back to a previous question unless you have marked it as a question you want to return to later. If you are truly stuck, make your best guess and move on.

▶ **Viewing the exam clock:** There is an exam clock on the screen that starts and stops while each question is loading, so the speed with which each question is loaded does not affect the time you have to complete the questions. (In other words, if you are completing the test on a slow computer you will not be penalized.) The total time you spend taking the exam will vary based on the speed of your computer, but the actual time you have to complete the exam will be consistent with anyone else taking the exam.

▶ **No Office Online Help:** You cannot use Office Online Help during the exam. The Help feature is disabled during the exam.

▶ **Dealing with problems:** If something happens to the exam environment—for instance, if the program freezes or if there is a power failure—contact the exam proctor. He or she will restart the exam and the exam clock where you were before the exam was interrupted. Such interruptions will not count against you. If there are other test-takers in the same room, it's best not to disturb them with questions.

Exam Tips

▶ **Pace yourself:** The overall exam is timed, although there is no time limit for each question. Most exams take 50 minutes or less and cover 30 to 35 questions, but the allotted time depends on the subject and level. If you do not complete all of the exam questions within the given timeframe, you will lose points for any unanswered questions. Because you have to complete the exam in a designated amount of time, you will want to consider the amount of time you have per question. You will not be graded on your efficiency (i.e., the time you take per question), but remember that if you spend a lot of time on one question, that leaves you with less time for other questions. Keep in mind that you can always save a particularly difficult question for the end of the test.

▶ **Complete each test item:** Each question is composed of one or more tasks listed in a pane at the bottom of the screen. You should complete the tasks in the order listed and make sure that you complete all of the tasks. You may need to scroll the pane to read all of the tasks in a question. It is a good idea to reread the entire question before advancing to the next question to ensure that you have completed all tasks. You will receive only partial credit for any question that you do not complete in its entirety.

▶ **Close dialog boxes:** Be sure you have closed all dialog boxes that you might have opened during the course of completing a task. Making the correct dialog box selections is not sufficient; you must always click OK or a similar button to close the dialog box(es) and fully complete the task.

▶ **Avoid additional tasks:** The end result of your actions is scored when you advance to the next question. You will not lose points for any extra mouse clicks or movements as they relate to the task, but you should undo any additional changes that are not part of the task that you might accidentally apply to the document. For example, if the task has you bold a word and you both bold and italicize it, you should undo the italicizing of the word. If you do start a test item with an incorrect action, remember that you can use the Reset button to begin that question again.

▶ **Type carefully:** If the task requires typing, you will lose points for spelling mistakes.

MICROSOFT WORD 2010
EXAM REFERENCE

Getting Started with Word 2010

The Word Microsoft Office Specialist exam assumes a basic level of proficiency in Word. This section is intended to help you reference these basic skills while you are preparing to take the Word exam.

> ▶ Starting and exiting Word
> ▶ Viewing the Word window
> ▶ Using the Ribbon
> ▶ Opening, saving, and closing documents
> ▶ Navigating in the document window
> ▶ Using views
> ▶ Using keyboard KeyTips
> ▶ Getting Help

START AND EXIT WORD

Start Word

Shortcut Method

▶ Click the **Start button** 🔵 on the Windows taskbar, then point to **All Programs**

▶ Click **Microsoft Office**, then click **Microsoft Word 2010**

OR

▶ Double-click the **Microsoft Word program icon** 🔳 on the desktop

OR

▶ Click the **Microsoft Word 2010 program icon** listed on the Start menu

Exit Word

Ribbon Method

▶ Click the **File tab** to open Backstage view, then click **Exit**

OR

▶ Click the **Close button** 🔳 on the Word program window title bar

Shortcut Method

▶ Press **[Alt][F4]**

VIEW THE WORD WINDOW

Figure WD-1 Word Program Window

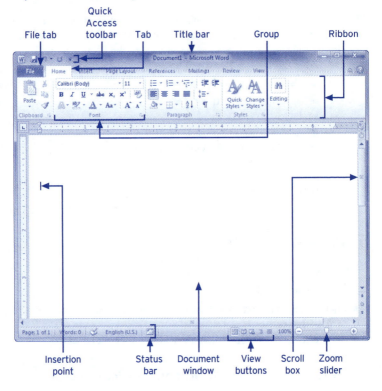

USE THE RIBBON

Display Tabs on the Ribbon

Ribbon Method
▶ Open a document, then click any tab

Hide the Ribbon

Ribbon Method
▶ Double-click the active tab to show only the tabs

Shortcut Method
▶ Right-click any tab, then click **Minimize the Ribbon** to select it

Work with the Ribbon

Ribbon Method

▶ Click a **button**, a **button list arrow**, or the **More button** ⊡ (when available) in any group, then click a command or gallery option, if necessary

OR

▶ Click a **launcher** ▣ to open a dialog box or a pane offering more options

Customize the Quick Access Toolbar

Ribbon Method

▶ Right-click any button on the Quick Access toolbar
▶ To hide that button, click **Remove from Quick Access Toolbar**
▶ To add or remove a button, click **Customize Quick Access Toolbar**, click a command in the left or right column of the Word Options dialog box, then click **Add** or **Remove** in the Word Options dialog box

Reposition the Quick Access Toolbar

Ribbon Method

▶ Right-click any button on the Quick Access toolbar
▶ Click **Show Quick Access Toolbar Below the Ribbon**

OPEN, SAVE, AND CLOSE DOCUMENTS

Open a New Document

Ribbon Method

▶ Click the **File tab** to open Backstage view, then click **New**
▶ Click **Blank document** under Available Templates, then click **Create**

Shortcut Method

▶ Press **[Ctrl][N]**

Open an Existing Document

Ribbon Method

▶ Click the **File tab** to open Backstage view, then click **Open**
▶ In the Open dialog box, navigate to the drive and folder where you stored your file
▶ Click the file, then click **Open**

Word

Shortcut Method

▶ Press **[Ctrl][O]**
▶ In the Open dialog box, navigate to the drive and folder where you stored your file
▶ Click the file, then click **Open**

Use Save As

Ribbon Method

▶ Click the **File tab** to open Backstage view, then click **Save As**
▶ In the Save As dialog box, navigate to the appropriate drive and folder, if necessary
▶ Type an appropriate filename in the File name text box, then click **Save**

Shortcut Method

▶ Press **[F12]**
▶ Follow the steps in bullets 2–3 in the Use Save As Ribbon Method

Save an Existing Document

Ribbon Method

▶ Click the **File tab** to open Backstage view, then click **Save**

Shortcut Method

▶ Press **[Ctrl][S]**
  OR
▶ Click the **Save button** 🖫 on the Quick Access toolbar

Close a Document

Ribbon Method

▶ Click the **File tab** to open Backstage view, then click **Close**
▶ If prompted to save the file, click **Save**, **Don't Save**, or **Cancel**, as appropriate

Shortcut Method

▶ Click the **Close button** [X] on the title bar
▶ If prompted to save the file, click **Save**, **Don't Save**, or **Cancel**, as appropriate
  OR
▶ Press **[Ctrl][W]** or **[Alt][F4]**
▶ If prompted to save the file, click **Save**, **Don't Save**, or **Cancel**, as appropriate

NAVIGATE IN THE DOCUMENT WINDOW

Ribbon Method

▶ Click the **Home tab**, click the **Find list arrow** in the Editing group, then click **Go To**
▶ In the Find and Replace dialog box, select an option in the Go to what list; in the related text box, type the go to identifier, then click **Go To**

Shortcut Method

▶ Press **[Ctrl][G]**
▶ Follow the step in bullet 2 in the Navigate in the Document Window Ribbon Method

  OR

▶ Use Table WD-1 as a reference to navigate through the document using keyboard shortcuts

Table WD-1 Navigation Keyboard Shortcuts

Key	Moves the insertion point
[Ctrl][Home]	To the beginning of the document
[Ctrl][End]	To the end of the document
[Home]	To the beginning of the current line
[End]	To the end of the current line
[Page Up]	One screen up
[Page Down]	One screen down
[→], [←]	To the right or left one character at a time
[Ctrl][→], [Ctrl][←]	To the right or left one word at a time
[↓], [↑]	Down or up one line at a time

Mouse Method

To change the view without moving the insertion point, do one of the following:

▶ Drag the **scroll box** in a scroll bar to move within the document
▶ Click above the scroll box in the vertical scroll bar to move up a screen without moving the insertion point
▶ Click below the scroll box in the vertical scroll bar to move down a screen without moving the insertion point
▶ Click the up scroll arrow in the vertical scroll bar to move up one line
▶ Click the down scroll arrow in the vertical scroll bar to move down one line

▶ Repeat bullets 2–5 using the horizontal scroll bar and replacing up and down with left and right

▶ Click the **Next Page button** 🔻 or the **Previous Page button** 🔺 on the vertical scroll bar to move to the next or previous page

USE VIEWS

Refer to Table WD-2 to change document views.

Table WD-2 Document Views

View	What you see	Ribbon Method: View tab	Shortcut Method: Status bar
Print Layout view	Displays a document as it will look on a printed page	Click the **Print Layout button**	Click the **Print Layout button** 📄
Full Screen Reading view	Displays document text so it is easy to read and annotate	Click the **Full Screen Reading button**	Click the **Full Screen Reading button** 📖
Web Layout view	Displays a document as it will appear when viewed in a Web browser	Click the **Web Layout button**	Click the **Web Layout button** 📑
Outline view	Displays the headings and their related subtext in hierarchical order	Click the **Outline View button**	Click the **Outline button**
Draft view	Displays a simplified layout of a document, without margins, etc.	Click the **Draft View button**	Click the **Draft button**

USE KEYBOARD KEYTIPS

Display KeyTips

Shortcut Method

▶ Press **[Alt]** to display the KeyTips for any active tab on the Ribbon and on the Quick Access toolbar

▶ Press the letter or number for the specific command for the active tab on the Ribbon

▶ Press additional letters or numbers as needed to complete the command sequence

▶ If two letters appear, press each one in order; for some commands, you will find that you have to click an option from a gallery or menu to complete the command sequence

▶ The KeyTips turn off automatically at the end of the command sequence

Hide KeyTips

Shortcut Method

▶ Press **[Alt]** to hide the KeyTips for each Ribbon command

GET HELP

Ribbon Method

▶ Click the **Microsoft Word Help button** to display the Word Help task pane

▶ Use Table WD-3 as a reference to select the most appropriate way to search for help using the Microsoft Word Help task pane

OR

▶ Point to any button on the Ribbon, then read the ScreenTip text

▶ If you see "Press F1 for more help." at the bottom of the ScreenTip, continue pointing to the button, then press **[F1]** to see targeted help on that button from Word Help

Shortcut Method

▶ Press **[F1]**

▶ Use Table WD-3 as a reference to select the most appropriate way to search for help using the Microsoft Word Help window

Word

Table WD-3 Microsoft Help Window Options

Option	To use
Getting started with Word 2010	Click a link representing a topic you want to read about; click subtopics that appear until you see help text for that topic
Browse Word 2010 support	Click a link representing a topic you want to read about; click subtopics that appear until you see help text for that topic
Back button	Click to return to the previously displayed information
Forward button	Click to go forward in the sequence of previously displayed information
Stop button	Click to stop searching on a topic
Refresh button	Click to refresh the Help window content
Home button	Click to return to the Word Help window
Print button	Click to print the current page
Change Font Size button	Click to enlarge or shrink the help text
Show Table of Contents	Click to show the Table of Contents pane, showing topic links you can click
Keep on Top	Click to keep the Help window on top as you work; button becomes the Not On Top button, which you click to let the Help window go behind the current window as you work
Type words to search for box	Type a word, then click the **Search button**
Search button list arrow	Click the **list arrow**, then click the area, such as Content from Office.com, All Word, or Word Help
Microsoft Office Search help using Bing	Type a word, then click the **Search button**; or type a word, then click the link to downloads, images, or templates to search for those items on Office.com

Word

Word 2010 Exam Reference

Core Objectives:

1. Sharing and maintaining documents
2. Formatting content
3. Applying page layout and reusable content
4. Including illustrations and graphics in a document
5. Proofreading documents
6. Applying references and hyperlinks
7. Performing mail merge operations

Expert Objectives:

1. Sharing and maintaining documents
2. Formatting content
3. Tracking and referencing documents
4. Performing mail merge operations
5. Managing macros and forms

Word Core Objectives

Word Core Objective 1: Sharing and Maintaining Documents

Apply Different Views to a Document

Select Zoom Options

Ribbon Method

▶ Click the **View tab**, then click the **Zoom button** in the Zoom group
▶ In the Zoom dialog box, select appropriate options, then click **OK**

Shortcut Method

▶ Click the **Zoom level button** `100%` on the status bar
▶ In the Zoom dialog box, select appropriate options, then click **OK**

Split Windows

Ribbon Method

▶ Click the **View tab**, then click the **Split button** in the Window group

▸ Drag the **horizontal split bar** to the location where you want to split the window

▸ To adjust the split, drag the **horizontal split bar** to a new location

▸ To remove the split, click the **Remove Split button** in the Window group

OR

▸ Double click the **horizontal split bar**

Arrange Windows

Ribbon Method

▸ Click the **View tab**, then click the **Arrange All button** in the Window group

▸ To view only one document, click the **Maximize button** on the title bar of that document

View Windows Side by Side

Ribbon Method

▸ Click the **View tab**, then click the **View Side by Side button** in the Window group

Use Synchronous Scrolling

Ribbon Method

▸ Click the **View tab**, click the **View Side by Side button** in the Window group, then click the **Synchronous Scrolling button** if it is not already active

Arrange Document Views

Ribbon Method

▸ Click the **View tab**, click the **View Side by Side button** in the Window group to open the View Side by Side dialog box, then click the filename of the document you want to view side by side with the active document

OR

▸ Click the **New Window button** in the Window group to open a new window

OR

▸ Click the **Arrange All button** in the Window group to arrange all open documents

OR

▸ Click the **Split button** in the Window group to split the current window at the location of the insertion point

OR

▶ Click the **Reset Window Position button** in the Window group to reset the Window

Reorganize a Document Outline

Ribbon Method

▶ Click the **View tab,** then click the **Outline button** in the Document Views group
▶ Use the options in the Outline Tools group to rearrange items in the document
▶ Click the **Close Outline View button** in the Close group

Shortcut Method

▶ Click the **Outline button** on the status bar
▶ Follow the steps in bullets 2–3 in the Reorganize a Document Outline Ribbon Method

View Master Documents

Ribbon Method

▶ Open a master document
▶ Click the **View tab,** then click the **Outline button** in the Document Views group
▶ Click the **Show Document button** in the Master Document group
▶ Use the commands in the Master Document group to work with the master document and its subdocuments

Shortcut Method

▶ Open a master document
▶ Click the **Outline button** on the status bar
▶ Follow the steps in bullets 3–4 in the View Master Documents Ribbon Method

View Subdocuments

Ribbon Method

▶ Open a master document
▶ Click the **View tab,** then click the **Outline button** in the Document Views group
▶ Click the **Collapse Subdocuments button** in the Master Document group to show the links containing the full paths to the subdocuments

OR

▶ Click the **Expand Subdocuments button** in the Master Document group to show the content of the subdocuments

Shortcut Method
▶ Open a master document
▶ Click the **Outline button** 🔳 on the status bar
▶ Follow the steps in bullets 3–4 in the View Subdocuments Ribbon Method

View a Document in Web Layout View

Ribbon Method
▶ Click the **View tab**, then click the **Web Layout button** in the Document Views group

Shortcut Method
▶ Click the **Web Layout button** 🔳 on the status bar

View a Document in Draft View

Ribbon Method
▶ Click the **View tab**, then click the **Draft button** in the Document Views group

Shortcut Method
▶ Click the **Draft button** 🔳 on the status bar

Switch Between Windows

Ribbon Method
▶ Click the **View tab**, click the **Switch Windows button** in the Window group, then click the document you want to view in the window from the available documents listed on the menu

Open a Document in a New Window

Ribbon Method
▶ Click the **View tab**, then click the **New Window button** in the Window group

---

APPLY PROTECTION TO A DOCUMENT

Apply Protection by Using the Microsoft Office Backstage View Commands

Ribbon Method
▶ Click the **File tab** to open Backstage view, then click the **Info tab** if it is not already selected
▶ Click the **Protect Document button**, then select an option on the menu to mark the document as final, encrypt the document with a password, restrict editing of the document, restrict permission to edit the document by people, or add a digital signature

Apply Controls and Restrictions to Document Access

Ribbon Method

▶ Click the **File tab** to open Backstage view, click the **Protect Document button**, then click **Restrict Editing**

▶ In the Restrict Formatting and Editing task pane, select the **Limiting formatting to a selection of styles check box** in the Formatting restrictions section, click **Settings**, select the appropriate options in the Formatting Restrictions dialog box, click **OK**, then click **Yes, Start Enforcing Protection**

▶ In the Start Enforcing Protection dialog box, click **OK** to start enforcement without protecting the document with a password; or type a password, press **[Tab]**, then type the password again to password-protect the document; or click the **User Authentication option** to encrypt the document and use Information Rights Management Service to authenticate the owners of the document and click **OK**, or click **Cancel** if you do not want to start enforcing protection

OR

▶ Click the **Review tab**, click the **Restrict Editing button** in the Protect group, then follow the steps in bullets 2–3 in the Apply Controls and Restrictions to Document Access Ribbon Method

Apply Editing Restrictions and Limit Access to a Document

Ribbon Method

▶ Click the **File tab** to open Backstage view, click the **Protect Document button**, then click **Restrict Editing**

▶ In the Restrict Formatting and Editing task pane, select the **Allow only this type of editing in the document check box** in the Editing restrictions section, click the **list arrow** to select the type of editing to allow, select the users to whom this editing restriction will apply, then click **Yes, Start Enforcing Protection**

▶ In the Start Enforcing Protection dialog box, click **OK** to start enforcement without protecting the document with a password; or type a password, press **[Tab]**, then type the password again to password-protect the document; or click the **User Authentication option** to encrypt the document and use Information Rights Management Service to authenticate the owners of the document and click **OK**, or click **Cancel** if you do not want to start enforcing protection

OR

Word

▶ Click the **Review tab**, click the **Restrict Editing button** in the Protect group, then follow the steps in bullets 2–3 in the Apply Editing Restrictions and Limit Access to a Document Ribbon Method

Password-Protect a Document

Ribbon Method

▶ Open a Word document, click the **File tab** to open Backstage view, click the **Protect Document button**, then click **Encrypt with a Password**

▶ Type a password in the Encrypt Document dialog box, then click **OK**

▶ Reenter the password in the Confirm Password dialog box, then click **OK**

   OR

▶ Follow the steps in bullets 1–3 in the Apply Editing Restrictions and Limit Access to a Document Ribbon Methods

Mark a Document as Final

Ribbon Method

▶ Click the **File tab** to open Backstage view, click the **Protect Document button**, click **Mark as Final**, then click **OK**

   OR

▶ Click the **File tab** to open Backstage view, click the **Protect Document button**, then click **Restrict Editing**

▶ In the Restrict Formatting and Editing task pane, select the **Allow only this type of editing in the document check box** in the Editing restrictions section, click the **list arrow** and select **No changes (Read only)**, then click **Yes, Start Enforcing Protection**

▶ In the Start Enforcing Protection dialog box, type a password, press **[Tab]**, then type the password again to password-protect the document; or click the **User Authentication option** and click **OK**, or click **Cancel** if you do not want to password-protect the document

   OR

▶ Click the **Review tab**, then click the **Restrict Editing button** in the Protect group

▶ Follow the steps in bullets 2–3 in the Mark a Document as Final Ribbon Method

Apply Protection by Using Ribbon Commands

Ribbon Method

▶ Click the **Review tab**, click the **Restrict Editing button** in the Protect group, then follow the steps in bullets 2–3 in the Apply Editing Restrictions and Limit Access to a Document Ribbon Method

OR

▶ Click the **Developer tab**, click the **Restrict Editing button** in the Protect group, then follow the steps in bullets 2–3 in the Apply Editing Restrictions and Limit Access to a Document Ribbon Method

MANAGE DOCUMENT VERSIONS

Modify AutoRecover Options

Ribbon Method

▶ Click the **File tab** to open Backstage view, click **Options**, then click **Save**
▶ In the Word Options dialog box, under the Save Documents section, click the **Save AutoRecover information check box** to turn on the feature or remove the check mark in the check box to turn off the feature, use the up and down arrows to change the number of minutes to have AutoRecover save information, choose whether or not to keep the last autosaved version of a file if you close without saving, or change the location where your AutoRecover files are saved

Note: Word's AutoRecover feature automatically saves your document at regular intervals so that you can recover at least some of your work in case of a power outage or other unexpected shutdown.

Recover Draft Versions

Ribbon Method

▶ Click the **File tab** to open Backstage view, click the **Manage Versions button**, then click **Recover Unsaved Documents**
▶ In the Open dialog box, click an unsaved document from the list, then click **Open** to open the document
▶ In the Recovered Unsaved File bar at the top of the document, click **Save As**
▶ In the Save As dialog box, type a filename, then click **Save**

Word

Delete All Draft Versions

Ribbon Method

▶ Click the **File tab** to open Backstage view, click the **Manage Versions button**, then click **Delete All Unsaved Documents**

▶ In the Microsoft message box, click **Yes** to delete all unsaved files

SHARE DOCUMENTS

Send Documents via E-mail

Ribbon Method

▶ Click the **File tab** to open Backstage view, click **Save & Send**, make sure **Send Using E-mail** is selected in the Save & Send pane, then click the **Send as Attachment button** in the Send Using E-mail pane to open a new e-mail message with the file attached and the filename in the subject line of the e-mail message

▶ Enter an e-mail address in the To: box, type a message in the box if necessary, then click the **Send button** to send the e-mail with the file attachment

Send Documents via SkyDrive

Ribbon Method

▶ Click the **File tab** to open Backstage view, click **Save & Send**, then click the **Save to Web button** in the Save & Send pane

▶ Click the **Sign In button** in the Save to Windows Live SkyDrive pane to sign in with your Windows Live ID and to gain access to Windows SkyDrive, or click the **Sign up for Windows Live SkyDrive link** to open the Welcome to Windows Live Web page where you can sign up for a Windows Live ID, then use it to sign in

▶ Click the folder where you want to save the file from the Personal Folders or Shared Folders list in the Save to Windows Live SkyDrive pane, then click the **Save As button**

▶ In the Save As dialog box, type an appropriate filename in the File name text box, click the **Save as type list arrow**, select the file format you want to save as, then click **Save**

Note: Windows Live SkyDrive is a free online storage service from Microsoft that makes documents accessible from any computer with Internet access.

Send Documents via Internet Fax

Ribbon Method

▶ Click the **File tab** to open Backstage view, click **Save & Send**, make sure **Send Using E-mail** is selected in the Save & Send pane, then click the **Send as Internet Fax button** in the Send Using E-mail pane

Note: A Microsoft Office message is displayed explaining that you need to choose an Internet Fax service in order to send a fax.

▶ Click OK to open a Web page that lists Internet Fax service providers
▶ Follow the instructions for choosing a provider, then repeat the steps in the first bullet

Change File Types

Ribbon Method

▶ Click the **File tab** to open Backstage view, click **Save & Send**, then click **Change File Type** in the File Types section of the center pane
▶ Click the appropriate file type in the Change File Type pane, then click the **Save As button**
▶ In the Save As dialog box, type an appropriate filename in the File name text box, click the **Save as type list arrow**, select the file format you want to save it as, then click **Save**
OR
▶ Click the **File tab** to open Backstage view, then click **Save As**
▶ In the Save As dialog box, type an appropriate filename in the File name text box, click the **Save as type list arrow**, select the file format you want to save it as, then click **Save**

Shortcut Method

▶ Press **F12**
▶ In the Save As dialog box, type an appropriate filename in the File name text box, click the **Save as type list arrow**, select the file format you want to save it as, then click **Save**

Create PDF Documents

Ribbon Method

▶ Click the **File tab** to open Backstage view, click **Save & Send**, click **Create PDF/XPS document** in the File Types section of the center pane, then click the **Create PDF/XPS button** in the Create PDF/XPS Document pane

Word

▶ In the Publish As PDF or XPS dialog box, type an appropriate filename in the File name text box, click the appropriate **Optimize for button**, change any other options to meet your needs, then click **Publish**

OR

▶ Click the **File tab** to open Backstage view, then click **Save As**
▶ In the Save As dialog box, type an appropriate filename in the File name text box, click the **Save as type list arrow** and click the **PDF (.pdf*) file type**, click the appropriate **Optimize for button**, change any other options as necessary, then click **Save**

Shortcut Method

▶ Press **F12**
▶ In the Save As dialog box, type an appropriate filename in the File name text box, click the **Save as type list arrow** and click the **PDF (.pdf*) file type**, click the appropriate **Optimize for button**, change any other options as necessary, then click **Save**

Create a Shared Document

Ribbon Method

▶ Create or open a document you want to share
▶ Click the **File tab** to open Backstage view, click **Save & Send**, click **Save to SharePoint** in the Save & Send section of the center pane, then click **Browse for Location** in the Save to SharePoint pane to locate the SharePoint server on your network
▶ Click the **Save As button** in the Save to SharePoint pane
▶ In the Save As dialog box, type an appropriate filename in the File name text box, click the **Save as type list arrow**, select the file format you want to save it as, then click **Save**

Note: Saving to an organization's SharePoint site provides opportunities for collaboration, such as multiple people editing documents at the same time.

Register a Blog Account

Ribbon Method

▶ Set up a blog account with an Internet blog provider that is compatible with Microsoft Word
▶ Open an existing blog post or create a new one using the steps in bullets 1–2 in the Create and Publish a Blog Post Ribbon Method on the next page
▶ Click the **Publish button** in the Blog group, then click **Register Now** in the Register New Blog Account dialog box or click the **Manage Accounts button** in the Blog group, then click **New**

▶ In the New Blog Account dialog box, click the **down arrow** to choose your blog provider, then click the **Next button**

▶ Follow the directions to register the account with Word, usually by entering the username and password you use to log in to the blog account and specifying picture options, then click **OK**

▶ In the Microsoft Office message box that states that other people may be able to see your information when it is sent, click **Yes**

▶ Click **OK** in the Microsoft Office message box that states that your account registration was successful

Note: You must create an account with an Internet blog provider that is compatible with Microsoft Word, then register that account with Word to be able to publish blog posts using Microsoft Word.

Create and Publish a Blog Post

Ribbon Method

▶ Click the **File tab** to open Backstage view, click **New**, click **Blog post** in the Available Templates section of the center pane, then click the **Create button** in the right pane

▶ In the new blog post, click **Enter Post Title Here** and type a title for the blog post, type the text of the blog post below the line, then save the document

▶ Click the **Publish button** in the Blog group, enter the username and password for access to your blogging space, then click **OK**

▶ In the **Microsoft Office message box** that states that other people may be able to see your information when it is sent, click **Yes** to publish the blog anyway (or click **No** to cancel publishing); a date and time stamp will appear at the top of the blog post stating the time, date, and location of the blog post

OR

▶ Open the document you would like to post as a blog

▶ Click the **File tab** to open Backstage view, click **Save & Send**, click **Publish as Blog Post** in the Save & Send section of the center pane, then click the **Publish as Blog Post button** in the right pane

▶ Follow the steps in bullets 2–4 in the Create and Publish a Blog Post Ribbon Method

Note: Word cannot publish blog posts saved with the .doc extension, so be sure to save blog posts in the .docx format. Also, be sure to include a title for your blog post, because some Internet blog providers require it.

Word

SAVE A DOCUMENT

Use Compatibility Mode

Ribbon Method

▶ Open a document saved with the .docx extension, click the **File tab** to open Backstage view, click **Save As**, click **Word 97-2003 Document** in the Save as type list, type a name for the document in the File name box, then click **Save** to save the document as a .doc file that can be used in an earlier version of Word

  OR

▶ Open a .doc file, click the **File tab** to open Backstage view, click the **Convert button**, then click **OK** to convert the .doc file to a .docx file that enables the new features in Word 2010

Use Protected Mode

Ribbon Method

▶ Click the **File tab** to open Backstage view, then click **Options** to open the Word Options dialog box
▶ Click **Trust Center** in the left pane, then click the **Trust Center Settings button** in the right pane to open the Trust Center dialog box
▶ Click **Protected View** in the right pane, select appropriate options to disable or enable protected view options in the right pane, then click **OK**

Note: When a file from the Internet or other potentially unsafe location is opened on your computer, it is opened in Protected View. Click the Enable Editing button on the Protected View message bar to exit Protected View.

Use Save As Options

Ribbon Method

▶ Click the **File tab** to open Backstage view, then click **Save As**
▶ In the Save As dialog box, type an appropriate filename in the File name text box, click the **Save as type list arrow**, select the file format you want to save as, such as .dotx for a Word Template or .pdf for a PDF file format, then click **Save**

Shortcut Method

▶ Press **[F12]**
▶ Follow the steps in bullet 2 in the Use Save As Options Ribbon Method

  OR

▶ To select the Save As file format for a file that has not been saved previously, click the **Save button** 💾 on the Quick Access toolbar, then follow the steps in bullet 2 in the Use Save As Options Ribbon Method

OR

▶ To select the Save As file format for a file that has not been saved previously, press **[Ctrl][S]**, then follow the steps in bullet 2 in the Use Save As Options Ribbon Method

APPLY A TEMPLATE TO A DOCUMENT

Find Templates

Ribbon Method

▶ Click the **File tab** to open Backstage view, click **New**, click **Sample Templates** in the Available Templates pane, click an appropriate template in the center pane, click the **Document button** or **Template button** in the right pane to select whether to open it as a document or a template, then click the **Create button**

OR

▶ Click the **File tab** to open Backstage view, click **New**, click **My Templates** in the Available Templates pane, click an appropriate template from the Personal Templates tab in the New dialog box, click the **Document button** or **Template button** to select whether to open it as a document or a template, then click **OK**

Locate a Template on Your Disk

Ribbon Method

▶ Click the **File tab** to open Backstage view, click **New**, click **Sample Templates** in the Available Templates pane, click an appropriate template in the center pane, click the **Document button** or **Template button** in the right pane to select whether to open it as a document or a template, then click the **Create button**

OR

▶ Click the **File tab** to open Backstage view, click **New**, click **My Templates** in the Available Templates pane, click an appropriate template from the Personal Templates tab in the New dialog box, click the **Document button** or **Template button** to select whether to open it as a document or a template, then click **OK**

Find Templates on the Web

Ribbon Method

▶ Click the **File tab** to open Backstage view, click **New**, click a category from the Office.com section of the center pane, click an appropriate template, then click **Download** to download a template from Office.com

OR

▶ Click the **File tab** to open Backstage view, click **New**, type a keyword in the Search Office.com for templates box, click the **Start searching button** ⊕, click an appropriate template from the center pane, then click the **Download button** to download the template from Office.com

Replace Placeholder Text in a Template

Ribbon Method

▶ Locate and open a template following the steps in bullets 1–2 in the Locate a Template on Your Disk Ribbon Method or Find Templates on the Web Ribbon Method

▶ Click the placeholder text in brackets, such as [Type the document title] and type your own text

Note: Some placeholders, such as those for the date, may have an arrow you can click to choose the date from a calendar.

WORD CORE OBJECTIVE 2: FORMATTING CONTENT

APPLY FONT AND PARAGRAPH ATTRIBUTES

Apply Character Attributes

Ribbon Method

▶ Select the text to which you want to apply a character format, then use Table WD 2-1 as a reference to apply the character formatting you want

Table WD 2-1 Applying Character Attributes

Attribute to apply	Ribbon Method: Home tab/ Font group	Shortcut Method: Mini toolbar	Shortcut Method: Keyboard	Launcher in the Font group: Font dialog box
Apply a new font	Click the **Font list arrow**, then click a font	Click the **Font list arrow**, then click a font	Press **[Ctrl] [Shift][F]**, click the **Font list arrow**, then click a font	Click the **Font list arrow**, then click a font
Apply a new font size	Click the **Font Size list arrow**, then click a font size, or type a value in the Font Size text box	Click the **Font Size list arrow**, then click a font size, or type a value in the Font Size text box	Press **[Ctrl] [Shift][P]**, then click the **Font Size list arrow** and click a font size; or type the value in the Font Size text box	Click the **Font Size list arrow**, then click a font size; or type the value in the Font Size text box
Increase the font size one increment	Click the **Grow Font button** A˄	Click the **Grow Font button** ▼	Press **[Ctrl][>]**	
Decrease the font size one increment	Click the **Shrink Font button** A˅	Click the **Shrink Font button** A˅	Press **[Ctrl][<]**	
Clear formatting	Click the **Clear Formatting button** 🔏		Right-click, click the **Styles command** on the Shortcut menu, then click **Clear Formatting**	
Apply bold	Click the **Bold button** **B**	Click the **Bold button** **B**	Press **[Ctrl][B]**	Click **Bold** in the Font style list

(continued)

Word

Word

Table WD 2-1 Applying Character Attributes (continued)

Attribute to apply	Ribbon Method: Home tab/ Font group	Shortcut Method: Mini toolbar	Shortcut Method: Keyboard	Launcher in the Font group: Font dialog box
Apply italic	Click the **Italic button** I	Click the **Italic button** I	Press **[Ctrl][I]**	Click **Italic** in the Font style list
Apply underlining	Click the **Underline button** $\underline{U}$, or click the **Underline list arrow** $\underline{U}$ ▾, select a preformatted underline or click **More Underlines** to open the Font dialog box, then refer to the directions in the last column	Click the **Underline button** $\underline{U}$	Press **[Ctrl][U]**	Click the **Underline style list arrow** and select a style; next, click the **Underline color list arrow**, select a color, then click **OK**
Apply strike-through	Click the **Strikethrough button** a̶b̶c̶			Click the **Strikethrough check box** in the Effects section
Apply subscript	Click the **Subscript button** x_2		Press **[Ctrl][=]**	Click the **Subscript check box** in the Effects section
Apply superscript	Click the **Superscript button** x^2		Press **[Ctrl] [Shift][+]**	Click the **Superscript check box** in the Effects section

(continued)

Table WD 2-1 Applying Character Attributes (continued)

Attribute to apply	Ribbon Method: Home tab/ Font group	Shortcut Method: Mini toolbar	Shortcut Method: Keyboard	Launcher in the Font group: Font dialog box
Apply high-lighting to text	Click the **Text Highlight Color button** to apply the active highlight color or click the **Text Highlight Color list arrow** , then select a new color	Click the **Text Highlight Color button** to apply the active high-light color or click the **Text Highlight Color list arrow** , then select a new color		
Apply a new font color	Click the **Font Color button** to apply the active font color or click the **Font Color list arrow** , then select a color from a palette of available colors; or click **More Colors**, then create a custom color	Click the **Font Color button** to apply the active font color or click the **Font Color list arrow** , then select a color from a palette of available colors; or click **More Colors**, then create a cus-tom color		Click the **Font Color list arrow** to select a color from a palette of available colors; or click **More Colors** to create a custom color

Word

(continued)

Table WD 2-1 Applying Character Attributes (continued)

Attribute to apply	Ribbon Method: Home tab/ Font group	Shortcut Method: Mini toolbar	Shortcut Method: Keyboard	Launcher in the Font group: Font dialog box
Change Case	Click the **Change Case button** Aa▾			Click an option in the Effects section, then click **OK**
Text Effects	Click the **Text Effects button**			Click the **Text Effects button** and choose options in the Format Text Effects dialog box, click **Close**, then click **OK**

Apply Styles

Ribbon Method

▶ Select the text, click the **Home tab**, click the **More button** in the Styles group, then click an appropriate Quick Style from the gallery

OR

▶ Click the **Home tab**, click the **Change Styles button** in the Styles group, click **Style Set**, then click an appropriate style set

OR

▶ Select the text, click the **Home tab**, then click the **launcher** in the Styles group to open the Styles task pane

▶ Scroll the list of available styles, then click an appropriate style

Shortcut Method

▶ Select the text, right-click, then click the **Styles command** on the shortcut menu

▶ Click a Quick Style in the gallery that opens or click **Apply Styles** at the bottom of the gallery to open the Apply Styles dialog box, click the **Style Name list arrow**, select a style, then close the dialog box

Use the Format Painter

Ribbon Method

▶ Select the text that has the formatting you want to copy, then click the **Home tab**

▶ Click the **Format Painter button** 🖌 in the Clipboard group one time, then select the text you want to format

OR

▶ Click the **Format Painter button** 🖌 in the Clipboard group two times, select the text you want to format and apply the same formatting to multiple places in the document, then click 🖌 to turn off the Format Painter

Shortcut Method

▶ Select the text that has the formatting you want to copy, then press **[Ctrl][Shift][C]** to copy the formatting

▶ Select the text you want to format, then press **[Ctrl][Shift][V]** to apply the formatting

▶ Repeat for each instance

Cut and Paste Text

Ribbon Method

▶ Select the text you want to cut, click the **Home tab**, then click the **Cut button** ✂

▶ Position the insertion point where you want to paste the text, then click the **Paste button**

Shortcut Method

▶ Select the text you want to cut, right-click, then click **Cut** on the shortcut menu

▶ Position the insertion point where you want to paste the text, right-click, click **Paste Options** on the shortcut menu, then click **Keep Source Formatting**, **Merge Formatting**, or **Keep Text Only** depending on how you want the pasted text to be formatted

OR

▶ Select the text you want to cut, then press **[Ctrl][X]**

▶ Position the insertion point where you want to paste the text, then press **[Ctrl][V]**

Copy and Paste Text

Ribbon Method

▶ Select the text you want to copy, click the **Home tab**, then click the **Copy button** 📋

▶ Position the insertion point where you want to paste the text, then click the **Paste button**

Shortcut Method

▶ Select the text you want to copy, right-click, then click **Copy** on the shortcut menu

▶ Position the insertion point where you want to paste the text, right-click, then click **Paste** on the shortcut menu

OR

▶ Select the text you want to copy, then press **[Ctrl][C]**

▶ Position the insertion point where you want to paste the text, then press **[Ctrl][V]**

NAVIGATE AND SEARCH THROUGH A DOCUMENT

Use the Navigation Pane

Ribbon Method

▶ Click the **View tab**, then click the **Navigation Pane check box** in the Show group

OR

▶ Click the **Home tab**, then click the **Find button** in the Editing group

▶ Use the tabs in the Navigation pane to browse document headings, document pages, or search results

Shortcut Method

▶ Press **[Ctrl][F]** to open the Navigation pane, then follow the steps in bullet 3 in the Use the Navigation Pane Ribbon Method

Use the Navigation Pane to Browse Document Headings

Ribbon Method

▶ Make sure your document's headings are formatted with heading styles

▶ Display the Navigation pane, then follow the steps in bullets 1–3 in the Use the Navigation Pane Ribbon Method

▶ Click the **Browse the headings in your document tab** 🗒

▶ Click a heading listed in the Navigation pane to display that section of the document on the right side of the window

Use the Navigation Pane to Browse Document Pages

Ribbon Method

▶ Display the Navigation pane, then follow the steps in bullets 1–3 in the Use the Navigation Pane Ribbon Method

▶ Click the **Browse the pages in your document tab** ▦

▶ Click a page thumbnail in the Navigation pane to display that page on the right side of the window

Note: A thumbnail is a small picture of a page.

Use the Navigation Pane to Browse the Results of a Search

Ribbon Method

▶ Click the **Home tab**, then click the **Find button** in the Editing group

▶ Type a keyword in the **Search Document text box**

▶ Click the **Browse the results from your current search tab** ▤ to display the results of the search in the navigation pane if that is not the current tab

Note: All instances of the keyword are highlighted in the document.

▶ Click a result in the Navigation pane to display that page on the right side of the window

Shortcut Method

▶ Press **[Ctrl][F]** to open the Navigation pane

▶ Follow the steps in bullets 2–4 in the Use the Navigation Pane to Browse the Results of a Search Ribbon Method

Use Go To

Ribbon Method

▶ Click the **Home tab**, click the **Find list arrow** in the Editing group, then click **Go To**

▶ Select an option in the Go to what list, type the go to identifier in the related text box, then click **Go To**

Shortcut Method

▶ Press **[Ctrl][G]** to open the Find and Replace dialog box with the Go To tab active

▶ Follow the step in bullet 2 in the Use Go To Ribbon Method

Word

Use the Browse by Button

Ribbon Method

▶ Click the **Select Browse Object button** ⊙
▶ Click a button on the menu to move quickly to the next occurrence of that object or to display the Find and Replace dialog box in the case of Find and Go To

Find Text

Ribbon Method

▶ Click the **Home tab**, click the **Find list arrow** in the Editing group, then click **Advanced Find** to open the Find and Replace dialog box with the Find tab active
▶ Type the text you want to find in the Find what text box
▶ Click the **More button** to view and select additional search options
▶ Click the **Find Next button** to view in the document each instance of the text in the Find what text box
▶ Click **Cancel** to close the Find and Replace dialog box

Shortcut Method

▶ Press **[Ctrl][F]** to open the Find and Replace dialog box with the Find tab active
▶ Follow the steps in bullets 2–5 in the Find Text Ribbon Method

Find and Replace Text

Ribbon Method

▶ Click the **Home tab**, then click the **Replace button** in the Editing group to open the Find and Replace dialog box with the Replace tab active
▶ Type the text you want to find and replace in the **Find what text box**
▶ Type the replacement text in the Replace with text box
▶ Click the **More button** to view additional search options, then select the appropriate search options
▶ Click the **Find Next button** to view in the document the next instance of the text in the Find what text box, review the selected text, then click **Replace** to replace the selected text or click **Find Next** to leave the selected text as is and move to the next instance
▶ Click **Cancel** to close the Find and Replace dialog box

Shortcut Method
▶ Press **[Ctrl][H]** to open the Find and Replace dialog box with the Replace tab active
▶ Follow the steps in bullets 2–6 in the Find and Replace Text Ribbon Method

Use Replace All

Ribbon Method
▶ Follow the steps in bullets 1–4 in the Find and Replace Text Ribbon Method
▶ Click **Replace All** to replace all instances without preview
▶ Click **Cancel** to close the Find and Replace dialog box

Use Highlight Features

Ribbon Method
▶ Click the **Home tab**, click the **Find list arrow** in the Editing group, then click **Advanced Find**
▶ In the Find and Replace dialog box, type a keyword in the **Find what box**, then click the **Reading Highlight button** and click **Highlight All** to highlight all occurrences of the keyword in the document
▶ Click the **Find Next button** to move to the next occurrence of the highlighted word

  OR

▶ Follow the steps in bullets 1–4 in the Use the Navigation Pane to Browse the Results of a Search Ribbon Method

Set Find and Replace Options Using the Format Button

Ribbon Method
▶ Click the **Home tab**, then click the **Replace button** in the Editing group to open the Find and Replace dialog box with the Replace tab active
▶ Click the **More button** to view additional search options
▶ Click in the **Find what box** to make it the active box, then leave it blank because you are searching for a format only
▶ Click the **Format button** near the bottom of the Find and Replace dialog box, then click a format from the list
▶ Click in the **Replace with box** to make it the active box, then leave it blank because you are replacing a format

Word

▶ Click the **Format button** near the bottom of the Find and Replace dialog box, then click a format from the list

▶ Click the **Find Next button** to view the next instance of the format you are searching for, review the selection, then click **Replace** to replace the selected format or click **Find Next** to leave the selected format as is and move to the next instance

▶ Click **Cancel** to close the Find and Replace dialog box

Shortcut Method

▶ Press **[Ctrl][H]** to open the Find and Replace dialog box with the Replace tab active

▶ Follow the steps in bullets 2–8 in the Find and Replace Options Using the Format Button Ribbon Method

Find and Replace Text with Specific Formatting

Ribbon Method

▶ Click the **Home tab**, then click the **Replace button** in the Editing group to open the Find and Replace dialog box with the Replace tab active

▶ Click the **More button** to view additional search options

▶ Type the text that you want to find in the Find what box

▶ Click the **Format button** near the bottom of the Find and Replace dialog box, then click a format from the list

▶ Type the replacement text in the Replace with box

▶ Click the **Format button** near the bottom of the Find and Replace dialog box, then click a format from the list

▶ Click the **Find Next button** to view the next instance of the text with the format you are searching for, review the selection, then click **Replace** to replace the selected text with the new text and the new format or click **Find Next** to leave the selection as is and move to the next instance

▶ Click **Cancel** to close the Find and Replace dialog box

Shortcut Method

▶ Press **[Ctrl][H]** to open the Find and Replace dialog box with the Replace tab active

▶ Follow the steps in bullets 2–8 in the Find and Replace Text with Specific Formatting Ribbon Method

Set Find and Replace Options Using the Special Button

Ribbon Method

▶ Click the **Home tab**, then click the **Replace button** in the Editing group to open the Find and Replace dialog box with the Replace tab active

▶ Click the **More button** to view additional search options

▶ Click in the **Find what text box** to make it the active box, then leave the box blank

▶ Click the **Special button** near the bottom of the Find and Replace dialog box, then click a format or special character from the list

▶ Click in the **Replace with text box** to make it the active box, then leave the box blank

▶ Click the **Special button** near the bottom of the Find and Replace dialog box, then click a format or character from the list

▶ Click the **Find Next button** to view the next instance of the format or special character, review the selection, then click **Replace** to replace the selection or click **Find Next** to leave the selection as is and move to the next instance

▶ Click **Cancel** to close the Find and Replace dialog box

Shortcut Method

▶ Press **[Ctrl][H]** to open the Find and Replace dialog box with the Replace tab active

▶ Follow the steps in bullets 2–8 in the Find and Replace Options Using the Special Button Ribbon Method

APPLY INDENTATION AND TAB SETTINGS TO PARAGRAPHS

Apply Indents

▶ Click anywhere in the paragraph you want to indent, then use Table WD 2-2 as a reference to apply the indent formatting you want

Table WD 2-2 Applying Indentation Formatting

Indent formatting to apply	Ribbon Method	Shortcut Method: Mini toolbar	Shortcut Method: Ruler	Paragraph dialog box/ Indents and Spacing tab*
Increase indent by preset .5"	Click the **Home tab**, then click the **Increase indent button** in the Paragraph group	Click the **Increase indent button**		
Decrease indent by preset .5"	Click the **Home tab**, then click the **Decrease indent button** in the Paragraph group	Click the **Decrease indent button**		
Left indent	Click the **Page Layout tab**, then use the arrows or enter a value in the Indent Left text box in the Paragraph group		Drag the **Left Indent marker** to the desired position (*Note*: The Left Indent Marker and the Hanging Indent Marker move together when you move the Left Indent Marker.)	Use the arrows or enter a value in the Left text box in the Indentation section

* Click the launcher in the Paragraph group on the Home tab or on the Page Layout tab to open the Paragraph dialog box.

(continued)

Table WD 2-2   Applying Indentation Formatting (continued)

Indent formatting to apply	Ribbon Method	Shortcut Method: Mini toolbar	Shortcut Method: Ruler	Paragraph dialog box/ Indents and Spacing tab*
Right indent	Click the **Page Layout tab**, then use the arrows or enter a value in the Indent Right text box in the Paragraph group		Drag the **Right Indent marker** △ to the desired position	Use the arrows or enter a value in the Right text box in the Indentation section
First Line Indent			Drag the **First Line Indent marker** ▽ to the desired position or scroll to the **First Line Indent marker** ▽ in the tab indicator, click the **First Line Indent marker** ▽ to select it, then click the **ruler** at the desired position	Click the list arrow under Special, click **First Line**, then if necessary, use the arrows or enter a value in the By text box in the Indentation section

* Click the launcher ⬚ in the Paragraph group on the Home tab or on the Page Layout tab to open the Paragraph dialog box.

(continued)

Table WD 2-2 Applying Indentation Formatting (continued)

Indent formatting to apply	Ribbon Method	Shortcut Method: Mini toolbar	Shortcut Method: Ruler	Paragraph dialog box/ Indents and Spacing tab*
Hanging Indent			Drag the **Hanging Indent marker** to the desired position or scroll to the Hanging Indent marker in the tab indicator, click the **Hanging Indent marker** to select it, then click the **ruler** at the desired position	Click the **list arrow** under Special, click **Hanging**, then if necessary, use the arrows or enter a value in the By text box in the Indentation section
Negative Indent (Outdent)	Click the **Page Layout tab**, then use the arrows or enter a negative value in the Indent Left text box in the Paragraph group		Drag the **Left Indent marker** to the desired position on the ruler (the position is to the left of the current paragraph)	Use the arrows or enter a negative value in the Left text box in the Indentation section

* Click the launcher in the Paragraph group on the Home tab or on the Page Layout tab to open the Paragraph dialog box.

Set Tabs

Use Table WD 2-3 as a reference on how to set tabs.

Table WD 2-3 Setting Tabs

Tab setting to apply	Ribbon Method	Shortcut Method: Ruler
	To open the Tabs dialog box: Click the **launcher** [icon] in the Paragraph group on the Home tab or the Page Layout tab to open the Paragraph dialog box, then click the **Tabs button**; click the appropriate Alignment option button in the Tabs dialog box	To use the tab indicators: Click the **View Ruler button** [icon] at the top of the vertical scroll bar to display the rulers if necessary, click the **tab indicator** at the left end of the horizontal ruler until the desired tab indicator is active, then position the pointer on the horizontal ruler at the location where you want the tab to be placed
[icon] Left tab	Type the value in the Tab stop position text box, then click **OK**	With the Left tab indicator active, click the **horizontal ruler**
[icon] Center tab	Type the value in the Tab stop position text box, then click **OK**	With the Center tab indicator active, click the **horizontal ruler**
[icon] Right tab	Type the value in the Tab stop position text box, then click **OK**	With the Right tab indicator active, click the **horizontal ruler**
[icon] Decimal tab	Type the value in the Tab stop position text box, then click **OK**	With the Decimal tab indicator active, click the **horizontal ruler**
[icon] Bar tab	Type the value in the Tab stop position text box, then click **OK**	With the Bar tab indicator active, click the **horizontal ruler**

Use the Tabs Dialog Box

Ribbon Method

▶ Click the **launcher** in the Paragraph group on the Home tab or the Page Layout tab to open the Paragraph dialog box, then click the **Tabs button** in the Paragraph dialog box to open the Tabs dialog box

▶ Set options related to tab stop positions, alignment, and leaders, then click **OK** to close the Tabs dialog box

OR

▶ Double-click any tab on the ruler to open the Tabs dialog box, then follow the steps in bullet 2

Set Tab Stops

Ribbon Method

▶ Open the **Tabs dialog box** (refer to Table WD 2-3 as needed), type the location of the tab stop you want to set in the Tab stop position text box, then press **[Enter]**

Set Tabs with Leaders

Ribbon Method

▶ Open the **Tabs dialog box** (refer to Table WD 2-3 as needed), select the tab stop in the Tab stop position list box that you want to modify, click the **leader style option button** for an appropriate leader style, then click **OK**

Clear a Tab

Ribbon Method

▶ Open the **Tabs dialog box** (refer to Table WD 2-3 as needed), select the tab stop in the Tab stop position list box that you want to modify, click the **Clear button**, then click **OK**

Mouse Method

▶ Position the pointer over the tab stop you want to remove
▶ Use the pointer to drag the tab stop off the horizontal ruler

Clear All Tabs

Ribbon Method

▶ Open the **Tabs dialog box** (refer to Table WD 2-3 as needed), click the **Clear All button**, then click **OK**

Set Tab Stops on the Ruler

Ribbon Method

▶ Click the **tab indicator** to scroll through the tab types, then click the tab type you want to set

▶ Click the tab type you want to select, position the pointer ⃕ over the location on the ruler where you want to set the tab, then click to place the tab indicator on the ruler

Move a Tab Stop

Mouse Method

▶ Position the pointer ⃕ over the tab stop you want to move

▶ Drag the **tab stop** to its new location on the horizontal ruler and release the mouse button

APPLY SPACING SETTINGS TO TEXT AND PARAGRAPHS

Set Line Spacing

Ribbon Method

▶ Click anywhere in the paragraph you want to format

▶ Click the **Line and Paragraph Spacing list arrow** ⃔≡⃕, then click a preset line spacing option or click **Line Spacing Options**

▶ On the Indents and Spacing tab in the Paragraph dialog box, click the appropriate line spacing option, then click **OK**

OR

▶ Click the **launcher** ⃔ in the Paragraph group on the Home tab or the Page Layout tab, click the **Indents and Spacing tab** if it is not the active tab, select the appropriate line spacing option, then click **OK**

Set Paragraph Spacing

Ribbon Method

▶ Click the **Page Layout tab**

▶ Click the **Spacing Before arrows** in the Paragraph group to increase or decrease the amount of space before a paragraph, or type the value in the Before text box

▶ Click the **Spacing After arrows** in the Paragraph group to increase or decrease the amount of space after a paragraph, or type the value in the After text box

OR

▶ Click the **launcher** ⃔ in the Paragraph group on the Page Layout tab or the Home tab to open the Paragraph dialog box

▶ Click the **Indents and Spacing tab** if it is not the active tab, select the appropriate Before and After options in the Spacing section of the dialog box, then click **OK**

Note: If you do not want to change paragraph spacing between paragraphs with the same style, click the Don't add spacing between paragraphs of the same style check box.

Apply Alignment

▶ Click anywhere in the paragraph you want to align, then use Table WD 2-4 as a reference to apply the alignment formatting you want

Table WD 2-4 Applying Alignment

Alignment to apply or modify	Ribbon Method: Home tab/ Paragraph group	Shortcut Method: Mini toolbar	Shortcut Method: Keyboard	Paragraph dialog box/ Indents and Spacing tab*
Left	Click the **Align Text Left button** ≡		Press **[Ctrl][L]**	In the General section, click the **Alignment list arrow**, then click **Left**
Center	Click the **Center button** ≡	Click the **Center button** ≡	Press **[Ctrl][E]**	In the General section, click the **Alignment list arrow**, then click **Centered**
Right	Click the **Align Text Right button** ≡		Press **[Ctrl][R]**	In the General section, click the **Alignment list arrow**, then click **Right**

(continued)

Table WD 2-4 Applying Alignment (continued)

Alignment to apply or modify	Ribbon Method: Home tab/ Paragraph group	Shortcut Method: Mini toolbar	Shortcut Method: Keyboard	Paragraph dialog box/ Indents and Spacing tab*
Justify	Click the **Justify button** ▤		Press **[Ctrl][J]**	In the General section, click the **Alignment list arrow**, then click **Justified**

* Click the launcher 🔲 in the Paragraph group on the Home tab or on the Page Layout tab to open the Paragraph dialog box.

CREATE TABLES

Create a Table Using the Insert Table Dialog Box
Ribbon Method
- ▶ Click the **Insert tab**, click the **Table button** in the Tables group, then click **Insert Table** to display the Insert Table dialog box
- ▶ Type a number in the Number of columns text box, then type a number in the Number of rows text box
- ▶ Set other options as appropriate, then click **OK**

Create a Table Using the Table Button and Grid
Ribbon Method
- ▶ Click the **Insert tab**, click the **Table button** in the Tables group, drag over the grid to select the number of columns and rows, then click the mouse

Draw a Table
Ribbon Method
- ▶ Click the **Insert tab**, click the **Table button** in the Tables group, then click **Draw Table**
- ▶ Use the **Draw Table pencil** ✏ to draw a rectangular boundary, then draw vertical and horizontal lines to create columns and rows

Word

Note: Use the Table Eraser tool in the Draw Borders group on the Table Tools Design tab to erase table lines and borders.

Insert a Quick Table

Ribbon Method

▶ Click the **Insert tab**, click the **Table button** in the Tables group, point to **Quick Tables**, then click a table option from the Built-in gallery

Convert Text to a Table

Ribbon Method

▶ Select the desired text, then click the **Insert tab**
▶ Click the **Table button** in the Tables group, then click **Convert Text to Table**
▶ Enter the appropriate options in the Convert Text to Table dialog box, then click **OK**

Use a Table to Control Page Layout

▶ Click the **Insert tab**, click the **Table button** in the Tables group, then click **Insert Table**
▶ In the Insert Table dialog box, specify the number of rows and columns appropriate for the content and orientation of the page
▶ Insert text, graphics, and other content in separate table cells instead of using tabs to align content
▶ Select the table, click the **Bottom Border List Arrow** ⊞ ▾, then click **No Borders** to remove table borders from view, if desired

Note: Tables are often used to control page layout in Web pages; for example, adding text in one table cell and a graphic in the cell beside it to keep them aligned on the page.

MANIPULATE TABLES IN A DOCUMENT

Apply Quick Styles to Tables

Ribbon Method

▶ Click anywhere in a table, click the **Table Tools Design tab**, then click the **More button** ▾ in the Table Styles group
▶ In the Table Styles gallery, click the Quick Style you want to apply or click **Modify Table Style**
▶ In the Modify Style dialog box, select appropriate options, then click **OK**

Sort Content

Ribbon Method

- ▶ Click anywhere in the table you want to sort, click the **Table Tools Layout tab**, then click the **Sort button** in the Data group
- ▶ In the Sort dialog box, choose appropriate options to identify primary, secondary, and tertiary criteria, then click **OK**

Add a Row to a Table

Ribbon Method

- ▶ Click in a table row
- ▶ Click the **Table Tools Layout tab**, then click the **Insert Above button** or **Insert Below button** in the Rows & Columns group

  OR

- ▶ To insert multiple rows, select the number of rows in the table that correspond to the number of rows you want to add (for example, select five rows if you want to add five rows)
- ▶ Click the **Table Tools Layout tab**, then click the **Insert Above button** or **Insert Below button** in the Rows & Columns group to add that number of rows above or below the selected rows

Shortcut Method

- ▶ Right-click in a table row
- ▶ Point to **Insert** on the shortcut menu, then click **Insert Rows Above** or **Insert Rows Below** from the submenu

Add a Column to a Table

Ribbon Method

- ▶ Click in a table column
- ▶ Click the **Table Tools Layout tab**, then click the **Insert Left button** or **Insert Right button** in the Rows & Columns group

  OR

- ▶ To add multiple columns at a time, select the number of columns in the table that correspond to the number of columns you want to add
- ▶ Click the **Table Tools Layout tab**, then click the **Insert Left button** or **Insert Right button** in the Rows & Columns group to add the number of columns to the right or left of the selected columns

Shortcut Method

- ▶ Right-click in a table column
- ▶ Point to **Insert** on the shortcut menu, then click **Insert Columns to the Left** or **Insert Columns to the Right** on the submenu

Word

Merge Table Cells in Rows or Columns

Ribbon Method

▶ Select the cells you want to merge into one cell, click the **Table Tools Layout tab**, then click the **Merge Cells button** in the Merge group

Shortcut Method

▶ Select the cells you want to merge into one cell, right-click, then click **Merge Cells** on the shortcut menu

Note: A cell is the intersection of a row and column.

Split Table Cells in Rows or Columns

Ribbon Method

▶ Click the cell you want to split, click the **Table Tools Layout tab**, then click the **Split Cells button** in the Merge group
▶ In the Split Cells dialog box, enter the appropriate options, then click **OK**

Shortcut Method

▶ Select the cell you want to split, right-click, then click **Split Cells** on the shortcut menu
▶ In the Split Cells dialog box, enter the appropriate options, then click **OK**

Move Columns and Rows

Ribbon Method

▶ Select the row(s) or column(s) that you want to move, click the **Home tab**, then click the **Cut button** in the Clipboard group
▶ Select a row or a column in the table, then click the **Paste button** to insert the row(s) above the selected row or to insert the column(s) to the left of the selected column

Mouse Method

▶ Select the row(s) or column(s) that you want to move, press and hold the pointer until you see the **Drag and drop pointer**, drag the dotted insertion point to the new location, then release the mouse button to insert the row(s) above the row with the dotted insertion point or to insert the column(s) to the left of the column with the dotted insertion point

Resize Columns and Rows

Ribbon Method

▶ Click in the column or row, click the **Table Tools Layout tab**, then click the **up arrow** and the **down arrow** in the Table Row

Height text box or the Table Column Width text box in the Cell
Size group to increase or decrease the height of a row or width of
a column

OR

▶ Click in the column or row, click the **Table Tools Layout tab**,
then click the **AutoFit list arrow** and click an option for automatically resizing the column width to the size of the contents,
window, or a fixed width

Mouse Method

▶ Position the mouse pointer on a vertical or horizontal cell border,
then drag the **Resize pointer** ⁺‖⁺ vertically or horizontally to
increase or decrease the size of the column or row

Delete Columns and Rows

Ribbon Method

▶ Select the column(s) or row(s), click the **Table Tools Layout tab**,
click the **Delete button** in the Rows & Columns group, then
click **Delete Columns** or **Delete Rows**

Shortcut Method

▶ Select the column(s) or row(s), right-click, then click **Delete
Rows** or **Delete Columns** on the shortcut menu

OR

▶ Select the column(s) or row(s), then press **[Shift][Delete]**

Define the Header Row

Ribbon Method

▶ Click in the table, click the **Table Tools Design tab**, then click the
Header Row check box in the Table Style Options dialog box

Convert Tables to Text

Ribbon Method

▶ Click anywhere in the table you want to convert to text, then
click the **Table Tools Layout tab**
▶ Click the **Convert to Text button** in the Data group, enter the
appropriate options in the Convert Table to Text dialog box, then
click **OK**

View Gridlines

Ribbon Method

▶ Click anywhere in the table, click the **Table Tools Layout tab**,
then click **View Table Gridlines** in the Table group

Note: It is most helpful to view gridlines on tables without borders.

Word

APPLY BULLETS TO A DOCUMENT

Apply Bullets to Existing Text

Ribbon Method

- ▶ Select the text you want to convert to a list
- ▶ Click the **Home tab**, then click the **Bullets button** ⊞ in the Paragraph group to apply the current bullet style

  OR
- ▶ Click the **Home tab**, then click the **Numbering button** ⊞ in the Paragraph group to apply the current numbering

Shortcut Method

- ▶ Select the text you want to convert to a bulleted list, right-click, point to **Bullets** on the shortcut menu, then click a bullet format from the Bullet Library

  OR
- ▶ Select the text you want to convert to a numbered list, right-click, point to **Numbering** on the shortcut menu, then click a number format from the Numbering Library

Select a New Symbol Format for Bullets

Ribbon Method

- ▶ Click anywhere in the list, click the **Home tab**, then click the **Bullets list arrow** ⊞ ▾ in the Paragraph group
- ▶ Click a new bullet style from the Bullet Library or click **Define New Bullet**
- ▶ In the Define New Bullet dialog box, click **Symbol** to open the Symbol dialog box, click a new bullet style, then click **OK**

Define a Picture to Be Used as a Bullet

Ribbon Method

- ▶ Click anywhere in the list, click the **Home tab**, then click the **Bullets list arrow** ⊞ ▾ in the Paragraph group
- ▶ Click a new bullet style from the Bullet Library or click **Define New Bullet**
- ▶ In the Define New Bullet dialog box, click **Picture** to open the Picture Bullet dialog box of options, click a new bullet style or click **Import** to select a picture to import as a bullet, then click **OK**

Shortcut Method

- ▶ Select the bulleted list, right-click, point to **Bullets** on the menu, then click **Define New Bullet**

▶ In the Define New Bullet dialog box, click **Picture** to open the Picture Bullet dialog box of options, click a new bullet style or click **Import** to select a picture to import as a bullet, then click **OK**

Use AutoFormat to Create a Bulleted, Numbered, or Multilevel List

Ribbon Method

▶ Position the insertion point where you want a list to begin
▶ Click the **Home tab**, then click the **Bullets button** :≡ in the Paragraph group to apply the current bullet style

OR

▶ Click the **Home tab**, then click the **Numbering button** ¦≡ in the Paragraph group to apply the current numbering style

OR

▶ Click the **Home tab**, then click the **Multilevel List button** ⁙☰ in the Paragraph group to apply the current style
▶ Type a list item, then press **[Enter]** at the end of each item
▶ Follow the steps in bullets 1–2 in the Demote and Promote List Items Ribbon Method below to change the level of an item in a list

Shortcut Method

▶ Right-click where you want to create a bulleted list, point to **Bullets** on the shortcut menu, then click a bullet format from the Bullet Library

OR

▶ Right-click where you want to create a bulleted list, point to **Numbering** on the shortcut menu, then click a numbering format from the Numbering Library
▶ Type a list item, then press **[Enter]** at the end of each item

Demote and Promote List Items

Ribbon Method

▶ To demote a list item, click anywhere in the item you want to demote, click the **Home tab**, then click the **Increase Indent button** ☰ in the Paragraph group
▶ To promote a list item, click anywhere in the item you want to promote, click the **Home tab**, then click the **Decrease Indent button** ☰ in the Paragraph group

Shortcut Method

▶ Select the item you want to demote or promote, then click the **Increase Indent button** ☰ or the **Decrease Indent button** ☰ on the Mini toolbar

Word

OR

▶ Position the insertion point in front of the item you want to demote or promote, then press **[Tab]** to demote the item or press **[Shift][Tab]** to promote the item

Sort List Items

Ribbon Method

▶ Select the appropriate items to sort, click the **Home tab**, then click the **Sort button** in the Paragraph group
▶ In the Sort dialog box, choose appropriate options to identify primary, secondary, and tertiary criteria, then click **OK**

WORD CORE OBJECTIVE 3: APPLYING PAGE LAYOUT AND REUSABLE CONTENT

APPLY AND MANIPULATE PAGE SETUP SETTINGS

Set Margins

Ribbon Method

▶ Click the **Page Layout tab**, then click the **Margins button** in the Page Setup group
▶ Click a **preset margin option** or click **Custom Margins**; enter values in the Top, Bottom, Left, and Right text boxes of the Page Setup dialog box; then click **OK**

OR

▶ Click the **Page Layout tab**, click the **launcher** in the Page Setup group, then click the **Margins tab** in the Page Setup dialog box if it is not the active tab
▶ Enter values in the Top, Bottom, Left, and Right text boxes, then click **OK**

Mouse Method

▶ Click the **View Ruler button** at the top of the vertical scroll bar to display the rulers if they are not already displayed, then select appropriate text to apply new margins

Note: Press [Ctrl][A] to select the entire document or drag the mouse over text you want to select.

▶ Drag the **Left Indent marker** to an appropriate location on the horizontal ruler

Note: The Left Indent Marker and the Hanging Indent Marker move together when you move the Left Indent Marker.

▶ Drag the **Right Indent marker** △ to an appropriate location on the horizontal ruler

Insert Nonbreaking Spaces

Ribbon Method

▶ Position the insertion point in the location where you want to insert a nonbreaking space

▶ Click the **Insert tab**, click the **Symbol button** in the Symbols group, then click **More Symbols**

▶ In the Symbol dialog box, click the **Special Characters tab**, click **Nonbreaking Space**, then click **Insert**

Shortcut Method

▶ Position the insertion point in the location where you want to insert a nonbreaking space

▶ Press **[Ctrl][Shift][Spacebar]**

Add Hyphenation

Ribbon Method

▶ Click the **Page Layout tab**, click the **Hyphenation button** in the Page Setup group, then click **Automatic** to turn on hyphenation; or click **Hyphenation Options** to open the Hyphenation dialog box, specify hyphenation settings, then click **OK**

Note: Turning on hyphenation lets Word break lines between syllables, creating more uniform line length and spacing between words.

Add Columns

Ribbon Method

▶ Select the text you want to format as columns

▶ Click the **Page Layout tab**, then click the **Columns button** in the Page Setup group

▶ Select one of the predefined options on the menu that opens or click **More Columns** to open the Columns dialog box, select the desired settings, then click **OK**

Note: To format a section of a document in columns, position the insertion point at the beginning of the section before selecting column formatting options.

Change Column Width and Spacing

Ribbon Method

▶ Position the insertion point in the text you want to change

Word

▶ Click the **Page Layout tab**, click the **Columns button** in the Page Setup group, then click **More Columns** to open the Columns dialog box
▶ Enter the desired settings in the width and spacing text boxes, then click **OK**

Mouse Method

▶ Position the insertion point in the text you want to change
▶ Drag the column markers on the horizontal ruler to the new location(s)

Set Page Orientation

Ribbon Method

▶ Click the **Page Layout tab**, click the **Orientation button**, then click **Portrait** or **Landscape**
OR
▶ Click the **Page Layout tab**, click the **launcher** in the Page Setup group to open the Page Setup dialog box, click the **Margins tab** if it is not the active tab, then click **Portrait** or **Landscape**

Set Paper Size

Ribbon Method

▶ Click the **Page Layout tab**, click the **Size button** in the Page Setup group, then select a paper size on the menu
OR
▶ Click the **Page Layout tab**, click the **launcher** in the Page Setup group to open the Page Setup dialog box, click the **Paper tab** if it is not the active tab, click the **Paper Size list arrow**, then select a paper size or enter values in the Width and Height text boxes

Force a Page Break

Ribbon Method

▶ Position the insertion point where you want the page break to occur
▶ Click the **Page Layout tab**, click the **Breaks button** in the Page Setup group, then click **Page** in the Page Breaks section

Shortcut Method

▶ Position the insertion point where you want the page break to occur, then press **[Ctrl][Enter]**

Remove a Page Break

Shortcut Method

▶ Click the **Home tab,** then click the **Show/Hide button** ¶ in the Paragraph group to display formatting marks

▶ Use the Selection pointer ⌀ to click to the left of the page break to select it, then press **[Delete]**

OR

▶ Double-click a page break to select it, then press **[Delete]**

Insert a Section Break: Continuous, Next Page, Next Odd, or Next Even

Ribbon Method

▶ Position the insertion point where you want the section break to occur

▶ Click the **Page Layout tab,** click the **Breaks button,** then click the type of break you want to insert—Continuous, Next Page, Next Odd, or Next Even—from the Section Breaks area on the menu

Remove a Section Break

Ribbon Method

▶ Click the **Home tab,** then click the **Show/Hide button** ¶ in the Paragraph group to display formatting marks

▶ Position the insertion point to the left of the section break, then press **[Delete]** as many times as needed to delete the section break

Insert a Blank Page into a Document

Ribbon Method

▶ Click the **Insert tab,** then click **Blank Page** in the Pages group to add a blank page at the location of the insertion point

Shortcut Method

▶ Position the insertion point where you want the blank page to be inserted, then press **[Ctrl][Enter]**

APPLY THEMES

Use a Theme to Apply Formatting

Ribbon Method

▶ Click the **Page Layout tab,** click the **Themes button** in the Themes group to display a gallery of options, then move the pointer over each theme in the gallery to preview the theme

▶ Click an appropriate theme

Customize Theme Effects

Ribbon Method

▶ Click the **Page Layout tab**, then click the **Theme Effects button** ▣▾ in the Themes group
▶ Click an appropriate option

Customize Theme Fonts

Ribbon Method

▶ Click the **Page Layout tab**, then click the **Theme Fonts button** Ⓐ▾ in the Themes group
▶ Click an appropriate option

   OR

▶ Click **Create New Theme Fonts**, select a Heading font and a Body font, type a name in the Name text box, then click **Save**

Customize Theme Colors

Ribbon Method

▶ Click the **Page Layout tab**, then click the **Theme Colors button** ▣▾ in the Themes group
▶ Click an appropriate option

   OR

▶ Click **Create New Theme Colors**, select appropriate options, type a name in the Name text box, then click **Save**

CONSTRUCT CONTENT IN A DOCUMENT BY USING THE QUICK PARTS TOOLS

Add Built-in Building Blocks

Ribbon Method

▶ Click the **Insert tab**, then click the **Quick Parts button** in the Text group
▶ Click **Building Blocks Organizer** on the Quick Parts menu, select the building block you want to insert, then click **Insert**

Insert Pull Quotes

Ribbon Method

▶ Position the insertion point in the location where you want the pull quote to appear, click the **Insert tab**, then click the **Text Box button** in the Text group
▶ Click a preformatted quote style from the gallery
▶ Replace the placeholder text with appropriate text

Insert a Text Box

Ribbon Method

▶ Position the insertion point where you want the text box to appear, click the **Insert tab**, then click the **Text Box button** in the Text group
▶ Select a preformatted text box from the gallery
▶ Replace the placeholder text with appropriate text

Insert a Header

Ribbon Method

▶ Click the **Insert tab**, then click the **Header button** in the Header & Footer group
▶ Scroll the Header gallery, then click the built-in Header Quick Part you want to insert
▶ Replace the placeholder text with your content
▶ Click the **Close Header and Footer button**

Insert a Footer

Ribbon Method

▶ Click the **Insert tab**, then click the **Footer button** in the Header & Footer group
▶ Scroll the Footer gallery, then click the built-in Footer Quick Part you want to insert
▶ Replace the placeholder text with your content
▶ Click the **Close Header and Footer button**

Insert a Cover Page

Ribbon Method

▶ Click the **Insert tab**, click **Cover Page**, scroll through the gallery of choices, then click an appropriate cover page to be inserted at the beginning of the document
▶ Replace the placeholder text with your content

Insert a Watermark

Ribbon Method

▶ Click the **Page Layout tab**, then click **Watermark** in the Page Background group
▶ Scroll to see the preset watermarks available, then click an appropriate watermark from the gallery

Note: A watermark is shaded text or a graphic that appears behind text in a document.

Word

Insert Equations

Ribbon Method

▶ Click the **Insert tab**, click the **Equation list arrow** in the Symbols group, then click an appropriate equation from the gallery

---

CREATE AND MANIPULATE PAGE BACKGROUNDS

Format a Document's Background

Ribbon Method

▶ Click the **Page Layout tab**, click the **Page Color button** in the Page Background group, then click **Fill Effects**
▶ In the Fill Effects dialog box, click the **Gradient**, **Texture**, **Pattern**, or **Picture tab**; select appropriate options; then click **OK**

Set a Colored Background

Ribbon Method

▶ Click the **Page Layout tab**, click **Page Color** in the Page Background group, then click an appropriate color

Add a Custom Watermark

Ribbon Method

▶ Click the **Page Layout tab**, click **Watermark** in the Page Background group, then click **Custom Watermark** to display the Printed Watermark dialog box
▶ Click the **Picture watermark option button**, click **Select Picture**, navigate to an appropriate drive and folder, double-click the picture, click **Apply**, then click **Close**
  OR
▶ Click the **Text watermark option button**, use the list arrows to select appropriate options, click **Apply**, then click **Close**

Set Page Borders

Ribbon Method

▶ Click the **Page Layout tab**, click **Page Borders** in the Page Background group, click appropriate options from the Borders & Shading dialog box, then click **OK**

CREATE AND MODIFY HEADERS AND FOOTERS

Insert Page Numbers

Ribbon Method

▶ Click the **Insert tab**, click the **Page Number button**, point to the location (Top of Page, Bottom of Page, Page Margins, or Current Position) where you want the page number to appear, view the options in the gallery that opens, then click the option you want

OR

▶ Double-click in the Header or Footer area, click the **Page Number button** in the Header & Footer group, point to the location (Top of Page, Bottom of Page, Page Margins, or Current Position) where you want the page number to appear, view the options in the gallery that opens, then click the option you want

OR

▶ Click the **Insert tab**, click the **Header** or **Footer button**, then select a header or footer option from the gallery that contains a page number

Format Page Numbers

Ribbon Method

▶ Click the **Insert tab**, click the **Page Number button** in the Header & Footer group, then click **Format Page Numbers** to open the Page Number Format dialog box
▶ Choose appropriate options, then click **OK**

Shortcut Method

▶ Select a page number in a Header or Footer area, right-click, then click **Format Page Numbers** on the shortcut menu
▶ In the Format Page Number dialog box, select appropriate options, then click **OK**

Insert the Current Date and Time

Ribbon Method

▶ Click the **Insert tab**, then click the **Date & Time button** in the Text group
▶ In the Date and Time dialog box, select an appropriate format in the Available formats list
▶ Check the **Update automatically check box** to automatically update the date and time stamp each time the document is opened
▶ Click **OK**

OR

Word

▶ Double-click in a Header or Footer area, click the **Date & Time button** in the Insert group
▶ Follow the steps in bullets 2–4 in the Insert the Current Date and Time Ribbon Method

Insert a Built-in Header or Footer

Ribbon Method

▶ Click the **Insert tab**, then click the **Header** or **Footer button** in the Header & Footer group
▶ Click a built-in Quick Part from the Header or Footer gallery
▶ Replace the placeholder text with your content
▶ Click the **Close Header and Footer button**

Add Content to a Header or Footer

Ribbon Method

▶ Insert a built-in header or footer using the steps in bullets 1–4 in the Insert a Built-in Header or Footer Ribbon Method
▶ Click the placeholder text in brackets, such as [Type the document title], and type your own text

Note: Some placeholders, such as those for the date, may have an arrow you can click to choose the date from a calendar.

Custom Dialog Box

Ribbon Method

▶ Open the Building Blocks Organizer dialog box, select the footer you want to edit, then click the **Edit Properties button**
▶ Make changes in the Modify Building Blocks dialog box, then click **OK**

Manual Entry

Shortcut Method

▶ Open the Header or Footer area, then type the content or insert Quick Parts and images in the Header or Footer area
▶ Click the document to close the Header and Footer areas

Delete a Header or Footer

Ribbon Method

▶ Click the **Insert tab**, then click the **Header** or **Footer button** in the Header & Footer group
▶ Click **Remove Header** or **Remove Footer**

Change the Margins of a Header or Footer

Ribbon Method

▶ Double-click in a Header or Footer area
▶ Move the **left indent marker** ▦ or **right indent marker** ⌂ to change the header margins
▶ Click the **Close Header and Footer button**

Apply a Different First Page Attribute

Ribbon Method

▶ Press **[Ctrl][Home]** to move to the beginning of the document, click the **Insert tab**, click the **Header button**, then click one of the built-in headers or click **Edit Header** to open the Header area or click the **Footer button**, then click one of the built-in footers or click **Edit Footer** to open the Footer area
▶ Click the **Different First Page check box** in the Options group to select it
▶ Type the text or insert the content you want to appear in the first page header, if any
▶ Click **Next Section**, then type the text or insert the content you want to appear in the header for the remaining pages in the section

WORD CORE OBJECTIVE 4: INCLUDING ILLUSTRATIONS AND GRAPHICS IN A DOCUMENT

INSERT AND FORMAT PICTURES IN A DOCUMENT

Insert and Format Pictures in a Document

Ribbon Method

▶ Position the insertion point in the desired location
▶ Click the **Insert tab**, then click the **Insert Picture from File button** in the Illustrations group
▶ In the Insert Picture dialog box, navigate to the appropriate drive and folder, then select an appropriate picture
▶ Click **Insert**

Shortcut Method

▶ Follow the steps in bullets 1–3 in the Insert and Format Pictures in a Document Ribbon Method
▶ Double-click an appropriate picture

Add Captions

Ribbon Method

▶ Select a picture in the document
▶ Click the **References tab**, then click **Insert Caption** from the Captions group
▶ In the Caption dialog box, click the **Label list arrow** to choose a label or click **New Label** to type the name of a new label, then click **OK**

OR

▶ Click the **Exclude label from caption check box** to remove the label
▶ Click the **Location list arrow** to choose a position for the label, type a caption in the Caption text box, choose any other options as necessary, then click **OK**

Shortcut Method

▶ Right-click a **picture** in your document, then click **Insert Caption** from the shortcut menu
▶ In the Caption dialog box, click the **Label list arrow** to choose a label or click **New Label** to type the name of a new label, then click **OK**

OR

▶ Click the **Exclude label from caption check box** to remove the label
▶ Click the **Location list arrow** to choose a position for the label, type a caption in the Caption text box, choose any other options as necessary, then click **OK**

Apply Artistic Effects

Ribbon Method

▶ Click the picture to select it, then click the **Picture Tools Format tab**
▶ Click the **Artistic Effects button** in the Adjust group, then click the effect you want to apply from the gallery

OR

▶ Click the **launcher** in the Picture Styles group to open the Format Picture dialog box
▶ Click **Artistic Effects** in the left pane, click the **Artistic Effects list arrow**, click the effect you want to apply, then click **Close**

Shortcut Method

▶ Right-click the picture, then click **Format Picture** on the short-cut menu to open the Format Picture dialog box

▶ Click **Artistic Effects** in the left pane, click the **Artistic Effects list arrow** in the right pane, click the effect you want to apply, then click **Close**

Apply Picture Styles

Ribbon Method

▶ Click the picture to select it, then click the **Picture Tools Format tab**

▶ Click the **More button** ⮟ in the Picture Styles group to display the gallery, then select a Quick Style

OR

▶ Select a picture

▶ Click the **Picture Tools Format tab**, then click the **launcher** 🔲 in the Picture Styles group to open the Format Picture dialog box

▶ Click a category in the left pane, then select specific options in the right pane

OR

▶ Select a picture

▶ Click the **Picture Tools Format tab**

▶ Click the **Picture Border button** in the Picture Styles group and click an option from the palette to change the picture's border color, or click the **Picture Effects button** and click an option from the effects menu

Shortcut Method

▶ Right-click a **picture**, then click **Format Picture** on the shortcut menu to open the Format Picture dialog box

▶ Click a category in the left pane, then select specific options in the right pane

Apply Corrections and Color to a Picture

Ribbon Method

▶ Click the picture to select it, then click the **Picture Tools Format tab**

▶ Click the **Corrections list arrow** in the Adjust group on the Picture Tools Format tab, then click a Soften and Sharpen option or a Brightness and Contrast option from the gallery

OR

▶ Click the **Color list arrow** in the Adjust group, then click an option from the gallery

OR

▶ Click the **launcher** [icon] in the Picture Styles group to open the Format Picture dialog box

▶ Click **Picture Corrections** or **Picture Color** in the left pane to meet your needs, then select the appropriate options in the right pane

Compress Pictures

Ribbon Method

▶ Select the picture to compress, then click the **Picture Tools Format tab**

▶ Click the **Compress Pictures button** [icon] in the Adjust group to open the Compress Pictures dialog box

▶ Click the **Apply only to this picture check box** if necessary to select it

▶ Select a Target output option, then click **OK**

Modify the Shape of a Picture Using the Crop Tool

Ribbon Method

▶ Click the picture to select it, then click the **Picture Tools Format tab**

▶ Click the **Crop button** in the Size group to display cropping handles on the sides and corners of the picture

▶ Position the **Crop Tool pointer** **T** over a cropping handle (solid black line), then drag the cropping handle inward and repeat with the other cropping handles as necessary to specify unwanted parts of the picture

▶ Click the **Crop button** in the Size group to remove the unwanted parts of the picture

OR

▶ Click the picture to select it, then click the **Picture Tools Format tab**

▶ Click the **Crop button list arrow** in the Size group, click **Crop to Shape**, then click a shape from the gallery

Shortcut Method

▶ Right-click the picture, then click the **Crop button** [icon] on the Mini toolbar to display the cropping handles on the sides and corners of the picture

▶ Position the **Crop Tool pointer** **T** over a cropping handle (solid black line), then drag the cropping handle inward and repeat with the other cropping handles as necessary to specify unwanted parts of the picture

▶ Click the **Crop button** in the Size group on the Picture Tools Format tab to remove the unwanted parts of the picture

Adjust Position

Ribbon Method

▶ Click the **picture**, then click the **Picture Tools Format tab**
▶ Click the **Position button** in the Arrange group, then click an appropriate option on the menu or click **More Layout Options** to open the Layout dialog box and apply advanced options

Shortcut Method

▶ Right-click the picture, then click **Size and Position** on the shortcut menu
▶ In the Layout dialog box, click the **Position tab** to specify horizontal, vertical, and additional position options, then click **OK**

Adjust Size

Ribbon Method

▶ Click the picture to select it, then click the **Picture Tools Format tab**
▶ Type values in the Shape Height and Shape Width text boxes in the Size group

OR

▶ On the Picture Tools Format tab, click the **launcher** 🔲 in the Size group to open the Layout dialog box
▶ On the Size tab, enter appropriate values in the Height, Width, Rotate, and Scale sections, then click **OK** to resize the picture precisely

Shortcut Method

▶ Right-click the picture, then click **Size and Position** on the shortcut menu
▶ In the Layout dialog box, click the **Size tab**; enter appropriate values in the Height, Width, Rotate, and Scale sections; then click **OK**

Mouse Method

▶ Click a picture to select it, move the mouse over a corner sizing handle, then drag the **Diagonal Resize pointer** ⬉ or the **Diagonal Resize pointer** ⬈ to resize the graphic proportionally

OR

▶ Move the mouse over a side, top, or bottom sizing handle, then press **[Ctrl]** and drag the **Horizontal Resize pointer** ⟺ or the **Vertical Resize pointer** ↕ to resize the graphic vertically or horizontally while keeping the center position fixed

OR

▶ Move the mouse over a corner sizing handle, then press **[Ctrl]** and drag the **Diagonal Resize pointer** ↘ or the **Diagonal Resize pointer** ↗ to resize the graphic diagonally while keeping the center position fixed

OR

▶ Move the mouse over a corner sizing handle, then press **[Shift] [Ctrl]** and drag the **Diagonal Resize pointer** ↘ or the **Diagonal Resize pointer** ↗ to resize the graphic proportionally while keeping the center position fixed

Insert Screenshots

Ribbon Method

▶ Open the document or window that you would like to use in a screenshot; make sure it is not minimized
▶ Position the insertion point in the document where you want to insert the screenshot
▶ Click the **Insert tab**, click the **Screenshot button** in the Illustrations group, then click a thumbnail from the Available Windows gallery to insert it

Insert Screen Clippings

Ribbon Method

▶ Open the document or window that you would like to use in a screen clipping; make sure it is not minimized
▶ Position the insertion point in the document where you want to insert the screenshot clipping
▶ Click the **Insert tab**, click the **Screenshot button** in the Illustrations group, then click **Screen Clipping**
▶ Use the **Crosshair pointer** ┼ to draw a rectangle around the area of the window that you want to cut out and insert into your document
▶ Release the mouse button to insert the screen clipping into your document

Note: A screenshot is a picture of a computer screen; a screen clipping is a picture of part of a screen, such as a window or button.

INSERT AND FORMAT SHAPES, WORDART, AND SMARTART

Insert Shapes

Ribbon Method

▶ Position the insertion point in the desired location

▶ Click the **Insert tab**, then click the **Shapes button** in the Illustrations group

▶ In the gallery of shapes, click an appropriate shape, then use the Crosshair pointer ╋ to draw the shape

Insert WordArt

Ribbon Method

▶ Click the **Insert tab**, then click the **WordArt button** in the Text group

▶ Select a WordArt style from the gallery, type the text in the text box that appears, then drag the **WordArt** into position in your document

▶ Use the Drawing Tools Format tab as needed to format and customize the WordArt graphic

Modify WordArt

Ribbon Method

▶ Click the **WordArt object**, then click the **Drawing Tools Format tab** if it is not the active tab

▶ Use the buttons in the Text group to edit the text, change the spacing, set the letter height as even, or change the text direction

▶ Use the buttons in the WordArt Styles group to change the style, text fill color, text outline color, or text effects

▶ Use the buttons in the Shape Styles group to change the style, shape fill, shape outline, or shape effects

▶ Use the buttons in the Arrange group to position and add text wrapping

▶ Use the buttons in the Size group to resize the WordArt object

Insert SmartArt Graphics

Ribbon Method

▶ Position the insertion point where you want the SmartArt graphic to be inserted in the document

▶ Click the **Insert tab**, then click the **SmartArt button** in the Illustrations group

▶ In the Choose a SmartArt Graphic dialog box, click the category of diagram in the left pane, select a specific diagram layout and design in the middle pane, then preview your selection in the right pane

▶ Click **OK**

▶ Replace the placeholder text and use the SmartArt Tools Design and Format tabs as needed to format and customize the SmartArt graphic

Word

Modify SmartArt Graphics

Ribbon Method

▶ Click the **SmartArt graphic**, then click the **SmartArt Tools Design tab** if it is not the active tab
▶ Use the buttons in the Create Graphic group to move and arrange SmartArt shapes
▶ Use the buttons in the Layouts group to change the SmartArt graphic layout
▶ Use the buttons in the SmartArt Styles group to change colors and styles
▶ Use the buttons in the Arrange group to position and add text wrapping
▶ Click the **SmartArt Tools Format tab** to modify shapes, shape styles, WordArt styles, arrangement, and size

Insert Text in SmartArt Graphics

Shortcut Method

▶ Click the **placeholder box**, then type appropriate text
▶ Press **[Shift][Enter]** to move to a new line in a placeholder box
OR
▶ Click the **text pane arrow** to expand the text pane, then type appropriate text
▶ Press **[↓]** or **[↑]** to move between placeholder boxes, or click the **placeholder box**
▶ Press **[Shift][Enter]** to move to a new line in a placeholder box

Add Text to a Shape

Mouse Method

▶ Click the **Insert tab**, click the **Shapes button**, then select a shape to insert at the location of the insertion point
▶ Double-click the **shape**, then type the text

Shortcut Method

▶ Right-click the **shape**, then click **Add Text** on the shortcut menu
▶ Type the text

Modify Text on a Shape

Ribbon Method

▶ Select the text
▶ Click the **Home tab**, then click buttons in the Font group to apply formatting characteristics
OR

▶ Select the text, click the **Drawing Tools Format tab**, then select options in the WordArt Styles group to apply formatting characteristics

Shortcut Method

▶ Select the text in a shape
▶ Point to a button on the Mini toolbar to modify the text

OR

▶ Select text in a WordArt or SmartArt shape
▶ Right-click the text, click **Font** on the Shortcut menu to open the Font dialog box, then specify formatting options

Add Captions

Ribbon Method

▶ Select a shape, WordArt graphic, or SmartArt graphic
▶ Click the **References tab**, then click **Insert Caption** in the Captions group
▶ In the Caption dialog box, click the **Label list arrow** to choose a label or click **New Label** to type the name of a new label and click **OK**

OR

▶ Click the **Exclude label from caption check box** to remove the label
▶ Click the **Location list arrow** to choose a position for the label, type a caption in the Caption text box, choose any other options as necessary, then click **OK**

Shortcut Method

▶ Right-click a shape, WordArt graphic, or SmartArt graphic in your document, then click **Insert Caption** on the shortcut menu
▶ In the Caption dialog box, click the **Label list arrow** to choose a label or click **New Label** to type the name of a new label, then click **OK**

OR

▶ Click the **Exclude label from caption check box** to remove the label
▶ Click the **Location list arrow** to choose a position for the label, type a caption in the Caption text box, choose any other options as necessary, then click **OK**

Set Shape Styles: Fill and Border

Ribbon Method

▶ Select a shape

Word

▶ Click the **Drawing Tools Format tab**, click the **More button** ⯆ in the Shape Styles group, then click a style from the gallery

OR

▶ Select a shape
▶ Click the **Drawing Tools Format tab**, then click the **launcher** 🡒 in the Shape Styles group to open the Format Shape dialog box
▶ Click a category in the left pane, then select specific options in the right pane

OR

▶ Select a shape
▶ Click the **Drawing Tools Format tab**
▶ Click the **Shape Fill list arrow** in the Shape Styles group and click an option from the palette to change the shape fill, click the **Shape Outline list arrow** and click an option from the palette to change the shape's border, or click the **Shape Effects list arrow** to choose an effect on the menu

Shortcut Method
▶ Right-click a shape, then click **Format Shape** on the shortcut menu to open the Format Shapes dialog box
▶ Click a category in the left pane, then select specific options in the right pane

OR

▶ Right-click a shape, then click the **Shape Fill list arrow** 🖌 on the Mini toolbar and click an option from the palette to change the shape fill; or click the **Shape Outline list arrow** ✎ on the Mini toolbar and click an option from the palette to change the shape's border

Set Shape Styles: Text
Ribbon Method
▶ Click the shape, then select the text in the shape
▶ Click the **Text Effects list arrow**, then select the effect you want to apply to the text in the shape

Adjust Position
Ribbon Method
▶ Select the shape or WordArt graphic, then click the **Drawing Tools Format tab**, or select a SmartArt graphic and click the **SmartArt Tools Format tab**
▶ Click the **Position button** in the Arrange group, then click an appropriate option on the menu; or click **More Layout Options** to open the Layout dialog box and apply advanced options

OR

▶ On the Drawing Tools Format tab or the SmartArt Tools Format tab, click the **launcher** 🖳 in the Size group to open the Layout dialog box

▶ Click the **Position tab** to specify horizontal, vertical, and additional position options, then click **OK**

Shortcut Method

▶ Right-click the shape, WordArt, or SmartArt graphic, then click **More Layout Options** on the shortcut menu

▶ In the Layout dialog box, click the **Position tab** to specify horizontal, vertical, and additional position options, then click **OK**

Note: Use the Text Wrapping options to specify the way text flows around an object.

Adjust Size

Ribbon Method

▶ Select the WordArt graphic or shape, then click the **Drawing Tools Format tab** or select a SmartArt graphic and click the **SmartArt Tools Format tab**

▶ Type values in the Shape Height and Shape Width text boxes in the Size group

OR

▶ On the Drawing Tools Format tab or the SmartArt Tools Format tab, click the **launcher** 🖳 in the Size group to open the Layout dialog box

▶ On the Size tab, enter appropriate values in the Height, Width, Rotate, and Scale sections, then click **OK** to resize the graphic precisely

Shortcut Method

▶ Right-click the shape, WordArt, or SmartArt graphic, then click **More Layout Options** on the shortcut menu

▶ In the Layout dialog box, click the **Size tab**; enter appropriate values in the Height, Width, Rotate, and Scale sections; then click **OK**

Mouse Method

▶ Select the shape, WordArt, or SmartArt graphic, move the mouse over a corner sizing handle, then drag the **Diagonal Resize pointer** ⬂ or the **Diagonal Resize pointer** ⬀ to resize the graphic proportionally

OR

▶ Move the mouse over a side, top, or bottom sizing handle, then press **[Ctrl]** and drag the **Horizontal Resize pointer** ⟺ or the **Vertical Resize pointer** ↨ to resize the graphic vertically or horizontally while keeping the center position fixed

OR

▶ Move the mouse over a corner sizing handle, then press **[Ctrl]** and drag the **Diagonal Resize pointer** ⬉ or the **Diagonal Resize pointer** ⬈ to resize the graphic diagonally while keeping the center position fixed

OR

▶ Move the mouse over a corner sizing handle, then press **[Shift] [Ctrl]** and drag the **Diagonal Resize pointer** ⬉ or the **Diagonal Resize pointer** ⬈ to resize the graphic proportionally while keeping the center position fixed

INSERT AND FORMAT CLIP ART

Insert Clip Art

Ribbon Method

▶ Position the insertion point in the desired location
▶ Click the **Insert tab**, then click the **Clip Art button** in the Illustrations group
▶ In the Clip Art task pane, type the search criteria in the Search for text box, use the **Results should be list arrow** to identify the format to find, click the **Include Office.com content check box** if you want to search for clip art on Office.com, then click **Go**
▶ Position the ⬚ pointer over the image you want to insert
▶ Click the list arrow that appears, then click **Insert**, or click an image to insert it

Organize Clip Art

▶ In the Clip Art task pane, position the pointer ⬚ over the online image that you want to add to the Clip Organizer
▶ Click the list arrow that appears, then click **Make Available Offline**
▶ In the Copy to Collection dialog box, click a collection folder in which to store the clip art, then click **OK**; or click **New** to create and name a new folder, then click **OK**

Add Clip Art to a Collection in the Clip Organizer

▶ In the Clip Art task pane, position the pointer ⬚ over the image that you want to add to a collection in the Clip Organizer
▶ Click the list arrow that appears, then click **Copy to Collection**

▶ In the Copy to Collection dialog box, click a collection folder in which to store the clip art, then click **OK**; or click **New** to create and name a new folder, then click **OK**

Remove Clip Art from the Clip Organizer

▶ In the Clip Art task pane, position the pointer over the image you want to remove from the Clip Organizer
▶ Click the list arrow that appears, then click **Delete from Clip Organizer**
▶ Click **OK** in the Microsoft Clip Organizer message box that appears stating that "This will delete the selected clip(s) from all collections" in the Clip Organizer

Add Captions

Ribbon Method

▶ Select a graphic
▶ Click the **References tab**, then click **Insert Caption** from the Captions group
▶ In the Caption dialog box, click the **Label list arrow** to choose a label or click **New Label** to type the name of a new label, then click **OK**

OR

▶ Click the **Exclude label from caption check box** to remove the label
▶ Click the **Location list arrow** to choose a position for the label, type a caption in the Caption text box, choose any other options as necessary, then click **OK**

Shortcut Method

▶ Right-click a graphic in your document, then click **Insert Caption** on the shortcut menu
▶ In the Caption dialog box, click the **Label list arrow** to choose a label or click **New Label** to type the name of a new label and click **OK**

OR

▶ Click the **Exclude label from caption check box** to remove the label
▶ Click the **Location list arrow** to choose a position for the label, type a caption in the Caption text box, choose any other options as necessary, then click **OK**

Apply Artistic Effects to Photographs

Ribbon Method

▶ Click the **Insert tab**, click the **Picture button** in the Illustrations group, navigate to the location where the picture you want to insert is stored, click the picture, then click **Insert**

▶ Click the picture, then click the **Artistic Effects button** in the Adjust group on the Picture Tools Format tab

▶ Click the artistic effect you want to apply to the picture

OR

▶ Click the **Artistic Effects button** in the Adjust group on the Picture Tools Format tab, then click **Artistic Effects Options** to open the Format Shape dialog box

▶ Click the **Artistic Effect list arrow**, select an effect, then adjust the transparency and intensity as needed or reset the picture

Compress Pictures

Ribbon Method

▶ Select the clip art graphic to compress, then click the **Picture Tools Format tab**

▶ Click the **Compress Pictures button** 🖼 in the Adjust group to open the Compress Pictures dialog box

▶ Click the **Apply only to this picture check box** if necessary to select it

▶ Select a Target output option, then click **OK** to reduce the file size of the graphic

Adjust Position

Ribbon Method

▶ Follow the steps in bullets 1–4 in the Adjust Position Ribbon Method under Insert and Format Pictures in a Document Ribbon Method

Shortcut Method

▶ Follow the steps in bullets 1–4 in the Adjust Position Shortcut Method under Insert and Format Pictures in a Document Ribbon Method

Adjust Size

Ribbon Method

▶ Follow the steps in bullets 1–4 in the Adjust Size Ribbon Method under Insert and Format Pictures in a Document Ribbon Method

Shortcut Method

▶ Follow the steps in bullets 1–2 in the Adjust Size Shortcut Method under Insert and Format Pictures in a Document Ribbon Method

Mouse Method

▶ Follow the steps in bullets 1–2 in the Adjust Size Shortcut Method under Insert and Format Pictures in a Document Ribbon Method

ROTATE A GRAPHIC

Ribbon Method

▶ Click the graphic to select it, then click the **Picture Tools Format tab** or **Drawing Tools Format tab** depending on the graphic type selected

▶ Click the **launcher** 🔲 in the Size group to open the Layout dialog box, enter appropriate values in the Rotate section on the Size tab, then click **OK** to rotate the graphic precisely

OR

▶ Click the **Rotate button** 🔄▾ in the Arrange group, click the appropriate option or click **More Rotation Options** to open the Layout dialog box, then enter the rotation value

Mouse Method

▶ Click the graphic, position the pointer over the green rotation handle, then use the Rotation pointer 🔄 to drag the green rotation handle

OR

▶ Press **[Shift]**, then use the Rotation pointer 🔄 to drag the green rotation handle in 15-degree increments

APPLY AND MANIPULATE TEXT BOXES

Insert a Text Box

Ribbon Method

▶ Position the insertion point where you want the text box to appear, click the **Insert tab**, then click the **Text Box button** in the Text group

▶ Select a preformatted text box from the gallery

OR

▶ Position the insertion point where you want the text box to appear, click the **Insert tab**, click the **Text Box button** in the Text group, click **Draw Text Box**, or click the **Shapes button** in the Illustrations group, then click the **Text Box icon** 🔲

▶ Use the crosshair pointer ┼ to draw a text box, then type text

Format a Text Box

Ribbon Method

- ▶ Select a text box
- ▶ Click the **Drawing Tools Format tab**, then click the **launcher** ☒ in the Shape Styles group to open the Format Shape dialog box
- ▶ Click **Text Box** in the left pane, then select Text layout, Autofit, and Internal margin options in the right pane

Shortcut Method

- ▶ Right-click a text box, then click **Format Shape** on the shortcut menu to open the Format Shapes dialog box
- ▶ Click **Text Box** in the left pane, then select Text layout, Autofit, and Internal margin options in the right pane

Save a Selection to the Text Box Gallery

Ribbon Method

- ▶ Select a text box you'd like to save to the Text Box gallery
- ▶ Click the **Insert tab**, click the **Text Box button**, then click **Save Selection to Text Box Gallery**
- ▶ In the Create New Building Block dialog box, type a name for the text box in the Name box, select other options as desired, then click **OK**

  OR

- ▶ Select a text box you'd like to save to the Text Box gallery
- ▶ Click the **Insert tab**, click the **Quick Parts button**, then click **Save Selection to Quick Part Gallery**
- ▶ In the Create New Building Block dialog box, type a name for the text box in the Name box, click the **Gallery list arrow** and click **Text Boxes**, select other options as desired, then click **OK**

Note: Building blocks are reusable parts accessible in galleries and stored in the Building Blocks Organizer.

Apply Text Box Styles

Ribbon Method

- ▶ Select a text box
- ▶ Click the **Drawing Tools Format tab**, click the **More button** ☒ in the Shape Styles group, then click a style from the gallery

  OR

- ▶ Select a text box
- ▶ Click the **Drawing Tools Format tab**, then click the **launcher** ☒ in the Shape Styles group to open the Format Shape dialog box
- ▶ Click a category in the left pane, such as Fill or Line Color, then select specific options in the right pane

OR
- ▶ Select a text box
- ▶ Click the **Drawing Tools Format tab**
- ▶ Click the **Shape Fill button** in the Shape Styles group and click an option from the palette to change the shape fill, click the **Shape Outline button** and click an option from the palette to change the shape's border, or click the **Shape Effects button** to choose an effect on the menu

Shortcut Method
- ▶ Right-click a text box, then click the **Shape Fill list arrow** 🎨 ▾ on the Mini toolbar and choose an option from the palette to change the fill of the text box; or click the **Shape Outline list arrow** ✏️ ▾ on the Mini toolbar and choose an option from the palette to change the text box outline
- ▶ Right-click a text box, then click **Format Shape** on the shortcut menu to open the Format Shapes dialog box
- ▶ Click a category in the left pane, then select specific options in the right pane

Change Text Direction

Ribbon Method
- ▶ Select a text box
- ▶ Click the **Drawing Tools Format tab**, click the **Text Direction button** in the Text group, click an option on the menu, or click **Text Direction Options** to open the Text Direction - Text Box dialog box and select additional options

Apply Shadow Effects

Ribbon Method
- ▶ Select a text box
- ▶ Click the **Drawing Tools Format tab**, click the **Shape Effects button** in the Shape Styles group, click **Shadow** on the menu, then click an option from the submenu or click **Shadow Options** to open the Format Shape dialog box where you can specify advanced options

  OR
- ▶ Select a text box
- ▶ Click the **Drawing Tools Format tab**, then click the **launcher** 🔲 in the Shape Styles group to open the Format Shape dialog box
- ▶ Click **Shadow** in the left pane, then select advanced options in the right pane

Shortcut Method

▶ Right-click a text box, then click **Format Shape** on the shortcut menu to open the Format Shape dialog box
▶ Click **Shadow** in the left pane, then select advanced options in the right pane

Apply 3-D Effects

Ribbon Method

▶ Select a text box
▶ Click the **Drawing Tools Format tab**, click the **Shape Effects button** in the Shape Styles group, click **Bevel** on the menu, then click an option on the menu or click **3-D Options** to open the Format Shape dialog box
▶ In the left pane, click **3-D Format** or **3-D Rotation**, then select advanced options in the right pane

OR

▶ Select a text box
▶ Click the **Drawing Tools Format tab**, then click the **launcher** 🔲 in the Shape Styles group to open the Format Shape dialog box
▶ Click **3-D Format** or **3-D Rotation** in the left pane, then select advanced options in the right pane

Shortcut Method

▶ Right-click a text box, then click **Format Shape** on the shortcut menu to open the Format Shape dialog box
▶ Click **3-D Format** or **3-D Rotation** in the left pane, then select advanced options in the right pane

WORD CORE OBJECTIVE 5: PROOFREADING DOCUMENTS

VALIDATE CONTENT BY USING SPELLING AND GRAMMAR CHECKING OPTIONS

Check the Spelling and Grammar in a Document

Ribbon Method

▶ Click the **Review tab**, then click the **Spelling & Grammar button** in the Proofing group
▶ In the Spelling and Grammar dialog box, make appropriate selections and use the buttons to ignore or change possible spelling or grammar errors

Shortcut Method

▶ Press **[F7]** to open the Spelling and Grammar dialog box, then follow the steps in bullet 2 in the Check the Spelling and Grammar in a Document Ribbon Method

Note: Word automatically checks spelling and grammar as you type. Word flags words that might be misspelled with a red wavy underline and questionable grammatical construction with a wavy green underline. You can right-click a word that has a red or green wavy underline and see a shortcut menu with suggestions for corrections.

Turn Grammar Checking On or Off

Ribbon Method

▶ Click the **File tab** to open Backstage view, then click the **Options button** to display the Word Options dialog box
▶ Click **Proofing** in the left pane
▶ In the When correcting spelling and grammar section of the right pane, click the **Check grammar with spelling check box**, if necessary, to insert a check mark to turn on grammar checking or to remove the check mark to turn off grammar checking
▶ Click **OK**

   OR

▶ Click the **Review tab**, then click the **Spelling & Grammar button** in the Proofing group
▶ In the Spelling and Grammar dialog box, click the **Check grammar check box** to insert a check mark to turn on grammar checking or remove the check mark to turn off grammar checking

Set Grammar

Ribbon Method

▶ Click the **Review tab**, then click the **Spelling & Grammar button** in the Proofing group
▶ In the Spelling and Grammar dialog box, click the **Options button** to open the Word Options dialog box
▶ In the right pane, in the Correcting Spelling and Grammar section, click the **Writing Style list arrow** and choose **Grammar Only** if it is not already selected, then click the **Settings button**
▶ In the Grammar Settings dialog box, select appropriate options, then click **OK**
▶ Click **OK** in the Word Options dialog box to return to the Spelling and Grammar dialog box

   OR

Word

▶ Click the **File tab** to open Backstage view, then click the **Options button** to display the Word Options dialog box
▶ Click **Proofing** in the left pane
▶ In the When Correcting Spelling and Grammar section of the right pane, click the **Writing Style list arrow** and choose **Grammar & Style**, then click the **Settings button**
▶ In the Grammar Settings dialog box, select appropriate options, then click **OK**
▶ Click **OK** to close the Word Options dialog box

Set Style Options

Ribbon Method

▶ Click the **Review tab**, then click the **Spelling & Grammar button** in the Proofing group
▶ In the Spelling and Grammar dialog box, click the **Options button**
▶ In the When Correcting Spelling and Grammar section of the Word Options dialog box, click the **Writing Style list arrow** and choose **Grammar & Style**, then click the **Settings button**
▶ In the Grammar Settings dialog box, select appropriate options, then click **OK**
▶ Click **OK** in the Word Options dialog box to return to the Spelling and Grammar dialog box

OR

▶ Click the **File tab** to open Backstage view, then click the **Options button** to open the Word Options dialog box
▶ Click **Proofing** in the left pane
▶ In the When Correcting Spelling and Grammar section of the right pane, click the **Writing Style list arrow** and choose Grammar & Style, then click the **Settings button**
▶ In the Grammar Settings dialog box, select appropriate options, then click **OK**
▶ Click **OK** to close the Word Options dialog box

CONFIGURE AUTOCORRECT SETTINGS

Add or Remove Exceptions

Ribbon Method

▶ Click the **File tab** to open Backstage view, then click **Options** to open the Word Options dialog box
▶ Click **Proofing** in the left pane
▶ In the right pane, click the **AutoCorrect Options button**
▶ Click the **AutoCorrect tab** in the AutoCorrect dialog box if it is not the active tab

▶ Click the **Exceptions button** to open the Exceptions dialog box
▶ Make appropriate selections within each tab, then click **OK**
▶ Click **OK** in the AutoCorrect dialog box, then click **OK** in the Word Options dialog box

Turn AutoCorrect On and Off

Ribbon Method

▶ Click the **File tab** to open Backstage view, then click **Options** to display the Word Options dialog box
▶ Click **Proofing** in the left pane
▶ In the right pane, click the **AutoCorrect Options button** to open the AutoCorrect dialog box
▶ To turn off AutoCorrect, click the **Replace text as you type check box** to remove the check mark
▶ To turn AutoCorrect on, click the **Replace text as you type check box** to insert a check mark
▶ In the AutoCorrect dialog box, click **OK**, then click **OK** in the Word Options dialog box

INSERT AND MODIFY COMMENTS IN A DOCUMENT

Insert a Comment

Ribbon Method

▶ Select the text (or existing comment) that you want to comment on, click the **Review tab**, then click the **New Comment button** in the Comments group
▶ Type the text for your comment in the balloon

Edit a Comment

Ribbon Method

▶ Click the **Review tab**, click the **Track Changes list arrow** in the Tracking group, then click **Change Tracking Options**
▶ In the Markup section in the Track Changes Options dialog box, click the **Comments list arrow**, then select a color

OR

▶ In the Balloons section in the Track Changes Options dialog box, select appropriate options, then click **OK**

OR

▶ Click in a comment, then make text changes

Delete a Comment

Ribbon Method

▶ Click a comment to select it
▶ Click the **Review tab**, click the **Delete list arrow** in the Comments group, then click **Delete** or another appropriate option

Shortcut Method

▶ Right-click a comment
▶ Click **Delete Comment** on the shortcut menu

View a Comment from Another User

Ribbon Method

▶ Open a document that contains comments from another user
▶ If the comments are not displayed, click the **Review tab**, click the **Show Markup list arrow** in the Tracking group, then click **Comments** to insert a check mark beside it to indicate that comments should be displayed in the document

OR

▶ Click the **Review tab**, click the **Show Markup list arrow** in the Tracking group, point to **Reviewers**, then click **All Reviewers** to show all comments in the document or click the name of the reviewer whose comments you want to show

View Comments Inline

Ribbon Method

▶ Click the **Review tab**, click the **Show Markup list arrow** in the Tracking group, point to **Balloons**, then click **Show All Revisions Inline**

View Comments as Balloons

Ribbon Method

▶ Click the **Review tab**, click the **Show Markup list arrow** in the Tracking group, point to **Balloons**, then click **Show Only Comments and Formatting in Balloons**

Word Core Objective 6: Applying References and Hyperlinks

Apply a Hyperlink

Apply a Hyperlink to Text or a Graphic

Ribbon Method

- ▶ Select the text or picture you want to create as a hyperlink, click the **Insert tab**, then click the **Hyperlink button** in the Links group
- ▶ In the Insert Hyperlink dialog box, click the option you want to link to in the Link to list, complete the rest of the Insert Hyperlink dialog box based on the Link to option you selected, then click **OK**

Shortcut Method

- ▶ Right-click the text or picture you want to create as a hyperlink, then click **Hyperlink** on the shortcut menu that opens
- ▶ Follow the steps in bullet 2 in the Apply a Hyperlink to Text or a Graphic Ribbon Method

  OR

- ▶ Select the text or picture you want to create as a hyperlink, then press **[Ctrl][K]**
- ▶ Follow the steps in bullet 2 in the Apply a Hyperlink to Text or a Graphic Ribbon Method

Use a Hyperlink as a Bookmark

Ribbon Method

- ▶ Select the text you want to create as a hyperlink, click the **Insert tab**, then click the **Hyperlink button** in the Links group
- ▶ In the Insert Hyperlink dialog box, click the **Bookmark button** to open the Select Place in Document dialog box
- ▶ Click an option under Select an existing place in the document, click **OK**, then click **OK** in the Insert Hyperlink dialog box

Shortcut Method

- ▶ Right-click the text or picture you want to create as a hyperlink, then click **Hyperlink** on the shortcut menu that opens
- ▶ Follow the steps in bullets 2–3 in the Use a Hyperlink as a Bookmark Ribbon Method

  OR

- ▶ Select the text or picture you want to create as a hyperlink, then press **[Ctrl][K]**

▶ Follow the steps in bullets 2–3 in the Use a Hyperlink as a Bookmark Ribbon Method

Link a Hyperlink to an E-mail Address

Ribbon Method

▶ Select the text that you want to create as a hyperlink to an e-mail address, click the **Insert tab**, then click the **Hyperlink button** in the Links group
▶ In the Insert Hyperlink dialog box, click the **E-mail Address option** in the Link to list
▶ In the Insert Hyperlink dialog box, type the text to display in the Text to display text box, type the e-mail address that you want to link to in the E-mail address text box or choose one from the list of recently used e-mail addresses at the bottom of the text box, type a subject for the e-mail message in the Subject text box, then click **OK**

Shortcut Method

▶ Right-click the text or picture you want to create as a hyperlink to an e-mail address, then click **Hyperlink** on the shortcut menu that opens
▶ Follow the steps in bullets 2–3 in the Link a Hyperlink to an E-mail Address Ribbon Method

OR

▶ Select the text or picture you want to create as a hyperlink to an e-mail address, then press **[Ctrl][K]**
▶ Follow the steps in bullets 2–3 in the Link a Hyperlink to an E-mail Address Ribbon Method

CREATE ENDNOTES AND FOOTNOTES IN A DOCUMENT

Insert Endnotes and Footnotes

Ribbon Method

▶ Position the insertion point where you want to insert the note reference mark, click the **References tab**, then click the **Insert Footnote button** or **Insert Endnote button** in the Footnotes group
▶ Type the text for the endnote or footnote

Note: Footnotes are used to provide details about the text and are located below the text or at the bottom of the page. Endnotes are used to provide references for text and are located at the end of the section or end of the document.

Shortcut Method

▶ Position the insertion point where you want to insert the note reference mark

▶ To insert a footnote, press **[Ctrl][Alt][F]**

▶ To insert an endnote, press **[Ctrl][Alt][D]**

▶ Type the text for the endnote or footnote

Manage Footnote and Endnote Locations

Ribbon Method

▶ Click the **References tab**, then click the **launcher** in the Footnotes group to open the Footnote and Endnote dialog box

▶ To change the location, click the **list arrow** beside Footnotes or Endnotes and choose a new location

▶ Click **Apply**

Convert Footnotes to Endnotes or Endnotes to Footnotes

Ribbon Method

▶ Click the **References tab**, then click the **launcher** in the Footnotes group to open the Footnote and Endnote dialog box

▶ In the Location section of the dialog box, click the **Convert button** to open the Convert Notes dialog box

▶ Choose an appropriate option, then click **OK**

Configure Footnote and Endnote Formatting

Ribbon Method

▶ Click the **References tab**, then click the **launcher** in the Footnotes group to open the Footnote and Endnote dialog box

▶ In the Format section of the dialog box, click the **Number format list arrow** and choose a new format; or click the **Symbol button** to open the Symbol dialog box where you can select a symbol, then click **OK**

▶ Click **Insert**

View Endnotes and Footnotes for a Presentation

Ribbon Method

▶ Click the **View tab**, then click the **Two Pages button** to view two pages of the document at once in Page Layout view
OR

▶ Click the **View tab**, then click the **Full Screen Reading button** to view the document on the full screen and scroll through the document

Change Footnote and Endnote Numbering

Ribbon Method

▶ Click the **References tab**, then click the **launcher** 🔲 in the Footnotes group to open the Footnote and Endnote dialog box
▶ In the Format section of the dialog box, click the **Start at list arrow** and choose a new starting value; or click the **Numbering list arrow** to choose a different numbering method
▶ Click **Insert**

CREATE A TABLE OF CONTENTS IN A DOCUMENT

Create a Table of Contents and Use Default Formats

Ribbon Method

▶ Assign headings and subheadings to text in the document using the buttons in the Styles group
▶ Position the insertion point where you want the table of contents to appear
▶ Click the **References tab**, then click the **Table of Contents list arrow** in the Table of Contents group
▶ Select an option from the Table of Contents menu
  OR
▶ On the Table of Contents menu, click **Insert Table of Contents**
▶ In the Table of Contents dialog box, click **OK** to accept the default formatting options

Set Levels

Ribbon Method

▶ Click the **References tab**, then click the **Table of Contents button** in the Table of Contents group, and click **Insert Table of Contents** to open the Table of Contents dialog box
▶ In the General area, use the Show levels up and down arrows to change the number of levels to show in the table of contents, then click **OK**
▶ Click **OK** if a Microsoft Word box opens asking to replace the current table of contents
  OR
▶ Click the **References tab**, then click the **Table of Contents button** in the Table of Contents group, and click **Insert Table of Contents** to open the Table of Contents dialog box
▶ Click the **Options button** to open the Table of Contents Options dialog box

▶ Set the table of contents level in the right column that matches the style you want to use in the left column, then click **OK**

▶ Click **OK** in the Table of Contents dialog box, then click **OK** in the Microsoft Word box that opens asking to replace the current table of contents

Set Alignment

Ribbon Method

▶ Click the **References tab**, click the **Table of Contents button** in the Table of Contents group, then click **Insert Table of Contents** to open the Table of Contents dialog box

▶ In the General area, click the **Right align page numbers check box** to remove the check mark and align the page number after the heading in the table of contents, or click the **Right align page numbers check box** to insert a check mark and right-align the page numbers, then click **OK**

▶ Click **Yes** if a Microsoft Word dialog box opens asking to replace the current table of contents

Set Tab Leaders

Ribbon Method

▶ Click the **References tab**, click the **Table of Contents button** in the Table of Contents group, then click **Insert Table of Contents** to open the Table of Contents dialog box

▶ In the Print Preview area, make sure the **Right align page numbers check box** contains a check mark, click the **Tab Leader list arrow** and choose an appropriate option, then click **OK**

▶ Click **Yes** in the Microsoft Word dialog box to replace the selected table of contents

Modify Styles

Ribbon Method

▶ Use styles to assign headings and subheadings to text in your document

▶ Click the **References tab**, click the **Table of Contents button** in the Table of Contents group, then click **Insert Table of Contents** to open the Table of Contents dialog box

▶ Click the **Modify button** to open the Style dialog box

▶ Select the style you want to modify from the Styles list, then click the **Modify button** to open the Modify Style dialog box

▶ Select appropriate options, then click **OK**

▶ Click **OK** in the Style dialog box, then click **OK** in the Table of Contents dialog box

▸ Click **OK** in the Microsoft Word box asking to replace the current table of contents

Apply a Different Format to the Table of Contents

Ribbon Method

▸ Use styles to assign headings and subheadings to your document
▸ Click the **References tab**, click the **Table of Contents button** in the Table of Contents group, then click **Insert Table of Contents** to open the Table of Contents dialog box
▸ Click the **Formats list arrow** in the General section, scroll as needed to select a new format, click the format you want to apply, then click **OK**
▸ Click **OK** if a Microsoft Word dialog box opens asking to replace the current table of contents

Update a Table of Contents: Page Numbers or Entire Table

Ribbon Method

▸ Make changes to the document (such as changing page numbers or deleting heads and their subtext)
▸ Click an entry in the table of contents to select the table of contents, click the **References tab**, then click the **Update Table button** in the Table of Contents group
▸ In the Update Table of Contents dialog box, click **Update page numbers only** or **Update entire table**, then click **OK**
▸ Click the **Table of Contents head** (or anywhere in the document) to deselect the table of contents

Shortcut Method

▸ Make changes to the document (such as changing page numbers or deleting heads and their subtext)
▸ Right-click the **table of contents**, then click **Update Field** on the shortcut menu that opens
▸ Follow the steps in bullets 3–4 in the Update a Table of Contents: Page Numbers or Entire Table Ribbon Method
  OR
▸ Make changes to the document (such as changing page numbers or deleting heads and their subtext)
▸ Click the **table of contents** to select it, then click the **Update Field tab**
▸ Follow the steps in bullets 3–4 in the Update a Table of Contents: Page Numbers or Entire Table Ribbon Method

Word Core Objective 7: Performing Mail Merge Operations

Set Up Mail Merge

Perform a Mail Merge Using the Mail Merge Wizard

Ribbon Method

▶ Click the **Mailings tab**, click the **Start Mail Merge button** in the Start Mail Merge group, then click **Step by Step Mail Merge Wizard**

▶ In the Mail Merge task pane, click the **Letters option button** (or another type of document you are working on), then click **Next: Starting document**

▶ In Step 2 of 6, click the **option button** next to the description of your starting document; if you select Start from a template or Start from an existing document, follow the onscreen directions to navigate to the file you want to use, click it, then click **OK** or **Open**; then click **Next: Select Recipients**

▶ In Step 3 of 6, click the **option button** next to the recipient list you want to use, then follow the onscreen directions to create the list or navigate to and open an existing list, then click **Next: Write your letter**

▶ In Step 4 of 6, write your letter inserting merge fields where appropriate, click **More items** to select individual merge fields to insert, then click **Next: Preview your letters**

▶ In Step 5 of 6, use the **arrow buttons** in the task pane to preview your letters, make changes if necessary, then click **Next: Complete the merge**

▶ In Step 6 of 6, click **Print** to send the merged document directly to a printer or click **Edit individual letters** to create a merge file that you can edit if you'd like to personalize one or more of the letters before printing

▶ Click the **Close box** to close the task pane

Perform a Mail Merge Manually

Ribbon Method

▶ Click the **Mailings tab**, click the **Start Mail Merge button** in the Start Mail Merge group, then click **Letters**

▶ Click the **Select Recipients button** in the Start Mail Merge group, click **Type New List** and click **Create** to create a new list, click **Use Existing List** to use a list that was created previously, or click **Select from Outlook Contacts**, then create the list or navigate to the file, select the file, then click **OK**

▶ Position the insertion point where you want to insert a field in the document, then use the buttons in the Write & Insert Fields group to insert an Address Block, insert a Greeting Line, or select a field on the menu that opens when you click the Insert Merge Field button

▶ Repeat the step in bullet 3 until you have inserted all merge fields in your document

▶ Click the **Preview Results button** in the Preview Results group

▶ Click the **Finish and Merge button** in the Finish group, then click **Edit Individual Documents** to create a merge file that you can edit, click **Print Documents** to send the merged document directly to the printer, or click **Send E-mail Messages** to create e-mail messages

▶ Select appropriate options in the dialog box that opens, then click **OK**

Use Auto Check for Errors

Ribbon Method

▶ Click the **Mailings tab**, then click **Auto Check for Errors** in the Preview Results group

▶ In the Checking and Reporting Errors dialog box, select an appropriate option, then click **OK**

Shortcut Method

▶ Press **[Alt][Shift][K]**

▶ In the Checking and Reporting Errors dialog box, select an appropriate option, then click **OK**

Execute Mail Merge: Preview and Print a Mail Merge Operation

Ribbon Method

▶ Click the **Mailings tab**, click the **Start Mail Merge button** in the Start Mail Merge group, then click **Step by Step Mail Merge Wizard**

▶ In the Mail Merge task pane, follow the steps to set up the documents for the mail merge and to merge the documents

▶ In Step 6 of 6 in the Mail Merge task pane, click **Print** to send the merged document directly to a printer, or click **Edit individual letters** to create a merge file that you can edit if you'd like to personalize one or more of the letters before printing

OR

▶ Click the **Mailings tab**, then use the buttons in the Start Mail Merge group, the Write & Insert Fields group, and the Preview Results group to set up and merge the documents for the mail merge

▶ Click the **Finish & Merge button**, then click **Print Documents** to open the Merge to Printer dialog box

▶ Make appropriate selections in the Merge to Printer dialog box, then click **OK** to open the Print dialog box

▶ Make adjustments as needed to meet your needs, then click **OK** to print the merged file

WORD EXPERT OBJECTIVES

WORD EXPERT OBJECTIVE 1: SHARING AND MAINTAINING DOCUMENTS

CONFIGURE WORD OPTIONS

Change Default Program Options

Ribbon Method

▶ Click the **File tab** to open Backstage view, then click **Options** to open the Word Options dialog box
▶ Click a category (such as General, Display, Proofing, Advanced) in the left pane, then select options in the right pane associated with that category
▶ Click **OK** to accept the changes and close the dialog box

Change Spelling Options

Ribbon Method

▶ Click the **File tab** to open Backstage view, then click **Options** to open the Word Options dialog box
▶ Click **Proofing** in the left pane, then select the appropriate spelling options in the right pane
▶ Click **OK** to accept the changes and close the dialog box

Change Grammar Checking Options

Ribbon Method

▶ Click the **File tab** to open Backstage view, then click **Options** to open the Word Options dialog box
▶ Click **Proofing** in the left pane, then select the appropriate grammar checking options in the right pane
▶ Click **OK** to accept the changes and close the dialog box

APPLY PROTECTION TO A DOCUMENT

Restrict Editing

Ribbon Method

▶ Click the **File tab** to open Backstage view, then click **Options** to open the Word Options dialog box
▶ Click **Customize Ribbon** in the left pane, click the **Developer check box** in the Customize the Ribbon Main Tabs list box, then click **OK** to display the Developer tab on the Ribbon

▶ Click the **Developer tab**, click **Design Mode** in the Controls group if it is active to make it nonactive, then click the **Restrict Editing button** in the Project group to open the Restrict Formatting and Editing pane

▶ In the Editing restrictions area, click the **Allow only this type of editing in the document: check box**, then click the **list arrow** and select the type of editing you want to allow

▶ Click the **Yes, Start Enforcing Protection button**, then enter and confirm a password in the Start Enforcing Protection dialog box when prompted if you want the restrictions to be password-protected

▶ Click **OK** in the Start Enforcing Protection dialog box to close the dialog box and restrict the document

Apply Controls or Restrictions to a Document

Ribbon Method

▶ Click the **File tab** to open Backstage view, then click **Options** to open the Word Options dialog box

▶ Click **Customize Ribbon** in the left pane, click the **Developer check box** in the Customize the Ribbon Main Tabs list box, then click **OK** to display the Developer tab on the Ribbon

▶ Click the **Developer tab**, click **Design Mode** in the Controls group if it is active to make it nonactive, then click the **Restrict Editing button** in the Project group to open the Restrict Formatting and Editing pane

▶ In the Formatting restrictions area, click the **Limit formatting to a selection of styles: check box**, then click the **settings link** and select the type of restrictions you want

▶ Click the **Yes, Start Enforcing Protection button**, then enter and confirm a password in the Start Enforcing Protection dialog box when prompted if you want the restrictions to be password-protected

▶ Click **OK** in the Start Enforcing Protection dialog box to close the dialog box and restrict the document

APPLY A TEMPLATE TO A DOCUMENT

Modify an Existing Template

Ribbon Method

▶ Click the **File tab** to open Backstage view, click **Open**, navigate to the location where the template you want to modify is stored, click the template you want to modify, then click **Open** to close the Open dialog box and open the template in the Word window as a template

Word

▶ Make the changes you want to make to the template, then click the **Save button** on the Quick Access toolbar to save the template to its current location

Shortcut Method

▶ Click the **File tab** to open Backstage view, click **Open**, navigate to the location where the template you want to modify is stored, then double-click the template you want to modify and open in the Word window as a template
▶ Make the changes you want to make to the template, then click the **Save button** on the Quick Access toolbar to save the template to its current location

Create a New Template

Ribbon Method

▶ Click the **File tab** to open Backstage view, click **New**, click **Blank document**, then click the **Create button** to open a new blank document
▶ Make the changes you want to make to the document (such as headings, boilerplate text, or a logo), then click the **Save button** on the Quick Access toolbar to open the Save As dialog box
▶ In the Save As dialog box, navigate to the location where you want to save the template, type the name of the template in the File name text box, click the **Save as type list arrow**, then select **Word Template (*.dotx)**
▶ Click **Save** to close the Save as dialog box and to save the document as a template

Apply a Template to an Existing Document

Ribbon Method

▶ Open the Word document to which you want to apply a template, then show the **Developer tab:** Click the **File tab** to open Backstage view, click **Options** to open the Word Options dialog box, click **Customize Ribbon** in the left pane, click the **Developer check box** in the Main Tabs list box, then click **OK** to display the Developer tab on the Ribbon
▶ On the Developer tab, click the **Document Template button** in the Templates group to open the Templates and Add-ins dialog box with the Templates tab active
▶ In the Templates and Add-ins dialog box, click the **Attach button** in the Document template area, navigate to the location of the template you want to apply, click the template you want to apply, then click **Open** to close the Attach Template dialog box

▶ Click the **Automatically update document styles check box** in the Document template area to select it, then click **OK** to close the Templates and Add-ins dialog box and to attach the selected template

Manage Templates by Using the Organizer

Ribbon Method

▶ Click the **File tab** to open Backstage view, click **Open**, navigate to the location where the template you want to modify is stored, click the template you want to modify, then click **Open** to close the Open dialog box and open the template in the Word window

▶ Show the Developer tab: Click the **File tab** to open Backstage view, click **Options** to open the Word Options dialog box, click **Customize Ribbon** in the left pane, click the **Developer check box** in the Main Tabs list box, then click **OK** to display the Developer tab on the Ribbon

▶ Click the **Developer tab**, click the **Document Template button** in the Templates group to open the Templates and Add-ins dialog box with the Templates tab active, then click the **Organizer button**

▶ Verify the filename of the source document appears in the Styles available in list box in the left pane; if it does not, click the **Close File button**, navigate to the location of the template you want to be the source file, then double-click the file you want to be the source file

▶ Verify the filename of the destination document appears in the Styles available in list box in the right pane; if it does not, click the **Close File button**, navigate to the location of the template you want to be the destination file, then double-click the file you want to be the destination file

▶ Click the style you want to copy from the source file to the destination file, then click the **Copy button**

▶ Click the style you want to rename, click the **Rename button**, type the new name, then click **OK** to close the Rename dialog box

▶ Click the style you want to delete, click the **Delete button**, then click **Yes** to confirm the deletion

▶ When you are finished copying, naming, and deleting styles, click the **Close button** to close the Organizer dialog box

Word

Word Expert Objective 2: Formatting Content

Apply Advanced Font and Paragraph Attributes

Use Character Attributes

Ribbon Method

▶ Select the text to which you want to apply character attributes, then click the **launcher** ⊡ in the Font group on the Home tab to open the Font dialog box with the Font tab active

▶ On the Font tab in the Font dialog box, select the attributes you want to apply, including font, font style, size, font color, underline style, underline color, and effects (such as small caps, all caps, superscript, subscript)

▶ On the Advanced tab in the Font dialog box, select the attributes you want to apply including scale, spacing, position, and kerning

▶ On the Advanced tab in the Font dialog box, click the **Text Effects button** to open the Format Text Effects dialog box, select the text effects you want to apply, including text fill, text outline, outline style, shadow, reflection, glow and soft edges, and 3-D format, then click the **Close button** to close the Format Text Effects dialog box

▶ Click **OK** to close the Font dialog box and apply the settings you selected

Mouse Method

▶ Select the text to which you want to apply character attributes, right-click the selected text to open a menu, then on the menu, click **Font** to open the Font dialog box

▶ Follow the steps in bullets 2–5 in the Use Character Attributes Ribbon Method

Use Character-Specific Styles

Ribbon Method

▶ Select the text to which you want to apply character-specific styles, then click the **launcher** ⊡ in the Font group on the Home tab to open the Font dialog box with the Font tab active

▶ On the Advanced tab in the Font dialog box, select the character-specific attributes you want to apply, including OpenType features such as ligatures, number spacing, number forms, and stylistic sets

▶ Click **OK** to close the Font dialog box and apply the settings you selected

Mouse Method

▶ Select the text to which you want to apply character-specific styles, right-click the selected text to open a menu, then on the menu, click **Font** to open the Font dialog box with the Advanced tab active

▶ Follow the steps in bullets 2–3 in the Use Character-Specific Styles Ribbon Method

CREATE TABLES AND CHARTS

Insert Tables by Using Microsoft Excel Data in Tables

Ribbon Method

▶ Open the Word document you want to insert the table in

▶ Click the **Insert tab**, click the **Table button** in the Tables group, then click **Excel Spreadsheet** to open a blank spreadsheet in the document as an object

▶ Type data in the cells in the spreadsheet, then use the tools on the Excel Ribbon to format the data in the spreadsheet

▶ Click the document outside the spreadsheet to deselect the spreadsheet object and to make the Word Ribbon the active Ribbon

Apply Formulas or Calculations on a Table

Ribbon Method

▶ Open a Word document, create a table, then enter data in the table

▶ Position the insertion point in the column (or row) where you want to perform the calculation

▶ Click the **Layout tab** on the Table Tools tab, then click the **Formula button** in the data group to open the Formula dialog box

▶ Delete any text in the Formula dialog box, type **=**, click the **Paste function list arrow** in the Formula dialog box, select a function from the list, then, in parentheses, insert the cell references of the cells you want to include in the calculation

▶ Click **OK** to close the Formula dialog box and see the result of the calculation

Shortcut Method

▶ Follow the steps in bullets 1–5 in the Apply Formulas or Calculations on a Table *except* in bullet 4, type the formula in the Formula text box instead of selecting it using the Paste function list arrow

Modify Chart Data

Ribbon Method

▶ Open a document with a chart, then click the chart to select it
▶ Click the **Chart Tools Design tab**, then click the **Edit Data button** in the Data group to open the Excel worksheet
▶ Modify the chart data, exit Excel, and return to the Word document to view the modified chart data

Save a Chart as a Template

Ribbon Method

▶ Open a document with a chart that you want to save as a chart template, then modify the chart as needed to reflect what you want it to be in the template
▶ Be sure the chart is active, then click the **Chart Tools Design tab** if it is not the active tab
▶ Click the **Save as Template button** in the Type group to open the Save Chart Template dialog box, then navigate to the location where you want to save the template if that location is different from the default location, which should appear in the address box
▶ Type a name for the chart in the File name text box, then click **Save** to save the chart as a template

Modify Chart Layout

Ribbon Method

▶ Open a document with a chart whose chart layout you want to modify, select the chart, then click the **Chart Tools Layout tab**
▶ Use the buttons in the Labels group to make changes to the chart title, axis titles, legend, data labels, and data table
▶ Use the buttons in the Axes group to make changes to the horizontal and vertical axes and to the gridlines
▶ Use the buttons in the Background group to make adjustments to the plot area, the chart wall, the chart floor, and the 3-D rotation
▶ Save the document

CONSTRUCT REUSABLE CONTENT IN A DOCUMENT

Create Customized Building Blocks

Ribbon Method

▶ Select the content you want to use as a customized building block (such as a company letterhead or logo)
▶ Click the **Insert tab**, click the **Quick Parts button** in the Text group, then click **Save Selection to Quick Part Gallery**
▶ Type the name for the quick part in the Name text box

▶ Click the **Gallery list arrow** and select a different gallery if you want to save to a gallery other than the Quick Parts gallery (the one listed by default)

▶ Click the **Category list arrow** and select a different category if you want to save in a category other than the General category (the one listed by default)

▶ Click the **Description text box**, then type a description of the quick part

▶ Click **OK** to save the customized quick part with the settings you specified

Save a Selection as a Quick Part

Save a Header as a Quick Part

Ribbon Method

▶ Select the header you want to save as a quick part

▶ Click the **Header button** in the Header & Footer group on the Header & Footer Tools Design tab, then click **Save Selection to Header Gallery**

Save a Footer as a Quick Part

Ribbon Method

▶ Select the footer you want to save as a quick part

▶ Click the **Footer button** in the Header & Footer group on the Header & Footer Tools Design tab, then click **Save Selection to Footer Gallery**

Save Selected Content as a Quick Part

Ribbon Method

▶ Select the content you want to save as a quick part

▶ Follow the steps in bullets 2–7 in the Create Customized Building Blocks Ribbon Method

Save Quick Parts After a Document Is Saved

Ribbon Method

▶ Click the **Insert tab**, click the **Quick Parts button** in the Text group, then click **Building Blocks Organizer** to open the Building Blocks Organizer dialog box

▶ Select the building block you want in the list of Building blocks that you want to save

▶ Click the **Edit Properties button** in the Building Blocks Organizer dialog box to open the Modify Building Block dialog box

▶ Click the **Save in list arrow** in the Modify Building Block dialog box, then select the template in which you want to save the building block

▶ Click **OK** to close the Modify Building Block dialog box, then click **Yes** when prompted to save the building block in the selected template
▶ Click **Close** to close the Building Blocks Organizer dialog box

Insert Text as a Quick Part

Ribbon Method

▶ Click the location in the document where you want the Quick Part to appear
▶ Click the **Insert tab**, then click the **Quick Parts button** in the Text group to open the Quick Parts gallery
▶ Click the quick part text in the gallery that you want to insert in the document, or click **AutoText** and select the autotext quick part that you want to insert in the document

Add Content to a Header or Footer

Ribbon Method

▶ Click the **Insert tab**, then click the **Header button** in the Header & Footer group to open the Header gallery
▶ Click the header style of your choice to insert that header in the Header area
▶ Replace placeholder text in a content control with text of your choice, or select the content control and delete it

Note: To select and delete a content control, click the placeholder text, click the content control handle that appears, then press [Delete].

▶ Click the **Quick Parts button** in the Insert group on the Header & Footer Tools Design tab, click **Document Property**, select a document property on the menu that opens to insert a document property (such as author or company name) content control in the header, then replace the placeholder text in the document property content control with text of your choice
▶ Click the **Close Header and Footer button** in the Close group to close the Header area and return to the document

Mouse Method

▶ Double-click the header to open the header or footer
▶ Type text directly into the Header area, or click the **Quick Parts button** in the Insert group on the Header & Footer Tools Design tab, click **Document Property**, select a document property on the menu that opens to insert a document property (such as author or company name) content control in the header, then

replace the placeholder text in the document property content control with text of your choice
▶ Double-click in the document to close the Header area

Ribbon Method
▶ Click the **Insert tab**, then click the **Footer button** in the Header & Footer group to open the Footer gallery
▶ Click the footer style of your choice to insert that footer in the Footer area
▶ Replace placeholder text in a content control with text of your choice, or select the content control and delete it

Note: To select and delete a content control, click the placeholder text, click the content control handle that appears, then press [Delete].

▶ Click the **Quick Parts button** in the Insert group on the Header & Footer Tools Design tab, click **Document Property**, select a document property on the menu that opens to insert a document property (such as author or company name) content control in the Footer, then replace the placeholder text in the document property content control with text of your choice
▶ Click the **Close Header and Footer button** in the Close group to close the Footer area and return to the document

Mouse Method
▶ Double-click the Footer area to open the footer
▶ Type text directly into the Footer area, or click the **Quick Parts button** in the Insert group on the Header & Footer Tools Design tab, click **Document Property**, select a document property on the menu that opens to insert a document property (such as author or company name) content control in the Footer, then replace the placeholder text in the document property content control with text of your choice
▶ Double-click in the document to close the Footer area

LINK SECTIONS

Link Text Boxes

Ribbon Method
▶ Click the **Insert tab**, click the **Text Box button** in the Text group, then click **Draw Text Box** on the menu that opens
▶ Position the insertion point where you want the text box to appear in the document, click the pointer to draw a text box, then fill it with text
▶ Create a second empty text box

Word

▶ Select the **first text box**, click the **Create Link button** in the Text group on the Drawing Tools Format tab to activate the link pointer, then click the **second text box** with the link pointer to link the boxes so that overflow text from the first text box will flow into the second text box

Break Links Between Text Boxes

Ribbon Method

▶ Open a document with linked text boxes, then select the **first text box**
▶ Click the **Break Link button** in the Text group on the Drawing Tools Format tab to break the link

Link Different Sections

Via Header Area

Ribbon Method

▶ Open a document that contains sections, open the Header area on page 1 of the document, then click the **Next button** in the Navigation group to move to the next section
▶ Verify Link to Previous is active to link the sections

Note: To unlink sections, move to the second of two linked sections, then click Link to Previous so it is no longer active and to break the link between the two sections.

Via Footer Area

Ribbon Method

▶ Open a document that contains sections, open the Footer area on page 1 of the document, then click the **Next button** in the Navigation group to move to the next section
▶ Verify Link to Previous is active to link the sections

Note: To unlink sections, move to the second of two linked sections, then click Link to Previous so it is no longer active and to break the link between the two sections.

WORD EXPERT OBJECTIVE 3: TRACKING AND REFERENCING DOCUMENTS

REVIEW, COMPARE, AND COMBINE DOCUMENTS

Apply Tracking

Ribbon Method

▶ Open a document to which you want to apply tracked changes

▶ Click the **Review tab**, then click the **Track Changes button** in the Tracking group to make tracking active

Merge Different Versions of a Document

Ribbon Method

▶ Click the **File tab** to open Backstage view and see the list of autosaved versions of the active document

Note: Word autosaves the document at regular intervals as you work on the document.

▶ Click the version you want to view

Note: The version opens in a new document window.

▶ Click **Compare** on the Message bar at the top of the document window

Note: The version you selected is merged with the most current version, and changes between the two documents are shown as tracked changes.

Track Changes in a Combined Document

Ribbon Method

▶ Click the **Review tab**, click **Compare** in the Compare group, then click **Combine** to open the Combine Documents dialog box
▶ Click the **Browse button** in the Original document section, navigate to the location of the file you want to open and combine with another document, click the filename, then click **Open**
▶ Click the **Browse button** in the Revised document section, navigate to the location of the file you want to open and combine with the document you opened in bullet 2, click the filename, then click **Open**
▶ Click **OK** to close the Combine Documents dialog box and to open the two documents in a new document window with differences between the documents shown as tracked changes
▶ Use the tools in the Changes group on the Review tab to accept, reject, or add changes

Review Comments in a Combined Document

Ribbon Method

▶ Follow the steps in bullets 1–4 in the Track Changes in a Combined Document Ribbon Method
▶ Use the tools in the Comments group on the Review tab to accept, reject, or add comments

CREATE A REFERENCE PAGE

Add Citations

Ribbon Method

▶ Place the insertion point where you want the citation marker to appear
▶ Click the **References tab**, click the **Style list arrow** in the Citations & Bibliography group, then select the style you want to use for the citations (such as MLA Sixth Edition)
▶ Click the **Insert Citation button** in the Citations & Bibliography group, then click **Add New Source** to open the Create Source dialog box
▶ In the Create Source dialog box, click the **Type of Source list arrow**, then select the type of source (such as book)
▶ Enter information about your source in the Create Source dialog box, then click **OK** to close the Create Source dialog box and add the citation to the document
▶ Click the citation to select it, click the **Citation Options list arrow** on the right side of the citation, then click **Edit Citation**
▶ Make adjustments (such as suppressing the author, year, or title) in the Edit Citation dialog box, then click **OK**

Manage Sources

Ribbon Method

▶ Open a document with sources or add sources to an existing document
▶ Click the **References tab**, then click the **Manage Sources button** in the Citations & Bibliography group to open the Source Manager dialog box
▶ Use the tools in the Source Manager dialog box to copy, delete, or edit existing sources, or to create new sources

Note: You can move sources from the Master list, which contains all the sources stored on the computer, to the Current list, which are the sources specific to the active document and vice versa.

▶ Click **Close** to close the Source Manager dialog box

Compile a Bibliography

Ribbon Method

▶ Open a document with sources or add sources to an existing document
▶ Click the **Reference tab**, then position the insertion point where you want the bibliography to be inserted

▶ Click **Bibliography** in the Citations & Bibliography group, then click **Bibliography** on the menu (or Works Cited depending on the type of resources you plan to list)
▶ Use tools on the Home tab to make adjustments to the formatting (such as using the same font as the font used in the document)
▶ If changes are made to any of the sources in the document or if new sources are added after the bibliography is added, click the **Bibliography field** at the top of the bibliography, click **Update Citations and Bibliography** on the tab at the top of the Bibliography field, then click outside the Bibliography field to deselect the bibliography and confirm the changes

Apply Cross References

Ribbon Method

▶ Create the object you want to cross-reference (such as a picture with a caption or a numbered list)
▶ Position the insertion point where you want the cross-reference to be located in the document
▶ Click the **References tab**, click the **Cross-reference button** in the Captions group to open the Cross-reference dialog box
▶ Click the **Reference type list arrow**, then select the type of reference you are cross-referencing (such as a figure)
▶ Click the **Insert reference to list arrow**, then select what you want to reference (such as a figure caption)
▶ Select the **Insert as a hyperlink check box** if you want the cross-reference to be a hyperlink to the object you are referencing
▶ Click **Insert** to insert the cross-reference based on the specifications you set in the Cross-reference dialog box
▶ Click the **Close button** to close the Cross-reference dialog box

CREATE A TABLE OF AUTHORITIES IN A DOCUMENT

Apply Default Formats

Ribbon Method

▶ Open a document that has citations or add citations to a document, then click the **References tab**
▶ Select the first citation in the document that you want to include in the Table of Authorities, then click the **Mark Citation button** in the Table of Authorities group
▶ In the Mark Citations dialog box, click the citation you want to mark, then click the **Mark button** or the **Mark All button**
▶ Continue to mark citations using the Mark Citation dialog box

Word

▶ Position the insertion point where you want the Table of Authorities to appear in the document, then click the **Insert Table of Authorities button** in the Table of Authorities group to open the Table of Authorities dialog box

▶ Click **OK** to accept the default formats in the Table of Authorities dialog box and to insert the Table of Authorities based on the citations you marked in the document

Adjust Alignment

Ribbon Method

▶ Open a document with a Table of Authorities, then click in the **Table of Authorities** to select it

▶ Click the **Insert Table of Authorities button** in the Table of Authorities group on the References tab

▶ Click the **Formats list arrow** in the Table of Authorities dialog box, then click **From template**

Note: You must select the From Template format before you can modify the alignment or other styles in a Table of Authorities.

▶ Click the **Modify button** to open the Style dialog box

▶ Click **Table of Authorities** in the Styles list box, then click the **Modify button** to open the Modify Style dialog box

▶ Click the **Increase indent button**, click **OK** until the message asking you if you want to replace the Table of Authorities appears, then click **OK**

Apply a Tab Leader

Ribbon Method

▶ Open a document with a Table of Authorities, then click in the **Table of Authorities** to select it

▶ Click the **Insert Table of Authorities button** in the Table of Authorities group on the References tab

▶ Accept the default format or click the **Formats list arrow** and select a format for the Table of Authorities

Note: You must select a format for the Table of Authorities before you apply a leader line.

▶ Accept the default Tab leader style or click the **Tab leader list arrow** and select a Tab leader format

▶ Click **OK** to close the Table of Authorities dialog box and generate or update the Table of Authorities based on the settings in the Table of Authorities dialog box

Modify Styles

Ribbon Method

▶ Open a document with a Table of Authorities, then click in the **Table of Authorities** to select it
▶ Click the **Insert Table of Authorities button** in the Table of Authorities group on the References tab
▶ Click the **Formats list arrow** in the Table of Authorities dialog box, then click **From template**

Note: You must select the From Template format before you can modify the alignment or other styles in a Table of Authorities.

▶ Click the **Modify button** to open the Style dialog box
▶ Click **Table of Authorities** in the Styles list box, then click the **Modify button** to open the Modify Style dialog box
▶ Apply new formats (such as a different font, font size, alignment) to the entries in the Table of Authorities
▶ Click **OK** until the message asking you if you want to replace the Table of Authorities appears, then click **OK**

Mark Citations

Ribbon Method

▶ Open a document that has citations or add citations to a document, then click the **References tab**
▶ Select the first citation in the document that you want to include in the Table of Authorities, then click the **Mark Citation button** in the Table of Authorities group to open the Mark Citation dialog box
▶ Click the **Category list arrow**, then select the category with which the selected citation is associated (such as Cases)
▶ Type a short citation in the Short citation text box if you want to include one
▶ Click the **Mark button** or **Mark all button** to mark the citation in the document, then return to the document
▶ Follow the steps in bullets 2–5 to continue to mark citations until all citations are marked

Use Passim (Short Form)

Ribbon Method

▶ Open a document with a Table of Authorities, click the **Table of Authorities** to select it, then click the **Insert Table of Authorities button** in the Table of Authorities group on the References tab
▶ Click the **Use Passim check box** to select it

Note: The Passim check box must be checked and a short citation must be in the Short citation text box in the Mark Citation dialog box for the short citation to appear in the Table of Authorities.

CREATE AN INDEX IN A DOCUMENT

Specify an Index Type

Ribbon Method

▶ Open a document with an index, click the **index** to select it, click the **References tab**, then click **Insert Index** in the Index group to open the Insert dialog box

▶ Click the **Formats list arrow**, then select the format type in the list that you want to apply to the index

▶ Click the **Type Indented option button** or the **Type Run-in option button** to identify how subentries are listed, then click **OK** to close the Index dialog box and return to the modified index

Specify Columns

Ribbon Method

▶ Open a document with an index, click the **index** to select it, click the **References tab**, then click **Insert Index** in the Index group to open the Insert dialog box

▶ Click in the **Columns text box**, then type the number for the number of columns you want to apply to the index, or click the **up arrow** or the **down arrow** to identify the number of columns

▶ Click **OK** to close the Index dialog box and return to the modified index

Specify a Language

Ribbon Method

▶ Open a document with an index, click the **index** to select it, click the **References tab**, then click **Insert Index** in the Index group to open the Insert dialog box

▶ Click the **Language list arrow**, select the language in the list that you want to apply to the index, then click **OK** to close the Index dialog box and return to the modified index

Modify an Index

Ribbon Method

▶ Open a document with an index, click the **index** to select it, click the **References tab**, then click **Insert Index** in the Index group to open the Insert dialog box

▶ Follow the steps in bullets 1–3 in the Specify an Index Type Ribbon Method, the steps in bullets 1–3 in the Specify Columns Ribbon Method, and the steps in bullets 1–2 in the Specify a Language Ribbon Method to modify those features of an index

▶ Click the **Format list arrow**, then click **From template**

Note: The From template format must be applied in order for the Modify button to become available.

▶ Click the **Modify button** in the Index dialog box to open the Style dialog box, select an Index style in the Styles list, then click the **Modify button** to open the Modify Style dialog box

▶ Select settings in the Modify Style dialog box that you want to apply to the selected index style, then click **OK** when all settings are identified to return to the Style dialog box

▶ Select a different index style, then repeat the step in the preceding bullet

▶ Click **OK** to close all open dialog boxes, then click **Yes** when asked if you want to replace the selected index and return to the modified index

Mark Index Entries

To Mark Main Entries

Ribbon Method

▶ Open or create a document that contains words and phrases you want to include in an index

▶ Click **Find** in the Editing group on the Home tab to open the Navigation pane

▶ Type the word or phrase you want to mark as an index entry, click the first instance of that word or phrase in the results list in the Navigation pane, then select that word or phrase in the document

Note: The search highlights the word or phrase in yellow, but it is not selected; you need to select the word or phrase using the pointer.

▶ Click the **Reference tab**, click the **Mark Entry button** in the Index group to open the Mark Index Entry dialog box, then verify the word you selected appears in the Main entry text box

▶ Click the **Mark button** to identify the selected term as a main entry, or click the **Mark All button** to mark all instances of the selected word or phrase as a main entry

▶ Continue to follow the steps in bullets 3–5 to mark entries as main entries

Shortcut Method

▶ Follow the step in bullet 1 in the Ribbon Method to Mark Main Entries

Word

▶ Press **[Ctrl][F]** to open the Navigation pane
▶ Follow the steps in bullets 3–6 in the Ribbon Method to Mark Main Entries

To Mark Subentries

Ribbon Method

▶ Follow the steps in bullets 1–4 in the Ribbon Method to Mark Main Entries to identify the word or phrase you want to be a subentry
▶ Select the word or phrase in the Main Entry text box (such as "carrot"), then type the word or phrase you want to be the main entry (such as "Vegetable")
▶ Click the **Subentry text box**, then type the word or phrase that is currently selected in the document and that you deleted from the Main entry text box (such as "carrot," in the example above)
▶ Click the **Mark button** to identify the selected term as a subentry, or click the **Mark All button** to mark all instances of the selected word or phrase as a subentry
▶ Continue to follow the steps in bullets 1–4 to mark entries as subentries

Shortcut Method

▶ Follow the step in bullet 1 in the Ribbon Method to Mark Subentries, but press **[Ctrl][F]** to open the Navigation pane
▶ Select the word or phrase in the Main Entry text box (such as "carrot"), press **[Ctrl][X]** to delete the word or phrase, then type the word or phrase you want to be the main entry (such as "Vegetable")
▶ Click the **Subentry text box**, then press **[Ctrl][V]** to insert the word or phrase you deleted from the Main entry text box (such as "carrot," in the example above) in the Subentry text box
▶ Follow the steps in bullets 4–5 in the Ribbon Method to Mark Subentries

To Mark Cross-References

Ribbon Method

▶ Follow the steps in bullets 1–4 in the Ribbon Method to Mark Main Entries to identify the word or phrase you want to be a cross-reference
▶ Select the word or phrase in the Main Entry text box (such as "whole wheat bread"), then type the word or phrase you want to be the main entry (such as "Bread")
▶ Click the **Cross-reference option button**, then type the word or phrase that is currently selected in the document and that you deleted from the Main entry text box (such as "whole wheat

bread," in the example above) after the word *See* in the Cross-reference text box
► Click the **Mark button** to identify the selected term as a cross-reference
► Continue to follow the steps in bullets 2–4 to mark entries as cross-references

Shortcut Method

► Follow the step in bullet 1 in the Ribbon Method to Mark Cross-References, but press **[Ctrl][F]** to open the Navigation pane
► Select the word or phrase in the Main Entry text box (such as "whole wheat bread"), press **[Ctrl][X]** to delete the word or phrase, then type the word or phrase you want to be the main entry (such as "Bread")
► Click the **Cross-reference option button**, click after *See* in the Cross-reference text box, then press **[Ctrl][V]** to insert the word or phrase you deleted from the Main entry text box (such as "whole wheat bread," in the example above) in the Subentry text box
► Follow the steps in bullets 4–5 in the Ribbon Method to Mark Cross-References

Word Expert Objective 4: Performing Mail Merge Operations

Execute Mail Merge

Merge Rules

Ribbon Method

► Use commands on the Mailings tab to create a mail merge main document, or open the mail merge main document if saved previously, then position the insertion point in the location in the document where you want the rule to apply
► Click the **Mailings tab** if it is not the active tab, then click the **Rules button** in the Write & Insert Fields group
► In the list that opens, click the rule you want to insert in the main document

Send Personalized E-mail Messages to Multiple Recipients

Ribbon Method

► Open a new blank document, click the **Mailings tab**, click the **Start Mail Merge button** in the Start Mail Merge group, then click **Step by Step Mail Merge Wizard** to open the Mail Merge task pane

▶ Select the **E-mail messages option button** in the Step 1 of 6 Mail Merge task pane, then click **Next: Starting document**

▶ Select the option button for the type of starting document you want to use in the Step 2 of 6 Mail Merge task pane

▶ Click **Next: Select recipients** when you are finished, then as directed in the Step 3 of 6 Mail Merge task pane, select the option button for the type of recipients list (data source) you want to use

Note: If you choose to use an existing list, click Browse, navigate to the data source file you want to use, select the file, then click OK. You can use one of your Outlook contacts lists as a data source, or create a new data source. To perform an e-mail merge, the data source you use must include a field for e-mail addresses.

▶ Click **Next: Write your e-mail message** when you are finished, then as directed in the Step 4 of 6 Mail Merge task pane, type the body text of the message in the document window

Note: If you want the body text of your e-mail message to contain customized data (a greeting line, for example), make sure to add the merge fields to the body text. You do not need to add a merge field for the e-mail address to the body text of the e-mail message.

▶ Click **Next: Preview the message** when you are finished, then as directed in the Step 5 of 6 Mail Merge task pane, preview the merged data in the e-mail message

▶ Click **Next: Complete the Merge** when you are finished, then as directed in the Step 6 of 6 Mail Merge task pane, click **Electronic Mail** to complete the merge and open the Merge to E-mail dialog box

▶ Click the **To list arrow** in the Merge to E-mail dialog box, then select the **field name** for e-mail addresses in your data source

▶ Type a message subject in the Subject line text box, then click the **Mail format list arrow** to select the e-mail format you want to use for your e-mail messages

▶ Click **OK** when you are finished to send the merged e-mail messages through your default e-mail program

Shortcut Method

▶ Instead of using the Step by Step Mail Merge Wizard, use the commands on the Mailings tab to follow the steps in bullets 1–10 in the Send Personalized E-mail Messages to Multiple Recipients Ribbon Method

CREATE A MAIL MERGE BY USING OTHER DATA SOURCES

Use Microsoft Outlook Tables as a Data Source for a Mail Merge Operation

Ribbon Method

▶ Click the **Mailings tab**, click the **Start Mail Merge button** in the Start Mail Merge group, then click **Step by Step Mail Merge Wizard** to open the Mail Merge task pane
▶ Select the option button for the type of document you want to create in the Step 1 of 6 Mail Merge task pane
▶ Click **Next: Starting document** when you are finished, then as directed in the Step 2 of 6 Mail Merge task pane, click the **Select from Outlook Contacts option button** for the type of starting document you want to use
▶ Click **Next: Select recipients** when you are finished, then as directed in the Step 3 of 6 Mail Merge task pane, click the **Choose Contacts Folder option button** to open the Choose Profile dialog box if there is more than one profile stored on this computer
▶ In the Choose Profile dialog box, click the **Profile Name list arrow** to select the profile you want to use, then click **OK** to open the Select Contacts dialog box
▶ In the Select Contacts dialog box, select the contact list you want to use as the data source, then click **OK** to open the Mail Merge Recipients dialog box
▶ In the Mail Merge Recipients dialog box, modify the list of recipients as needed, then click **OK** to close the Mail Merge Recipients dialog box
▶ Click **Next: Write your letter** when you are finished, then as directed in the Step 4 of 6 Mail Merge task pane, type the letter and insert the merge fields in the document
▶ Click **Next: Preview the letter** when you are finished, then as directed in the Step 5 of 6 Mail Merge task pane, preview the merged data in a letter
▶ Click **Next: Complete the merge** when you are finished, then in the Step 6 of 6 Mail Merge task pane, click **Print** to print the merged envelopes, or click **Edit individual letters** to merge to a new document, where you can modify the individual letters as needed, then print or save the merged document

Word

Shortcut Method

▶ Instead of using the Step by Step Mail Merge Wizard, use the commands on the Mailings tab to follow the steps in bullets 1–10 in the Use Microsoft Outlook Tables as a Data Source for a Mail Merge Operation Ribbon Method

Use Access Tables as a Data Source for a Mail Merge Operation

Ribbon Method

▶ Follow the steps in bullets 1–3 in the Use Microsoft Outlook Tables as a Data Source for a Mail Merge Operation Ribbon Method

▶ Click **Next: Select recipients** when you are finished, then as directed in the Step 3 of 6 Mail Merge task pane, click the **Use an existing list option button**, click **Browse**, navigate to the Access database file you want to use as your data source, select the file, then click **Open** to open the Access table in the Mail Merge Recipients dialog box

Note: If the database you are using has multiple tables, double-click the table you want to use.

▶ In the Mail Merge Recipients dialog box, modify the list of recipients as needed, then click **OK** to close the Mail Merge Recipients dialog box

▶ Follow the steps in bullets 8–10 in the Use Microsoft Outlook Tables as a Data Source for a Mail Merge Operation Ribbon Method

Shortcut Method

▶ Instead of using the Step by Step Mail Merge Wizard, use the commands on the Mailings tab to follow the steps in bullets 1–4 in the Use Access Tables as a Data Source for a Mail Merge Operation Ribbon Method

Use Excel Tables as a Data Source for a Mail Merge Operation

Ribbon Method

▶ Follow the steps in bullets 1–3 in the Use Microsoft Outlook Tables as a Data Source for a Mail Merge Operation Ribbon Method

▶ Click **Next: Select recipients** when you are finished, then as directed in the Step 3 of 6 Mail Merge task pane, click the **Existing list option button**, click **Browse**, navigate to the Excel file you want to use as your data source, select the file, then click **Open** to open the Select Table dialog box

▶ In the Select Table dialog box, select the sheet from the Excel file that you want to use as your data source, then click **OK** to open that sheet in the Mail Merge Recipients dialog box

▶ In the Mail Merge Recipients dialog box, modify the list of recipients as needed, then click **OK** to close the Mail Merge Recipients dialog box

▶ Follow the steps in bullets 8–10 in the Use Microsoft Outlook Tables as a Data Source for a Mail Merge Operation Ribbon Method

Shortcut Method

▶ Instead of using the Step by Step Mail Merge Wizard, use the commands on the Mailings tab to follow the steps in bullets 1–5 in the Use Excel Tables as a Data Source for a Mail Merge Operation Ribbon Method

Use Word Tables as a Data Source for a Mail Merge Operation

Ribbon Method

▶ Follow the steps in bullets 1–3 in the Use Microsoft Outlook Tables as a Data Source for a Mail Merge Operation Ribbon Method

▶ Click **Next: Select recipients** when you are finished, then as directed in the Step 3 of 6 Mail Merge task pane, click the **Existing list option button**, click **Browse**, navigate to the Word file you want to use as your data source, select the file, then click **Open** to open the Word data source in the Mail Merge Recipients dialog box

▶ In the Mail Merge Recipients dialog box, modify the list of recipients as needed, then click **OK** to close the Mail Merge Recipients dialog box

▶ Follow the steps in bullets 8–10 in the Use Microsoft Outlook Tables as a Data Source for a Mail Merge Operation Ribbon Method

Shortcut Method

▶ Instead of using the Step by Step Mail Merge Wizard, use the commands on the Mailings tab to follow the steps in bullets 1–4 in the Use Word Tables as a Data Source for a Mail Merge Operation Ribbon Method

Word

CREATE LABELS AND FORMS

Prepare Data

Ribbon Method

▶ Make sure Step 3 of 6 is displayed at the bottom of the Mail Merge task pane
▶ Select the **Type a new list option button**, then click **Create** to open the New Address List dialog box
▶ Click **Customize Columns**, then modify column field names to meet your needs

Note: You can add, delete, rename, and move column names in the Customize Address List dialog box.

▶ Click **OK** to close the Customize Address List dialog box and return to the New Address List dialog box
▶ In the New Address List dialog box, enter the data for each record, pressing **[Tab]** to move from field to field or to start a new record, then click **OK** when all records are entered to open the Mail Merge Recipients dialog box
▶ In the Mail Merge Recipients dialog box, modify records as needed to meet your needs

Note: You can perform actions such as sort, filter, and edit records.

▶ Click **OK** when you are satisfied with the data source to close the Mail Merge Recipients dialog box

Shortcut Method

▶ Instead of using the Step by Step Mail Merge Wizard, click the **Select Recipients button** in the Start Mail Merge group on the Mailings tab, click **Type New List**, then follow the steps in bullets 2–7 in the Prepare Data Ribbon Method

Create Mailing Labels

Ribbon Method

▶ Click the **Mailings tab**, click the **Start Mail Merge button** in the Start Mail Merge group, then click **Step by Step Mail Merge Wizard** to open the Mail Merge task pane
▶ Click the **Labels option button** in the Step 1 of 6 Mail Merge task pane
▶ Click **Next: Starting document** when you are finished, then as directed in the Step 2 of 6 Mail Merge task pane, select the option button for the type of starting document you want to use: the Change document layout option button or the Start from existing document option button

▶ If you select the Change document layout option button, click **Label options** to open the Label Options dialog box, select the printer information, select the label information including the vendor and product number, or click the **New Label button** to open the Label Details dialog box and create a custom label

▶ Click **OK** to close the Label Details dialog box if it is open, then click **OK** to close the Label Options dialog box

▶ Click **Next: Select recipients** when you are finished, then as directed in the Step 3 of 6 Mail Merge task pane, click the options to select your data; then in the Mail Merge Recipients dialog box, modify the list of recipients as needed and click **OK** to close the Mail Merge Recipients dialog box, OR if the Save Address List dialog box opens, navigate to the location where you want to save the list, then click **Save**

▶ Click **Next: Arrange your labels**, then as directed in the Step 4 of 6 Mail Merge task pane, insert the merge fields in the top-left label

Note: Be sure to use proper spacing and punctuation between fields, and be sure to select the chevrons surrounding a field if you want to format that field, such as to change the font of the field.

▶ When you are satisfied with the layout of the first label, click the **Update all labels button** to copy the layout from the first label to all labels on the page

▶ Click **Next: Preview your labels** when you are finished, then as directed in the Step 5 of 6 Mail Merge task pane, preview labels

▶ Click **Next: Complete the merge** when you are finished, then as directed in the Step 6 of 6 Mail Merge task pane, click **Print** to print the merged envelopes; or click **Edit individual letters** to merge to a new document, modify the individual letters as needed, then print or save the merged document

Shortcut Method

▶ Instead of using the Step by Step Mail Merge Wizard, click **Start Mail Merge** in the Start Mail Merge group on the Mailings tab, click **Labels** to open the Label Options dialog box, then follow the steps in bullets 4–5 in the Create Mailing Labels Ribbon Method

▶ Use the commands on the Mailings tab to follow the steps in bullets 6–10 in the Create Mailing Labels Ribbon Method to create the labels and complete the merge

Word

Create Envelope Forms

Ribbon Method

- ▶ Click the **Mailings tab**, click the **Start Mail Merge button** in the Start Mail Merge group, then click **Step by Step Mail Merge Wizard** to open the Mail Merge task pane
- ▶ Click the **Envelopes option button** in the Step 1 of 6 Mail Merge task pane, then click **Next: Starting document**
- ▶ Click **Envelope options** in the Step 2 of 6 Mail Merge task pane to open the Envelope Options dialog box
- ▶ In the Envelope Options dialog box, click the **Envelope Options tab**, if it is not the active tab, to select the envelope size and the formatting options for the return and delivery addresses
- ▶ Click **OK** in the Envelope Options dialog box when you are finished, then click **Next: Select recipients** in the Mail Merge task pane
- ▶ Select the options for the file you want to use as the data source in the Step 3 of 6 Mail Merge task pane, edit the recipient list as needed, click **OK** to close the Mail Merge Recipients dialog box, then click **Next: Arrange your envelope**
- ▶ Insert the merge field(s) for the recipient address in the envelope main document to arrange the layout of your envelope

Note: Be sure to insert the merge fields in the delivery address placeholder box. Format the merge fields to meet your needs.

- ▶ Click **Next: Preview your envelopes** when you are finished, then as directed in the Step 5 of 6 Mail Merge task pane, preview the merged data in the envelopes
- ▶ Click **Next: Complete the merge** when you are finished, then as directed in the Step 6 of 6 Mail Merge task pane, click **Print** to print the merged envelopes, or click **Edit individual letters** to merge to a new document, modify the individual labels as needed, then print or save the merged document

Shortcut Method

- ▶ Instead of using the Step by Step Mail Merge Wizard, click **Start Mail Merge** in the Start Mail Merge group on the Mailings tab, click **Envelopes** to open the Envelopes Options dialog box, then follow the steps in bullets 4–5 in the Create Envelope Forms Ribbon Method
- ▶ Use the commands on the Mailings tab to follow the steps in bullets 6–9 in the Create Envelope Forms Ribbon Method to create the labels and complete the merge

Create Label Forms

Ribbon Method

▶ Click the **Mailings tab**, then click **Labels** in the Create group to open the Envelope and Labels dialog box with the Labels tab as the active tab

▶ Type the **address** in the Address box, then click the **Options button** to open the Label Options dialog box

▶ In the Label Options dialog box, select the label information, including the vendor and product number, or click the **New Label button** to create a new label

▶ Click **OK** when you are finished, then preview the label in the Label area on the Labels tab of the Envelopes and Labels dialog box

▶ Select the print option that meets your needs, then click **Print** to print the label or click the **New Document button** to display the label in a new document that you can save

WORD EXPERT OBJECTIVE 5: MANAGE MACROS AND FORMS

APPLY AND MANIPULATE MACROS

Record a Macro

Ribbon Method

▶ Show the Developer tab on the Ribbon: Click the **File tab** to open Backstage view, click **Options**, click **Customize Ribbon**, click the **Developer check box** in the right list box to select it, then click **OK**

▶ Click the **Developer tab**, then click **Record Macro** in the Code group to open the Record Macro dialog box

▶ In the Record Macro dialog box, type a name for the macro (for example, Insert&FormatPicture), type a description for the macro, then click **OK**

▶ Perform each of the steps required for the macro

▶ After all the steps for the macro are complete, click the **Developer tab** if it is not the active tab, then click **Stop Recording** in the Code group

Run a Macro

Ribbon Method

▶ Position the insertion point at the location in the document where you want the macro applied, click the **Developer tab** if it is not the active tab, then click **Macros** in the Code group to open the Macros dialog box

▶ In the Macros dialog box, click the macro in the Macro name list box that you want to run, then click **Run**

Apply Macro Security

Ribbon Method

▶ Follow the steps in bullet 1 in the Run a Macro Ribbon Method to show the Developer tab if it is not available on the Ribbon
▶ Click the **Developer tab** if it is not the active tab, then click **Macro Security** in the Code group to open the Trust Center with the Macro Setting tab active
▶ In the Macro Settings area, select the macro settings you prefer, then click **OK** to close the Trust Center and return to the document window

Shortcut Method

▶ Click the **File tab** to open Backstage view, then click **Options** in the left pane to open the Word Options dialog box
▶ Click **Trust Center** in the left pane, then click the **Trust Center Settings button** in the right pane to open the Trust Center with the Macro Setting tab active
▶ Follow the steps in bullet 2 in the Apply Macro Security Ribbon Method

---

APPLY AND MANIPULATE MACROS OPTIONS

Run Macros When a Document Is Opened

Ribbon Method

▶ Create a new blank document in Word, click the **File tab** to open Backstage view, then click **Options**
▶ In the Word Options dialog box, click **Trust Center** in the left pane, click the **Trust Center Settings button** in the right pane, then click **Trusted Locations** in the left pane to open the Trusted Locations pane
▶ Add the trusted location where you want to store a template with the AutoExec and AutoOpen macros, then click **OK** two times to exit the Word Options dialog box and return to the document
▶ Create an AutoExec macro as follows:
  • Click the **Developer tab**, then click **Record Macro** in the Code group to open the Record Macro dialog box
  • Type **AutoExec** as the macro name in the Record Macro dialog box, then click **OK**
  • Click **Stop Recording** in the Code group

- Click **Macros** in the Code group, select **AutoExec** in the list of macros, then click the **Edit button** to open the Microsoft Visual Basic Editor
- In the Microsoft Visual Basic Editor, add the following code to the AutoExec macro: **MsgBox "You're seeing the AutoExec macro in action", vbMsgBoxSetForeground**, then press **[Enter]**
- Click **File** on the menu bar in the Microsoft Visual Basic Editor, click **Save Normal**, click **File** on the menu bar, then click **Close and Return to Microsoft Word** to close the Microsoft Visual Basic Editor and return to Word

▶ Follow the same steps that you used for the AutoExec macro to create an AutoOpen macro, but type **AutoOpen** to replace each instance of AutoExec in each step

▶ Save the document to the location of your choice, close the document, then exit Word

▶ Start Word, click **OK** to accept the message that appears, click the **File tab** to open Backstage view, click **Open**, open the file you saved in the previous bullet, then click **OK** in response to the message

▶ If using a shared computer or if the auto macros are no longer needed, delete the two macros you created as follows:
  - Click the **Developer tab**, then click **Macros** in the Code group
  - Click **AutoExec**, click **[Delete]**, then click **Yes**
  - Click **AutoOpen**, click **[Delete]**, then click **Yes**
  - Click the **Close button**

Run Macros When a Button Is Clicked

Ribbon Method

▶ Open a document with a macro, then be sure a button has been assigned to the macro (see the next skill: Assign a Macro to a Command Button Ribbon Method) and is placed on a Ribbon tab or the Quick Access toolbar

▶ Position the insertion point at the location in the document where you want the macro to run

▶ Click the button assigned to the macro to run the macro at the location of the insertion point

Shortcut Method

▶ If a key combination has been assigned to the macro, position the insertion point at the location in the document where you want the macro to run, then press the assigned key combination to run the macro at the location of the insertion point

Word

Assign a Macro to a Command Button

Ribbon Method

▶ Click the **File tab** to open Backstage view, click **Options**, then click **Customize Ribbon** in the left pane

▶ Click the **Choose commands from: Popular Commands list arrow** in the right pane, click **Macros** to see the list of all macros you have recorded, then click the macro you want to add to the Ribbon

▶ Click the **Customize the Ribbon: Main Tab list arrow** in the right pane, then click **Main Tabs** or **Tool Tabs**

▶ In the Customize the Ribbon Main Tabs (or Tool Tabs) list, click the **New Tab button**, click the new group that appears under the new tab, click the **Rename button**, then type a name for the new group in the Rename dialog box

Note: You can click the New Tab name, click the Rename button, then type a new name for the new tab in the Rename dialog box.

▶ Verify the macro you want to add to the Ribbon is selected in the left list box and the tab and group you want to add the macro to are selected in the right list box, then click the **Add button**

▶ Click the macro in the right pane to select it, then click the **Rename button** to open the Rename dialog box

▶ In the Rename dialog box, select the symbol you want to represent the macro, select the text in the Display name text box, then type the macro name you want to appear in a ScreenTip next to the button symbol

▶ Click **OK** to close the Rename dialog box and to view the symbol you assigned to the macro and the macro name in the list of buttons in the right pane

▶ Click **OK** to see the macro symbol in the group on the tab on the Ribbon that you assigned it to

▶ Click the **macro button** on the Ribbon to run the macro

▶ To remove the macro button from the Ribbon, click the **File tab** to open Backstage view, click **Options**, click **Customize Ribbon**, click the **macro** in the right pane, then click the **Remove button**

Create a Custom Macro Button on the Quick Access Toolbar

Ribbon Method

▶ Click the **File tab** to open Backstage view, click **Options**, then click **Quick Access Toolbar**

▶ Click the **Popular Commands list arrow** in the left pane, then click **Macros** to see a list of all the macros you have recorded

▶ Click the macro you want to add to the Quick Access toolbar, then click the **Add button** to see the macro added to the list of buttons included on the Quick Access toolbar

▶ Click the **Modify button** to open the Modify Button dialog box, then select the symbol you want to represent the macro

▶ Select the contents of the Display name text box, then type the macro name you want to appear in a ScreenTip next to the button symbol on the Quick Access toolbar

▶ Click **OK** to close the Modify Button dialog box to see the symbol you assigned to the macro and the macro name included in the list of buttons on the Quick Access toolbar

▶ Click **OK** to view the macro symbol on the Quick Access toolbar

▶ Click the **macro button** on the Quick Access toolbar to run the macro

▶ To remove the macro button from the Quick Access toolbar, right-click the **macro button**, then click **Remove from Quick Access Toolbar**

Shortcut Method

▶ Click the **Developer tab**, click the **Record Macro button** in the Code group to open the Record Macro dialog box, then click **Button** to open the Word Options dialog box with the Customize Quick Access Toolbar tab active

▶ Follow the steps in bullets 2–9 in the Create a Custom Macro Button on the Quick Access Toolbar Ribbon Method

CREATE FORMS

Use the Controls Group

Ribbon Method

▶ Open a document that you want to contain a form, click the **Insert tab**, click the **Table button**, click **Insert Table** on the menu that opens, then insert a table with the number of rows and columns needed for the form, merging and splitting cells as needed to define the structure of the form

▶ Click a cell in the table that you want to contain a control, click the **Developer tab**, then click the control in the Controls group you want to add, such as a Rich Text content control or a Date Picker content control

Note: The Legacy Tools button 🔲 in the Controls group includes Legacy Forms content controls as well as ActiveX Controls content controls.

▶ Add a label in a cell to the left or above the cell with the content control that clearly identifies the type of information that will be entered in the content control, such as First Name next to a Rich Text content control in which you want form users to enter their first names

▶ Click the control in the form to select it, click **Properties** in the Controls group to open the Content Control Properties dialog box, then type information (such as the title and tag for the content control) and make selections specific to that content control (such as the type of formatting that should be applied to the content of the content control)

Note: The choices available in the Content Control Properties dialog box vary depending on the content control associated with the choices.

▶ Continue to add content controls to the form following the steps in bullets 2–4

Add Help Content to Form Fields

Ribbon Method

▶ Follow the steps in bullets 1–3 in the Use the Controls Group Ribbon Method to add a Text Form Field content control using the Legacy Tools button 🖳▾

▶ Click the **Text Form Field content control**, then click **Properties** in the Controls group to open the Text Form Field Options dialog box

▶ In the Text Form Field Options dialog box, click the **Add Help Text button** to open the Form Field Help Text dialog box

▶ Click the **Type your own option button**, then type the help text in the text box below the selected option button

▶ Click **OK** to close the Form Field Help Text dialog box, then click **OK** to close the Text Form Field Options dialog box and return to the Word document

Note: You see the help text in the status bar when you open and complete the form as a user.

Shortcut Method

▶ Follow the steps in bullet 1 in the Add Help Content to Form Fields Ribbon Method

▶ Double-click the **Text Form Field content control** to open the Text Form Field Options dialog box

▶ Follow the steps in bullets 3–5 in the Add Help Content to Form Fields Ribbon Method

Link a Form to a Database

Ribbon Method

▶ Change the location where you store user templates to the location where you will store the form template that you wish to link to a database

▶ Click the **Developer tab**, click the **Design Mode button** in the Controls group to turn on Design Mode if it is not already active, then create a form that includes content controls

▶ Below the form, insert a command button such as "Submit" as follows: Click the **Legacy Tools button** in the Controls group to open a gallery, then click the **Command Button button** in the ActiveX Controls gallery

▶ Right-click the **Command Button button**, click **CommandButton Object**, click **Edit**, select the text "**CommandButton1**", press **[Delete]**, type **Submit**, then click away from the button

▶ Click the **Command Button button**, click the **Properties button** in the Controls group, select the text "**CommandButton1**" next to (Name), type **Submit**, then close the Properties dialog box

▶ Click the **Design Mode button** in the Controls group to turn off Design Mode, click the **Restrict Editing button** in the Protect group to open the Restrict Formatting and Editing pane, click the **No changes (Read only) list arrow**, then click **Filling in forms**

▶ Save the form as a Word Macro-Enabled Template (*.dotm) file to the location you set for user templates

▶ Open Access, then create an Access database that contains a table with the same labels you included in the Word form template

Note: The labels in the Word document are the fields in the Access database.

▶ Save the Access database to the same folder as the Word form template

▶ Return to Word, click the **Developer tab** if it is not the active tab, click the **Visual Basic button** in the Code group, click **Tools** on the menu bar in the Microsoft Visual Basic window, then click **References**

▶ Click the **Microsoft Office 14.0 Access Database Engine Object Library check box**, then click **OK**

Note: You will need to scroll down to the entries starting with "M".

▶ Click **View** on the menu bar in the Microsoft Visual Basic window, then click **Code**

▶ Type or paste the required Visual Basic code into the Visual Basic Editor

Word

Note: If you have Visual Basic experience, you can type the code directly in the Visual Basic Editor; otherwise, you can obtain the Visual Basic code from a programmer. Either way, the Visual Basic code must contain the name of the database, the name of the database table to which the form data will be added, and the names of the fields.

▶ Click the **Save button** on the menu bar in the Microsoft Visual Basic window, close the **Visual Basic Editor**, then save and close the Word template file, but do not exit Word

▶ Click the **File tab** to open Backstage view, click **Options**, click **Trust Center**, click **Trust Center Settings**, then verify that the Disable all macros with notification button is selected

▶ Click **Trusted Locations** in the left pane, add the location where you stored both the Word form and the Access database to the list of trusted locations, then click **OK** until you return to Word

▶ Click the **File tab** to open Backstage view, click **New**, click **My templates**, click the Word form template you created, then click **OK**

▶ Complete the form with the required information, then click **Submit**

▶ Open the Access database, then open the database table to confirm the data you entered in the Word form is in the Access table

Lock a Form

Ribbon Method

▶ Open a document with a form that you want to lock

▶ Click the **Developer tab** if it is not the active tab, then click the **Design Mode button** in the Controls group to turn off Design Mode

▶ Click the **Restrict Editing button** in the Protect group, click the check box in the Editing restrictions area, click the **No changes (Read only) list arrow**, then click **Filling in forms**

▶ Click **Yes, Start Enforcing Protection**

▶ Type a password in the Start Enforcing Protection dialog box if you want the document to be password-protected, renter the password, then click **OK**

Note: If you do not want the document to be password-protected, skip these directions and follow the step in the next bullet.

▶ Click **OK** in the Start Enforcing Protection dialog box without entering a password if you do not want the document to be password-protected

MANIPULATE FORMS

Unlock a Form

Ribbon Method

▶ Open a document with a form that is protected
▶ Click the **Developer tab** if it is not the active tab, then click the **Restrict Editing button** in the Protect group to open the Restrict Formatting and Editing pane
▶ In the Restrict Formatting and Editing pane, click the **Stop Protection button**

Note: The document is no longer protected if it is not password-protected; if the document is password-protected, the Unprotect Document dialog box opens—follow the steps in the next bullet to stop protection.

▶ In the Unprotect Document dialog box, type the password if the document is password-protected, then click **OK**

Add Fields to a Form

Ribbon Method

▶ Open a document with a form to which you want to add fields
▶ Click the **Developer tab** if it is not the active tab, then click the **Design Mode button** in the Controls group to turn Design Mode on if it is not currently active
▶ Click the cell in the form where you want to insert a field, click the **Legacy Tools button** in the Controls group, then click the **Text Form Field button** in the Legacy Forms group to insert a Text Form Field at the location of the insertion point
▶ Click the **Text Form Field**, then click the **Properties button** in the Controls group to open the Text Form Field Options dialog box
▶ Select the settings that meet your needs for the Text Form Field, then click **OK**

Note: Refer to the Add Help Content to Form Fields Ribbon Method if you want to add help text.

▶ Continue to follow the steps in bullets 3–5 to add additional Text Form Fields to the form

Remove Fields from a Form

Ribbon Method

▶ Open a document that contains a field you want to delete, then click the **Developer tab** if it is not the active tab

▶ Click a content control in the form to select it, click the **title tag** of the selected content control, then press **[Delete]**

Note: When the title tag of a content control is selected, the title tag turns dark blue and the rest of the content control is light blue.

▶ Click a Legacy Tools form control, such as a Text Form Field content control, to select it, then press **[Delete]**

Note: Legacy Tools content controls do not have title tags.

Word

MICROSOFT EXCEL 2010
EXAM REFERENCE
Getting Started with Excel 2010

The Excel Microsoft Office Specialist Core exam assumes a basic level of proficiency in Excel. The Expert exam covers more advanced skills. This section is intended to help you reference these basic and advanced skills while you are preparing to take the Excel exam.

▶ Starting and exiting Excel
▶ Viewing the Excel window
▶ Using the Ribbon
▶ Opening, saving, and closing workbooks
▶ Navigating in the worksheet window
▶ Using keyboard KeyTips
▶ Getting Help

START AND EXIT EXCEL

Start Excel

Mouse Method

▶ Click the **Start button** 🔵 on the Windows taskbar
▶ Point to **All Programs**
▶ Click **Microsoft Office**, then click **Microsoft Excel 2010**

OR

▶ Double-click the **Microsoft Excel program icon** 🔲 on the desktop

Exit Excel

Ribbon Method

▶ Click the **File tab** to open Backstage view, then click **Exit**

OR

▶ Click the **Close button** ⊠ on the Excel program window title bar

Shortcut Method

▶ Press **[Alt][F4]**

View the Excel Window

Figure EX-1 Excel Window

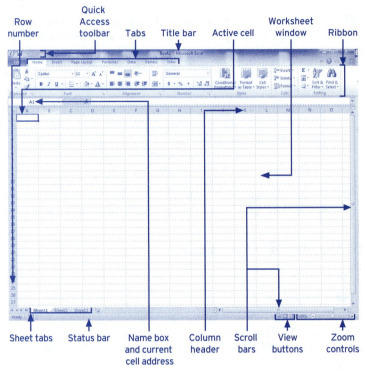

Row number | Quick Access toolbar | Tabs | Title bar | Active cell | Worksheet window | Ribbon

Sheet tabs | Status bar | Name box and current cell address | Column header | Scroll bars | View buttons | Zoom controls

Use the Ribbon

Display the Ribbon

Ribbon Method
▶ Double-click any tab or click the **Expand the Ribbon button**

Shortcut Method
▶ Right-click any tab, then click **Minimize the Ribbon** to deselect it

Hide the Ribbon

Ribbon Method
▶ Double-click the active tab or click the **Minimize the Ribbon button** 🔼

Shortcut Method

▶ Right-click any tab or any place on the Ribbon, then click **Minimize the Ribbon** to select it

Customize the Quick Access Toolbar

Shortcut Method

▶ Right-click any Quick Access toolbar button
▶ To remove that button, click **Remove from Quick Access Toolbar**
▶ To add or remove a button, right-click the **Quick Access Toolbar list arrow**, click **Customize Quick Access Toolbar**, click a command in the left or right column of the dialog box, then click **Add** or **Remove**

Reposition the Quick Access Toolbar

Shortcut Method

▶ Right-click any Quick Access toolbar button or any tab
▶ Click **Show Quick Access Toolbar Below the Ribbon**

OPEN, SAVE, AND CLOSE WORKBOOKS

Open a New Workbook

Ribbon Method

▶ Click the **File tab** to open Backstage view, then click **New**
▶ Verify that Blank workbook is selected under Available Templates, then click **Create** in the right pane

Shortcut Method

▶ Press **[Ctrl][N]**

Open an Existing Workbook

Ribbon Method

▶ Click the **File tab** to open Backstage view, then click **Open**
▶ In the Open dialog box, navigate to the drive and folder where the file is stored
▶ Click the file you want, then click **Open**

Shortcut Method

▶ Press **[Ctrl][O]**
▶ Follow the steps in bullets 2–3 of the Open an Existing Workbook Ribbon Method

Excel

Use Save As

Ribbon Method

▶ Click the **File tab** to open Backstage view, then click **Save As**
▶ In the Save As dialog box, navigate to the drive and folder where you want to store the workbook
▶ Type an appropriate **file name** in the File name text box, then click **Save**

Shortcut Method

▶ Press **[F12]**
▶ Follow the steps in bullets 2–3 of the Use Save As Ribbon Method

Save an Existing Workbook

Ribbon Method

▶ Click the **File tab** to open Backstage view, then click **Save**
   OR
▶ Click the **Save button** 🖫 on the Quick Access toolbar

Shortcut Method

▶ Press **[Ctrl][S]**

Close a Workbook

Ribbon Method

▶ Click the **File tab** to open Backstage view, then click **Close**
▶ If prompted to save the file, click **Yes** or **No** as appropriate
   OR
▶ Click the **Close Window button** 🗙 in the document window
▶ If prompted to save the file, click **Yes** or **No** as appropriate

Shortcut Method

▶ Press **[Ctrl][W]** or **[Alt][F4]**
▶ If prompted to save the file, click **Yes** or **No** as appropriate

NAVIGATE IN THE WORKSHEET WINDOW

Ribbon Method

▶ On the Home tab, click the **Find & Select button** in the Editing group
▶ Click **Go To**
▶ In the Reference text box in the Go To dialog box, type the **address** of the cell you want to go to, then click **OK**

Shortcut Method

▶ Press **[Ctrl][G]**

▶ In the Reference text box in the Go To dialog box, type the **address** of the cell you want to go to, then click **OK**

    OR

▶ Use Table EX-1 as a reference to navigate through the worksheet using keyboard shortcuts

Table EX-1 Navigation Keyboard Shortcuts

Keys	Moves the insertion point
[Ctrl][Home]	To the beginning of the worksheet (cell A1)
[Ctrl][End]	To the end of the worksheet area containing data
[Page Up]	One screen up
[Page Down]	One screen down
[Alt][Page Up]	One screen to the left
[Alt][Page Down]	One screen to the right

Mouse Method

To change the view without moving the insertion point, do one of the following:

▶ Drag the **scroll box** in a scroll bar to move within the worksheet

▶ Click above the scroll box in a scroll bar to jump up a screen

▶ Click below the scroll box in a scroll bar to jump down a screen

▶ Click the **up scroll arrow** in a scroll bar to move up one row

▶ Click the **down scroll arrow** in a scroll bar to move down one row

USE KEYBOARD KEYTIPS

Display KeyTips

▶ Press **[Alt]** to display the KeyTips (labels containing numbers or letters) on the active tab on the Ribbon and on the Quick Access toolbar

▶ Press the letter or number for a tab to open a tab, then press the letter or number for the specific command on the active tab to perform the command

▶ Press additional letters or numbers as needed to complete the command sequence

▶ If two letters appear, press each one in order

Excel

▶ For some commands, you have to click an option from a gallery or menu to complete the command sequence

▶ The KeyTips turn off automatically at the end of the command sequence

Hide KeyTips

▶ Press **[Alt]**

GET HELP

Ribbon Method

▶ Click the **Microsoft Excel Help button** on the Ribbon

▶ Enter the topic you want help with in the Search text box in the Excel Help dialog box, then click **Search**

Shortcut Method

▶ Press **[F1]**

▶ Enter the topic you want help with in the Search text box in the Excel Help dialog box

Excel 2010 Exam Reference

Core Objectives:

1. Managing the worksheet environment
2. Creating cell data
3. Formatting cells and worksheets
4. Managing worksheets and workbooks
5. Applying formulas and functions
6. Presenting data visually
7. Sharing worksheet data with other users
8. Analyzing and organizing data

Expert Objectives:

1. Sharing and maintaining workbooks
2. Applying formulas and functions
3. Presenting data visually
4. Working with macros and forms

Excel

Excel Core Objectives

Excel Core Objective 1: Managing the Worksheet Environment

Navigate Through a Worksheet

Use Hot Keys

Shortcut Method

▶ Use Table EX-2 as a guide for using a hot key combination

Table EX-2 Excel Hot Keys

Hot Keys	Function
[Ctrl][A]	Select the entire worksheet
[Ctrl][B]	Add or remove bold formatting
[Ctrl][C]	Copy the selected cell or range of cells
[Ctrl][D]	Fill down a selected range of cells using the top value
[Ctrl][F]	Open the Find and Replace dialog box to the Find tab
[Ctrl][G]	Open the Go To dialog box
[Ctrl][H]	Open the Find and Replace dialog box to the Replace tab
[Ctrl][I]	Add or remove italic
[Ctrl][O]	Open the dialog box to open a file
[Ctrl][S]	Save the workbook
[Ctrl][U]	Add or remove underline

Use the Name Box

Mouse Method

▶ Click the **Name Box arrow**, then select the name of a cell or range

PRINT A WORKSHEET OR WORKBOOK

Print Only Selected Worksheets

Ribbon Method

▶ Select the worksheets that you want to print
▶ Click the **File tab** to open Backstage view, then click **Print**

Shortcut Method

▶ Select the worksheets that you want to print
▶ Press **[Ctrl][P]**

Print an Entire Workbook

Ribbon Method

▶ Click the **File tab** to open Backstage view
▶ In the Settings section of the Print tab, choose **Print Entire Workbook**

Shortcut Method

▶ Press **[Ctrl][P]**
▶ In the Settings section of the Print tab, choose **Print Entire Workbook**

Construct Headers and Footers

Ribbon Method

▶ Click the **Insert tab**, then click the **Header & Footer button** in the Text group
▶ Click in the left, center, or right **header section** and type text, or click one of the **buttons** in the Header & Footer Elements group
▶ Click an **option** in the Options group if desired
▶ Click the **Go to Footer button** in the Navigation group
▶ Click a **footer section** and type text, or click one of the **buttons** in the Header & Footer Elements group
▶ Click the **Normal View button** ⊞ on the status bar

Shortcut Method

▶ Click the **Page Layout button** ▣ on the status bar
▶ Follow the steps in bullets 2–6 in the Construct Headers and Footers Ribbon Method

Apply Printing Options

Scale

Ribbon Method

▶ Click the **Page Layout tab**
▶ Click the **Width arrow button** in the Scale to Fit group, then click the desired number of pages
▶ Click the **Height arrow button** in the Scale to Fit group, then click the desired number of pages

OR

▶ Click the **Page Layout tab**, then click the **Size button** in the Page Setup group
▶ Click **More Paper Sizes**
▶ On the Page tab in the Page Setup dialog box, under Scaling, click the **Fit to option button**, then enter the desired number of pages in the pages(s) wide and tall text boxes
▶ Click **OK**

OR

▶ Click the **File tab** to open Backstage view
▶ In the Settings section of the Print tab, click the **No Scaling arrow**, then select the desired scaling option

Print Titles

Ribbon Method

▶ Click the **Page Layout tab**, then in the Page Setup group, click **Print Titles**

▶ On the Sheet tab, under Print titles, do one or both of the following:
  • In the Rows to repeat at top box, type the reference of the rows that contain the column labels
  • In the Columns to repeat at left box, type the reference of the columns that contain the row labels

Page Setup

Ribbon Method

▶ Click the **File tab** to open Backstage view
▶ In the Settings section of the Print tab, select options from the following: what to print, pages to print, collated or uncollated, page orientation, paper size, margins, and scaling options

OR

▶ Click the **Page Layout tab**
▶ In the Page Setup group, use the **Margins**, **Orientation**, **Size**, **Print Area**, **Breaks**, **Background**, and **Print Titles buttons** to select print options

Shortcut Method

▶ Press **[Ctrl][P]**
▶ In the Settings section of the Print tab, select options from the following: what you want to print, one- or two-sided printing, pages you want to print, collated or uncollated, page orientation, paper size, margins, and scaling options

Print Area

Ribbon Method

▶ Select the worksheet area you want to print
▶ Click the **Page Layout tab**, then click the **Print Area button** in the Page Setup group
▶ Click **Set Print Area** to set the print area

Gridlines

Ribbon Method

▶ Click the **Page Layout tab**
▶ Click the **Print check box** in the Gridlines section of the Sheet Options group to select the check box

OR

▶ Click the **File tab** to open Backstage view, click **Print**, then click **Page Setup**
▶ Click the **Sheet tab** in the Page Setup dialog box, click the **Gridlines check box** in the Print section, then click **OK**

PERSONALIZE THE ENVIRONMENT BY USING BACKSTAGE

Manipulate the Quick Access Toolbar

Ribbon Method

▶ Click the **File tab** to open Backstage view, click **Options**, then click **Quick Access Toolbar**
▶ To add a button to the Quick Access toolbar, click the command you want to add, click the **Add button**, then click **OK**
▶ To move a button on the Quick Access toolbar, click the command you want to move, then click the **Move Up** or **Move Down arrow**

Shortcut Method

▶ Right-click the **Quick Access toolbar**
▶ To reposition the Quick Access toolbar, click **Show Quick Access Toolbar Below the Ribbon**
▶ To add a button to the Quick Access toolbar, click **Customize Quick Access Toolbar**, click the command you want to add, click the **Add button**, then click **OK**
▶ To move a button on the Quick Access toolbar, click **Customize Quick Access Toolbar**, click the command you want to move, then click the **Move Up** or **Move Down arrow**

Mouse Method

▶ Click the **Customize Quick Access Toolbar button** 🔽 on the title bar
▶ To add a button to the Quick Access toolbar, click a button name or click **More Commands**, click the command you want to add, click the **Add button**, then click **OK**
▶ To reposition the Quick Access toolbar, click **Show Below the Ribbon**

Customize the Ribbon

Tabs

Ribbon Method

▶ Click the **File tab** to open Backstage view, click **Options**, then click **Customize Ribbon**
▶ To add an undisplayed tab to the Ribbon, click the **Customize the Ribbon arrow**, click **All Tabs**, if necessary, then click a check box to select an undisplayed tab
▶ To add a new tab to the Ribbon, click **New Tab**

Excel

Shortcut Method

▶ Right-click the **Quick Access toolbar** or the **Ribbon**, then click **Customize the Ribbon**

▶ Click **Customize Ribbon** in the left pane

▶ Follow the steps in bullets 2–3 in the Tabs Ribbon Method

Groups

Ribbon Method

▶ Click the **File tab** to open Backstage view, click **Options**, then click **Customize Ribbon**

▶ Click the tab that you want to add a group to, click **New Group**, click the command you want to add, click the **Add button**, then click **OK**

▶ Click **New Group (Custom)** to add commands, click the command you want to add, then click the **Add button**

▶ Click **Rename** to change the New Group or the New Tab name, then click **OK**

Shortcut Method

▶ Right-click the **Quick Access toolbar** or the **Ribbon**, then click **Customize the Ribbon**

▶ Click **Customize Ribbon** in the left pane

▶ Follow the steps in bullets 2–4 in the Groups Ribbon Method

Manipulate Excel Default Settings (Excel Options)

Ribbon Method

▶ Click the **File tab** to open Backstage view, then click **Options**

▶ Click **General**, **Formulas**, **Proofing**, **Save**, **Language**, **Advanced**, **Customize Ribbon**, **Quick Access Toolbar**, **Add-Ins**, or **Trust Center** to select Excel options for those categories

Manipulate Workbook Properties (Document Panel)

Ribbon Method

▶ Click the **File tab** to open Backstage view, then click **Info**

▶ Click **Properties** in the right pane, click **Show Document Panel**, enter information about the document in the panel, then close the panel

Manipulate Workbook Files and Folders

Manage Versions

Ribbon Method

▶ Click the **File tab** to open Backstage view, then click **Info**

▶ Click a **file icon** in the Versions list, or click the **Manage Versions button**, then click **Recover Unsaved Workbooks** to see a list of AutoRecovered files

AutoSave

Ribbon Method

▶ Click the **File tab** to open Backstage view, then click **Options**
▶ Click **Save** in the Excel Options dialog box, then verify that the Save AutoRecover information check box is selected
▶ Enter how often AutoRecover should save your files by clicking the **up/down arrows** to adjust the number of minutes
▶ Click **OK**

EXCEL CORE OBJECTIVE 2: CREATING CELL DATA

CONSTRUCT CELL DATA

Use Paste Special

Formats

Ribbon Method

▶ Select one or more cells, then click the **Copy button** 🗐 or the **Cut button** ✂ in the Clipboard group on the Home tab
▶ Click the destination cell, then click the **Paste button arrow**
▶ Click a Paste Special option that includes formatting, using Table EX-3 as a reference

Table EX-3 Paste Special Options

Command	Icon / Location	Result
Paste	📋	Pastes cell contents and formatting
Formulas	f_x	Pastes formulas
Formulas & Number Formatting		Pastes text and number formatting
Keep Source Formatting		Pastes source formatting
Transpose		Changes columns of data to rows or rows to columns
Values	123	Pastes displayed values

(continued)

Table EX-3 Paste Special Options (continued)

Command	Icon / Location	Result
Formatting	[icon]	Pastes cell formatting
Paste Link	[icon]	Links original data to the pasted data
Add	Paste Special dialog box	Adds the copied values to the values in the destination
Divide	Paste Special dialog box	Divides the copied values into the values in the destination
Comments	Paste Special dialog box	Pastes comments attached to a cell
Validation	Paste Special dialog box	Pastes data validation rules

Shortcut Method

▶ Select one or more cells, then press **[Ctrl][C]** or **[Ctrl][X]**
▶ Right-click the destination cell, then point to **Paste Special**
▶ Click a Paste Special option that includes formatting, using Table EX-3 as a reference

Formulas

Ribbon Method

▶ Select one or more cells, then click the **Copy button** [icon] or the **Cut button** [icon] in the Clipboard group on the Home tab
▶ Click the destination cell, then click the **Paste button arrow**
▶ Click a Paste Special option that includes formulas, using Table EX-3 as a reference

Shortcut Method

▶ Select one or more cells, then press **[Ctrl][C]** or **[Ctrl][X]**
▶ Right-click the destination cell, then point to **Paste Special**
▶ Click a Paste Special option that includes formulas, using Table EX-3 as a reference

Values

Ribbon Method

▶ Select one or more cells, then click the **Copy button** [icon] or the **Cut button** [icon] in the Clipboard group on the Home tab
▶ Click the destination cell, then click the **Paste button arrow**
▶ Click a Paste Special option that includes values, using Table EX-3 as a reference

Shortcut Method

▶ Select one or more cells, then press **[Ctrl][C]** or **[Ctrl][X]**
▶ Right-click the destination cell, then point to **Paste Special**
▶ Click a Paste Special option that includes values, using Table EX-3 as a reference

Preview Icons

Ribbon Method

▶ Select one or more cells, then click the **Copy button** 🖺 or the **Cut button** ✂ in the Clipboard group on the Home tab
▶ Click the destination cell, then click the **Paste button arrow**
▶ Move the mouse over the Paste Special icons shown in Table EX-3 to preview the results

Shortcut Method

▶ Select one or more cells, then press **[Ctrl][C]** or **[Ctrl][X]**
▶ Right-click the destination cell, then point to **Paste Special**
▶ Move the mouse over the Paste Special icons shown in Table EX-3 to preview the results

Transpose Rows

Ribbon Method

▶ Select one or more rows, then click the **Copy button** 🖺 or the **Cut button** ✂ in the Clipboard group on the Home tab
▶ Click the upper-left cell in the destination range, then click the **Paste button arrow**
▶ Click **Transpose**

Shortcut Method

▶ Select one or more rows, then press **[Ctrl][C]** or **[Ctrl][X]**
▶ Right-click the upper-left cell in the destination range, then point to **Paste Special**
▶ Click **Transpose**

Transpose Columns

Ribbon Method

▶ Select one or more columns, then click the **Copy button** 🖺 or the **Cut button** ✂ in the Clipboard group on the Home tab
▶ Click the upper-left cell in the destination range, then click the **Paste button arrow**
▶ Click **Transpose**

Shortcut Method

▶ Select one or more columns, then press **[Ctrl][C]** or **[Ctrl][X]**
▶ Right-click the upper-left cell in the destination range, then point to **Paste Special**

Excel

▶ Click **Transpose**

Operations: Add and Divide

Ribbon Method

▶ Select one or more cells, then click the **Copy button** 📋 or the **Cut button** ✂ in the Clipboard group on the Home tab
▶ Click the destination cell, then click the **Paste button arrow**
▶ Click **Paste Special**
▶ In the Paste Special dialog box, click the **Add option button** or the **Divide option button**, then click **OK**

Shortcut Method

▶ Select one or more cells, then press **[Ctrl][C]** or **[Ctrl][X]**
▶ Right-click the destination cell, then point to **Paste Special**
▶ Click **Paste Special**
▶ In the Paste Special dialog box, click the **Add option button** or the **Divide option button**, then click **OK**

Comments

Ribbon Method

▶ Select one or more cells, then click the **Copy button** 📋 or the **Cut button** ✂ in the Clipboard group on the Home tab
▶ Click the destination cell, then click the **Paste button arrow**
▶ Click **Paste Special**
▶ In the Paste Special dialog box, click the **Comments option button**, then click **OK**

Shortcut Method

▶ Select one or more cells, then press **[Ctrl][C]** or **[Ctrl][X]**
▶ Right-click the destination cell, then point to **Paste Special**
▶ Click **Paste Special**
▶ In the Paste Special dialog box, click the **Comments option button**, then click **OK**

Validation

Ribbon Method

▶ Select one or more cells, then click the **Copy button** 📋 or the **Cut button** ✂ in the Clipboard group on the Home tab
▶ Click the destination cell, then click the **Paste button arrow**
▶ Click **Paste Special**
▶ In the Paste Special dialog box, click the **Validation option button**, then click **OK**

Shortcut Method

▶ Select one or more cells, then press **[Ctrl][C]** or **[Ctrl][X]**
▶ Right-click the destination cell, then point to **Paste Special**

▶ Click **Paste Special**
▶ In the Paste Special dialog box, click the **Validation option button**, then click **OK**

Paste as a Link

Ribbon Method

▶ Select one or more cells, then click the **Copy button** 🗎 or the **Cut button** ✂ in the Clipboard group on the Home tab
▶ Click the destination cell, then click the **Paste button arrow**
▶ Click **Paste Link**

Shortcut Method

▶ Select one or more cells, then press **[Ctrl][C]** or **[Ctrl][X]**
▶ Right-click the destination cell, then click the **Paste button list arrow**
▶ Click **Paste Link**

Cut

Ribbon Method

▶ Select the **cell(s)** to cut
▶ On the Home tab, click the **Cut button** in the Clipboard group

Shortcut Method

▶ Select the **cell(s)** to cut
▶ Right-click the **selected cell(s)**, then click **Cut**
  OR
▶ Select the **cell(s)** to cut
▶ Press **[Ctrl][X]**

Move

Ribbon Method

▶ Select the **cell(s)** to move
▶ On the Home tab, click the **Cut button** in the Clipboard group
▶ Click where you want to move the cell(s)
▶ Click the **Paste button** in the Clipboard group

Shortcut Method

▶ Select the **cell(s)** to move
▶ Right-click the **selected cell(s)**, then click **Cut**
▶ Right-click where you want to move the cell(s), then click **Paste**
  OR
▶ Select the **cell(s)** to move
▶ Press **[Ctrl][X]**
▶ Click where you want to move the cell(s)
▶ Press **[Ctrl][V]**

Excel

Mouse Method

▶ Select the **cell(s)** to move
▶ Place the mouse pointer over any edge of the selected range until the pointer becomes ⟊
▶ Drag the selected range to the appropriate location, then release the mouse button

Select Cell Data

Mouse Method

Table EX-4 summarizes the actions to select cell data

Table EX-4 Cell Selection Actions

Select	Action
Single cell	Click the cell
Range of cells	Click the first cell, then drag to the last cell OR Press **[Shift]** and click the last cell in the range
All cells on a worksheet	Click the **Select All button** OR Press **[Ctrl][A]**

APPLY AUTOFILL

Copy Data

Ribbon Method

▶ Drag to select **data** in a cell, then continue dragging to include the range you want to copy in the selection
▶ On the Home tab, click the **Fill button** in the Editing group, then click **Down**, **Right**, **Up**, or **Left**

Mouse Method

▶ Drag to select one or more adjacent **cells**
▶ Drag the **fill handle** horizontally or vertically to copy the data to the range you choose
▶ Click the **AutoFill Options button** , then click **Copy Cells**

Shortcut Method

▶ Select the **cell(s)** to copy
▶ Right-click the **selected cell(s)**, then click **Copy**
   OR

▶ Select the **cell(s)** to cut
▶ Press **[Ctrl][C]**
   OR

▶ Click the **cell** whose value or formula you want to copy
▶ Press **[Shift][↓]** or **[Shift][→]** as necessary to select the fill range
▶ Press **[Ctrl][D]** to fill the range down or **[Ctrl][R]** to fill the range to the right

Fill a Series and Preserve Cell Format

Ribbon Method

▶ Drag to select two or more **cells** in a series you have started and continue dragging to include the range you want to fill, or select one **cell** containing the starting content in an AutoFill series, as described in Table EX-5, and the range you want to fill
▶ On the Home tab, click the **Fill button** 🔳▾ in the Editing group, then click **Series**
▶ In the Series dialog box, click the **AutoFill Options button** 🔳▾ in the Type section, then click **OK** to fill in the series with formatting intact

Mouse Method

▶ Select two or more **cells** in a series you have started, or click one **cell** containing the starting content in an AutoFill series, as described in Table EX-5
▶ Drag the **fill handle** horizontally or vertically to automatically fill in the appropriate values
▶ Click the **AutoFill Options button** 🔳▾, then click **Fill Series**, **Fill Formatting Only**, or **Fill Without Formatting**

Shortcut Method

▶ Click two or more **cells** in a series you have started, or click one **cell** containing the starting content in an AutoFill series, as described in Table EX-5
▶ Point to the cell's **fill handle** until the pointer changes to **+**
▶ Click and hold the **right mouse button**, then drag in the direction you want to fill
▶ On the shortcut menu, click **Fill Series**, **Fill Formatting Only**, or **Fill Without Formatting**

Excel

Table EX-5 Built-in AutoFill Series

To fill	Enter and select	Drag to display
Months	January	February, March, April,...
Quarters	Q1	Q2, Q3, Q4
Years	2012, 2013	2014, 2015, 2016,...
Times	8:00	9:00, 10:00, 11:00,...
Text + numbers	Student 1, Student 2	Student 3, Student 4, Student 5,...
Numeric sequence	1, 3	5, 7, 9,...

APPLY AND MANIPULATE HYPERLINKS

Create a Hyperlink in a Cell

Ribbon Method

▶ Select the appropriate **cell**, **range**, **chart**, or **graphic**
▶ Click the **Insert tab**, then click the **Hyperlink button** in the Links group
▶ In the Insert Hyperlink dialog box, specify the appropriate options using Table EX-6 as a reference, then click **OK**

Shortcut Method

▶ Select the appropriate **cell**, **range**, **chart**, or **graphic**
▶ Right-click the selection then click **Hyperlink**, or press **[Ctrl][K]**
▶ In the Insert Hyperlink dialog box, specify the appropriate options using Table EX-6 as a reference, then click **OK**

Table EX-6 Inserting Hyperlinks Using the Insert Hyperlink Dialog Box

Link to	Instructions
Another place in the document	Click **Place in This Document**, select a **location** in the "Or select a place in this document" list, then click **OK**
Another document	Click **Existing File or Web Page**, navigate to the appropriate drive and folder, click the **file name** in the list, then click **OK**
A new document	Click **Create New Document**, name the document and verify the drive and folder, choose to edit it now or later, then click **OK**

(continued)

Table EX-6 Inserting Hyperlinks Using the Insert Hyperlink
           Dialog Box (continued)

Link to	Instructions
A Web page	Click **Existing File or Web Page**, click the **Address text box**, type the **URL**, then click **OK**
An e-mail address	Click **E-mail Address**, type the **address** and any other text to display, then click **OK**

Modify Hyperlinks

Ribbon Method

▶ Move to the cell containing the hyperlink, click the **Insert tab**, then click the **Hyperlink button** in the Links group
▶ In the Edit Hyperlink dialog box, make modifications, then click **OK**

Shortcut Method

▶ Right-click the **hyperlink**, then click **Edit Hyperlink**
▶ In the Edit Hyperlink dialog box, make modifications, then click **OK**

Modify Hyperlinked Cell Attributes

Ribbon Method

▶ On the Home tab, click **Cell Styles** in the Styles group
▶ Under Data and Model, right-click **Hyperlink**, then click **Modify** (to modify existing hyperlinks, right-click **Followed Hyperlink**, then click **Modify**)
▶ In the Style dialog box, click **Format**
▶ On the Font tab and Fill tab, select the formatting options that you want, click **OK**, then click **OK**

Remove a Hyperlink

Ribbon Method

▶ Move to the cell containing the hyperlink, click the **Insert tab**, then click the **Hyperlink button** in the Links group
▶ Click **Remove Link** in the Edit Hyperlink dialog box

Shortcut Method

▶ Right-click the **hyperlink**, then click **Remove Hyperlink**

EXCEL CORE OBJECTIVE 3: FORMATTING CELLS AND WORKSHEETS

APPLY AND MODIFY CELL FORMATS

Align Cell Content

Ribbon Method
▶ Select the **cell(s)** to align
▶ Use the buttons in the Alignment group on the Home tab to apply the appropriate formats, using Table EX-7 as a reference

Shortcut Method
▶ Select the **cell(s)** to align
▶ Right-click the **selected range**, then use the buttons on the Mini toolbar to align the cell contents, using Table EX-7 as a reference

Table EX-7 Applying Cell Formats Using the Home Tab or Mini Toolbar

Button	Formatting	Effect
Calibri	Font	Changes font style
11	Font Size	Changes font size
B	Bold	**Bold**
I	Italic	*Italic*
U	Underline	<u>Underline</u>
	Align Text Left	Aligns to left cell edge
	Center	Aligns between left and right cell edges
	Align Text Right	Aligns to right cell edge
	Merge and Center	Merges selected cells and centers text in a merged cell
	Merge Across	Merges each row of the selected cells into a larger cell
	Merge Cells	Merges the selected cells into one cell

(continued)

Table EX-7   Applying Cell Formats Using the Home Tab or
Mini Toolbar (continued)

Button	Formatting	Effect
	Unmerge Cells	Splits the selected cells into multiple cells
\$	Accounting Number Format	\$1234.56
%	Percent Style	123456%
,	Comma Style	1,234.56
	Increase Decimal	1234.560
	Decrease Decimal	1234.6
	Decrease Indent	Decreases indentation from left cell edge
	Increase Indent	Indents from left cell edge
	Borders	Adds borders to edge(s) of selected cell(s)
	Fill Color	Fills cell(s) with color
A	Font Color	Changes font color

Apply a Number Format

Ribbon Method

▶ Select the **cell(s)** to format
▶ Use the buttons in the Font and Number groups on the Home tab to apply the appropriate formats, using Table EX-7 as a reference

Shortcut Method

▶ Select the **cell(s)** to format
▶ Right-click the **selected range**, then use the buttons on the Mini toolbar to format the cell contents, using Table EX-7 as a reference

Wrap Text in a Cell

Ribbon Method

▶ Select one or more cells
▶ On the Home tab, click the **Wrap Text button** in the Alignment group

Use the Format Painter

Ribbon Method

▶ Select one or more cells with formatting you want to copy, then click the **Format Painter button** 🖉 in the Clipboard group on the Home tab

▶ Select one or more cells you want to format

MERGE OR SPLIT CELLS

Use Merge & Center, Merge Across, Merge Cells, and Unmerge Cells

Ribbon Method

▶ Select the **cells** to merge or the **merged cell** to be split
▶ On the Home tab, click the **Merge and Center list arrow** in the Alignment group
▶ Click an option, using Table EX-8 as a reference

Table EX-8 Merge Options

Option	Action
Merge & Center	Merges selected cells and centers content in the newly merged cell
Merge Across	Merges cells in a range horizontally only
Merge Cells	Merges content across the selected cell range
Unmerge Cells	Removes a merge and restores the column or row structure

CREATE ROW AND COLUMN TITLES

Print Row and Column Headings

Ribbon Method

▶ Click the **Page Layout tab**
▶ Click the **Print check box** under Headings in the Sheet Options group
▶ Click the **File tab** to open Backstage view, click **Print**, then click **Print** again

   OR

▶ Click the **Page Setup dialog box launcher** 🖾

▶ Click the **Sheet tab** in the Page Setup dialog box, then click the **Row and column headings check box**

OR

▶ Click the **File tab** to open Backstage view, click **Print**, then click the **Page Setup link** in the middle pane
▶ Click the **Sheet tab** in the Page Setup dialog box, then click the **Row and column headings check box**

Shortcut Method
▶ Press **[Ctrl][P]**, then click the **Page Setup link** in the middle pane
▶ Click the **Sheet tab** in the Page Setup dialog box, then click the **Row and column headings check box**

Print Rows to Repeat with Titles
Ribbon Method
▶ Click the **Page Layout tab**
▶ In the Page Setup group, click the **Print Titles button**
▶ In the Page Setup dialog box, click the **Collapse button** 🔳 to the right of the Rows to repeat at top text box, drag the **row selection pointer** ➡ over the row headings you want repeated, then click the **Expand button** 🔳
▶ Click **OK**, click the **File tab** to open Backstage view, click **Print**, then click **Print** again

OR

▶ Click the **Page Setup dialog box launcher** 🔳
▶ Click the **Sheet tab** in the Page Setup dialog box, then follow the step in bullet 3 in the Print Rows to Repeat with Titles Ribbon Method

Shortcut Method
▶ Press **[Ctrl][P]**
▶ Click the **Page Setup link** in the middle pane
▶ Click the **Sheet tab**, then follow the step in bullet 3 in the Print Rows to Repeat with Titles Ribbon Method

Print Columns to Repeat with Titles
Ribbon Method
▶ Click the **Page Layout tab**
▶ In the Page Setup group, click the **Print Titles button**
▶ In the Page Setup dialog box, click the **Collapse button** 🔳 to the right of the Columns to repeat at left text box, drag the **column selection pointer** ⬇ over the column headings you want repeated, then click the **Expand button** 🔳

> ▶ Click **OK**, click the **File tab** to open Backstage view, click **Print**, then click **Print** again
> OR
> ▶ Click the **Page Setup dialog box launcher** 🔲
> ▶ Click the **Sheet tab** in the Page Setup dialog box, then follow the step in bullet 3 in the Print Columns to Repeat with Titles Ribbon Method

Shortcut Method

> ▶ Press **[Ctrl][P]**
> ▶ Click the **Page Setup link** in the middle pane
> ▶ Click the **Sheet tab**, then follow the step in bullet 3 in the Print Columns to Repeat with Titles Ribbon Method

Configure Titles to Print Only on Odd or Even Pages

Ribbon Method

> ▶ Click the **Insert tab**, then click the **Header & Footer button** in the Text group
> ▶ Click the **Different Odd & Even Pages check box** in the Options group on the Header & Footer Tools Design tab
> ▶ Enter the heading in the Odd or Even Page Header text box

Shortcut Method

> ▶ Click the **Page Layout button** 🔲 on the status bar
> ▶ Click in the Header area, then follow the steps in bullets 2–3 of the Configure Titles to Print Only on Odd or Even Pages Ribbon Method

Configure Titles to Skip the First Worksheet Page

Ribbon Method

> ▶ Click the **Insert tab**, then click the **Header & Footer button** in the Text group
> ▶ Click the **Different First Page check box** in the Options group on the Header & Footer Tools Design tab

Shortcut Method

> ▶ Click the **Page Layout button** 🔲 on the status bar
> ▶ Click in the Header area, click the **Header & Footer Tools Design tab**, then follow the step in bullet 2 of the Configure Titles to Skip the First Worksheet Page Ribbon Method

HIDE OR UNHIDE ROWS AND COLUMNS

Hide or Unhide a Column

Ribbon Method

▶ Click a **cell** in the column to hide, or select an entire **column**
▶ On the Home tab, click the **Format button** in the Cells group
▶ Point to **Hide & Unhide**, then click **Hide Columns**
▶ To unhide a column, drag to select two **cells** on either side of the hidden column, click the **Format button** in the Cells group, point to **Hide & Unhide**, then click **Unhide Columns**

Shortcut Method

▶ Right-click a column, then click **Hide**
▶ To unhide a column, drag to select the columns on either side of the hidden column, right-click the columns, then click **Unhide**

Hide or Unhide a Row

Ribbon Method

▶ Click a **cell** in the row to hide, or select an entire **row**
▶ On the Home tab, click the **Format button** in the Cells group
▶ Point to **Hide & Unhide**, then click **Hide Rows**
▶ To unhide a row, drag to select two **cells** on either side of the hidden row, click the **Format button** in the Cells group, point to **Hide & Unhide**, then click **Unhide Rows**

Shortcut Method

▶ Right-click a row, then click **Hide**
▶ To unhide a row, drag to select the rows on either side of the hidden row, right-click the rows, then click **Unhide**

Hide a Series of Columns

Ribbon Method

▶ Select a **range** of cells spanning the columns to hide or select two or more **columns**
▶ On the Home tab, click the **Format button** in the Cells group
▶ Point to **Hide & Unhide**, then click **Hide Columns**

Shortcut Method

▶ Select two or more **columns**
▶ Right-click a selected column, then click **Hide**

Excel

Hide a Series of Rows

Ribbon Method

▶ Select a **range** of cells spanning the rows to hide or select two or more **rows**
▶ On the Home tab, click the **Format button** in the Cells group
▶ Point to **Hide & Unhide**, then click **Hide Rows**

Shortcut Method

▶ Select two or more **rows**
▶ Right-click a selected row, then click **Hide**

MANIPULATE PAGE SETUP OPTIONS FOR WORKSHEETS

Configure Page Orientation

Ribbon Method

▶ Click the **Page Layout tab**, then click the **Orientation button** in the Page Setup group
▶ Click **Portrait** (to make the worksheet taller than it is wide) or **Landscape** (to make the worksheet wider than it is tall)

OR

▶ Click the **File tab** to open Backstage view, then click **Print**
▶ Click the **Portrait** or **Landscape Orientation button** in the Settings section, to change the orientation to Portrait (to make the worksheet taller than it is wide) or Landscape (to make the worksheet wider than it is tall)

Manage Page Scaling

Ribbon Method

▶ Click the **Page Layout tab**
▶ Click the **Width list arrow** in the Scale to Fit group, then click the number of desired pages you want to display
▶ Click the **Height list arrow** in the Scale to Fit group, then click the number of desired pages you want to display

OR

▶ Click the **Page Layout tab**, then click the **Size button** in the Page Setup group
▶ Click **More Paper Sizes**

▶ On the Page tab in the Page Setup dialog box, under Scaling, click **Fit to** then enter the number of desired pages in the pages(s) wide and tall text boxes

▶ Click **OK**

OR

▶ Click the **File tab** to open Backstage view, then click **Print**

▶ Click **No Scaling** then select the desired scaling option

Configure Page Margins

Ribbon Method

▶ Click the **Page Layout tab**, then click the **Margins button** in the Page Setup group

▶ Click **Custom Margins**

▶ On the Margins tab of the Page Setup dialog box, enter **values** for the Top, Left, Right, and Bottom margins, then click **OK**

OR

▶ Click the **File tab** to open Backstage view, then click **Print**

▶ Click **Normal Margins** then select the desired margin settings

Change Header and Footer Size

Ribbon Method

▶ Click the **Insert tab**, then click the **Header & Footer button** in the Text group

▶ Click the **Scale with Document check box** in the Options group on the Header & Footer Tools Design tab to scale the font of the headers and footers with the font size in the worksheet

Shortcut Method

▶ Click the **Page Layout button** on the status bar

▶ Click in the Header area, click the **Header & Footer Tools Design tab**, then follow the step in bullet 2 of the Change Header and Footer Size Ribbon Method

---

CREATE AND APPLY CELL STYLES

Apply Cell Styles

Ribbon Method

▶ Click the **cell(s)** to format, then on the Home tab, click the **Cell Styles button** in the Styles group

▶ Click the desired cell style

Construct New Cell Styles

Ribbon Method

▶ Click the **cell(s)** to format
▶ On the Home tab, click the **Cell Styles button** in the Styles group, then click **New Cell Style**
▶ Type a **name** in the Style name text box, then click **Format**
▶ Choose settings on the tabs of the Format Cells dialog box, then click **OK**
▶ Click any check box to not include that parameter, click **OK**, then click **OK** again

EXCEL CORE OBJECTIVE 4: MANAGING WORKSHEETS AND WORKBOOKS

CREATE AND FORMAT WORKSHEETS

Insert a Single Worksheet

Ribbon Method

▶ On the Home tab, click the **Insert button arrow** in the Cells group, then click **Insert Sheet**

Shortcut Method

▶ Right-click the **sheet tab** to the right of where you want the new worksheet to appear
▶ Click **Insert**
▶ In the Insert dialog box, click the **Worksheet icon** on the General tab if necessary, then click **OK**

Insert Multiple Worksheets

Ribbon Method

▶ Press and hold **[Shift]**, then click two or more worksheet tabs that correspond with the number of sheets you want to add
▶ On the Home tab, click the **Insert button arrow** in the Cells group, then click **Insert Sheet**

Shortcut Method

▶ Press and hold **[Shift]**, then click the number of worksheet tabs that you want to add to the workbook
▶ Right-click a **sheet tab**, click **Insert**, click **Worksheet**, then click **OK**

Delete a Single Worksheet

Ribbon Method

▶ On the Home tab, click the **Delete button arrow** in the Cells group, then click **Delete Sheet**

Shortcut Method

▶ Right-click the **sheet tab** to delete, then click **Delete**

Delete Multiple Worksheets

Ribbon Method

▶ Press and hold **[Shift]**, then click the number of worksheet tabs that you want to delete
▶ On the Home tab, click the **Delete button arrow** in the Cells group, then click **Delete Sheet**

Shortcut Method

▶ Select the worksheets to delete from the workbook
▶ Right-click a selected **sheet tab**, then click **Delete**

Reposition Worksheets

Ribbon Method

▶ On the Home tab, click the **Format button** in the Cells group, then, under Organize Sheets, click **Move or Copy Sheet**
▶ In the Before sheet section of the Move or Copy dialog box, select a **location**
▶ Click **OK**

Shortcut Method

▶ Right-click the **sheet tab** of the worksheet to copy, then click **Move or Copy**
▶ Follow the steps in bullets 1–3 of the Reposition Worksheets Ribbon Method

OR

▶ Position the pointer over the **sheet tab** to be moved or copied
▶ Use ⌖ to drag the tab to the appropriate location in the workbook, then release the mouse button

Copy Worksheets

Ribbon Method

▶ On the Home tab, click the **Format button** in the Cells group, then, under Organize Sheets, click **Move or Copy Sheet**
▶ In the Before sheet section of the Move or Copy dialog box, select a **location**

▶ Click the **Create a copy check box**
▶ Click **OK**

Shortcut Method

▶ Right-click the **sheet tab** of the worksheet to copy, then click **Move or Copy**
▶ Follow the steps in bullets 2–4 of the Copy Worksheets Ribbon Method

OR

▶ Position the pointer over the **sheet tab** to be copied
▶ Press **[Ctrl]** and use ⮯ to drag a worksheet copy to the desired location

Move Worksheets

Ribbon Method

▶ Open the source and destination workbooks
▶ In the source workbook, click the **sheet tab** of the sheet you want to move
▶ On the Home tab, click the **Format button** in the Cells group, then, under Organize Sheets, click **Move or Copy Sheet**
▶ In the Move or Copy dialog box, click the **To book arrow**, then click the destination workbook name
▶ Click **OK**

Mouse Method

▶ Open the source and destination workbooks
▶ Click the **View tab**, click the **Arrange All button** in the Window group, click the **Tiled option button**, then click **OK**
▶ Drag to move the source worksheet to the destination workbook window

Rename Worksheets

Ribbon Method

▶ On the Home tab, click the **Format button** in the Cells group, then, under Organize Sheets, click **Rename Sheet**
▶ Type the new worksheet name, then press **[Enter]**

Mouse Method

▶ Double-click a **sheet tab**
▶ Type a new worksheet **name**, then press **[Enter]**

Shortcut Method

▶ Right-click a **sheet tab**, then click **Rename**
▶ Type a new worksheet name, then press **[Enter]**

Group Worksheets

Shortcut Method

▶ To group worksheets, use Table EX-9 as a reference to selecting worksheets

Table EX-9 Sheet Selection Actions

To select	Action
Adjacent sheets	Click the first sheet tab, press and hold **[Shift]**, then click the last sheet tab
Nonadjacent sheets	Click the first sheet tab, press and hold **[Ctrl]**, then click the other sheet tabs

Apply Color to Worksheet Tabs

Ribbon Method

▶ On the Home tab, click the **Format button** in the Cells group, then, under Organize Sheets, click **Tab Color**
▶ Click a **theme color** or a **standard color**, or click **More Colors** to select a color from the Colors dialog box

Shortcut Method

▶ Right-click the **sheet tab** to change
▶ Point to **Tab Color**, then click a **theme color** or a **standard color**, or click **More Colors** to select a color from the Colors dialog box

Hide Worksheet Tabs

Ribbon Method

▶ On the Home tab, click the **Format button** in the Cells group
▶ Under Visibility, point to **Hide & Unhide**, then click **Hide Sheet**

Shortcut Method

▶ Right-click any **worksheet tab**
▶ Click **Hide**

Unhide Worksheet Tabs

Ribbon Method

▶ On the Home tab, click the **Format button** in the Cells group
▶ Under Visibility, point to **Hide & Unhide**, then click **Unhide Sheet**

Shortcut Method

▶ Right-click any **sheet tab**
▶ Click **Unhide**
▶ In the Unhide dialog box, click the **sheet** you want to unhide, then click **OK**

MANIPULATE WINDOW VIEWS

Split Window Views

Ribbon Method

▶ Click the **cell** below and to the right of where you want to split the worksheet
▶ Click the **View tab**, then click the **Split button** in the Window group to split the worksheet horizontally and vertically
▶ To remove the splits, click the **Split button** in the Window group again

Mouse Method

▶ Point to the split box to the right of the horizontal scroll bar or the split box above the vertical scroll bar until the pointer becomes ⬌ or ↔
▶ Drag left, right, up, or down, releasing the mouse button when the split bar is in the appropriate location
▶ To remove a split, double-click either **split bar**, or double-click the **intersection** of the horizontal and vertical split bars to remove both

Arrange Window Views

Ribbon Method

▶ With two or more workbooks open, click the **View tab**, then click the **Arrange All button** in the Window group
▶ Using Table EX-10 as a reference, click an **option button** in the Arrange Windows dialog box, then click **OK**

Table EX-10 Arrange Windows Dialog Box Options

Click this option button	To
Tiled	Arrange windows in blocks so all are visible at once
Horizontal	Arrange workbooks horizontally, one above another
Vertical	Arrange workbooks vertically, one next to another
Cascade	Arrange workbooks on top of each other, with title bars visible

Open a New Window with Contents from the Current Worksheet

Ribbon Method

▶ Click the **View tab**, then click the **New Window button** in the Window group

MANIPULATE WORKBOOK VIEWS

Use Normal Workbook View, Use Page Layout Workbook View, and Use Page Break Workbook View

▶ Refer to Table EX-11 to change worksheet views

Table EX-11 Worksheet Views

View	What you see	Ribbon method	Mouse method
Normal view	Worksheet without headers, footers, or some graphics; does not show worksheet as it would appear as printed	Click the **View tab**, then click the **Normal button** in the Workbook Views group	Click the **Normal button** ⊞ on the status bar

(continued)

Table EX-11 Worksheet Views (continued)

View	What you see	Ribbon method	Mouse method
Page Layout view	Worksheet with headers, footers, and vertical and horizontal rulers	Click the **View tab**, then click the **Page Layout button** in the Workbook Views group	Click the **Page Layout button** 🔲 on the status bar
Page Break Preview	Similar to Normal view, except with blue lines indicating page breaks; drag a page break using the resize pointers ↔, ↕ or ⬊	Click the **View tab**, then click the **Page Break Preview button** in the Workbook Views group	Click the Page **Break Preview button** 🔳 on the status bar
Custom views	Saved views	Click the **View tab**, then click the **Custom Views button** in the Workbook Views group	None

Create Custom Views

Ribbon Method

▶ Click the **View tab**, then click the **Custom Views button** in the Workbook Views group

▶ Click **Add** in the Custom Views dialog box, enter a name in the Name text box, then click **OK**

EXCEL CORE OBJECTIVE 5: APPLYING FORMULAS AND FUNCTIONS

CREATE FORMULAS

Use Basic Operators

Keyboard Method

▶ Enter operators using Table EX-12 as a guide

Table EX-12   Excel Operators

Operator	How it is used
+	Addition
- Or negation	Subtraction or to change the sign of a value
*	Multiplication
/	Division
^	Exponentiation
%	Percent

Revise Formulas

Keyboard Method

▶ Click the cell that contains the formula, then edit the formula in the formula bar

Shortcut Method

▶ Click the cell that contains the formula, press **[F2]**, edit the formula in the cell, then press **[Enter]**

ENFORCE PRECEDENCE

Order of Evaluation

Keyboard Method

▶ Refer to Table EX-13, which provides the operations from the highest precedence to the lowest

Table EX-13   Precedence of Operators

Operator	Function
-	Negation
%	Percent

(continued)

Table EX-13 Precedence of Operators (continued)

Operator	Function
^	Exponentiation
* and / (evaluated from left to right)	Multiplication and division
+ and - (evaluated from left to right)	Addition and subtraction
& (concatenates string values)	Connect text strings
= <> <= >= > <	Comparison

Precedence Using Parentheses

Keyboard Method

▶ Enclose in parentheses ( ) the operation you want to calculate first; this will change the order of evaluation of an expression because operations in parentheses are always calculated before other operations

Precedence of Operators for Percent vs. Exponentiation

Keyboard Method

▶ The Percent operator (%) has a higher precedence than the Exponentiation operator (^); to change the precedence, use parentheses ( ) as described in Precedence Using Parentheses

APPLY CELL REFERENCES IN FORMULAS

Relative and Absolute References

Shortcut Method

To use relative references in formulas:

▶ Click the appropriate **cell**, then click the **formula bar** and type **=**, or type **=** directly in the cell

▶ To insert a cell reference in the formula, type the **cell address** you want to reference in the formula bar or in the cell that contains the formula, or click the **cell** you want to reference

▶ Complete the formula using appropriate operators, values, and additional cell references, then click the **Enter button** ☑ on the formula bar

To use absolute references in formulas:

▶ Click a **cell** where you want to enter a formula, then enter the **formula** in the formula bar or type the **formula** directly in the cell

▶ In the formula bar, select the **cell reference** that you want to make an absolute reference

▶ Press **[F4]**, then verify that the cell reference now reads **A1** (where A1 is the cell address)

▶ Press **[Enter]** or **[Tab]**

To use mixed references in formulas:

▶ Click a **cell** where you want to enter a formula, then enter the **formula** in the formula bar or type the **formula** directly in the cell

▶ In the formula bar, select the **cell reference** that you want to make into a mixed reference

▶ Press **[F4]** until the cell reference reads **A$1** or **$A1** (where A1 is the cell address)

▶ Press **[Enter]** or **[Tab]**

Excel

APPLY CONDITIONAL LOGIC IN A FORMULA

Create a Formula with Values that Match Conditions

Ribbon Method

▶ Click the **cell** where you want the formula result to appear

▶ Click the **Formulas tab**, then click the **Insert Function button** in the Function Library group (or click the **Insert Function button** 𝑓𝑥 on the formula bar)

▶ In the Insert Function dialog box, select the appropriate function using Table EX-14 as a reference, then click **OK**

▶ In the Function Arguments dialog box, specify the appropriate settings or the appropriate cells if necessary, then click **OK**

OR

▶ Click the **Formulas tab**, click the **Logical button** in the Function Library group, then click the function name in the list, using Table EX-14 as a reference

▶ In the Function Arguments dialog box, specify the appropriate settings or the appropriate cells if necessary, then click **OK**

Table EX-14 Functions for Conditional Logic

Function	Example	Results
IF	=IF(*logical_ test,value_if_true, value_if_false*)	Performs the logical test, then returns (displays) a value if it is true or false, such as whether a budget is within limits
AND	=AND(A1>10,B1>25)	Checks two or more conditions; if all are true, then returns TRUE; if one of the conditions is not true, then returns FALSE
OR	=OR(A1>10,B1>25)	Checks two or more conditions; if any are true, then returns TRUE; if all of the conditions are not true, then returns FALSE
NOT	=NOT(A1=25)	Checks the condition; then reverses the TRUE result and reports FALSE
IFERROR	=IFERROR(*formula,* "*ERRORMESSAGE*")	Checks a formula for correctness; if it would result in an Excel error message (such as #DIV/0!), it displays your *ERRORMESSAGE* text instead of the Excel error

Edit Defined Conditions in a Formula

Keyboard Method

▶ Click the cell that contains the conditional formula, then edit the conditions in the formula bar

Shortcut Method

▶ Click the cell that contains the conditional formula, press **[F2]**, edit the conditions in the cell, then press **[Enter]**

Use a Series of Conditional Logic Values in a Formula

Keyboard Method

▶ Click the **formula bar**, then enter a nested IF statement using the syntax IF(*logical_test*, *value_if_true1*, IF(*logical_test 2*, *value_if_true2*, *value_if_false2*))

▶ Verify that the second IF statement is actually the *value_if_false* argument of the first IF statement

---

APPLY NAMED RANGES IN FORMULAS

Define Ranges in Formulas

Ribbon Method

▶ Click in the **cell** where the formula will appear

▶ Begin typing the formula, then when you need to insert the range name, click the **Formulas tab**

▶ Click the **Use in Formula button** in the Defined Names group, then click the **range name** in the list

▶ Complete the formula as appropriate

OR

▶ Click in the **cell** where the formula will appear

▶ Begin typing the formula, then when you need to insert the range name, click the **Formulas tab**

▶ Click the **Use in Formula button** in the Defined Names group, click **Paste Names**, then in the Paste Name dialog box, double-click the **range name**

▶ Complete the formula as appropriate

Shortcut Method

▶ Click the **cell** where the formula will appear

▶ As you type the formula in the cell, type the first letter of the range name, then use **[↓]** to select the range name that appears in the list

▶ Press **[Tab]**, then type the rest of the formula and press **[Enter]**

Edit Ranges in Formulas

Ribbon Method

▶ Click the **formula bar**, then click the named range you want to remove from the formula

▶ Click the **Formulas tab**, click the **Use in Formula button** in the Defined Names group, then click the **replacement range name** in the list

▶ Click the **Enter button** ✔ on the formula bar or press **[Enter]**

Rename a Named Range

Ribbon Method

▶ Click the **Formulas tab**, then click the **Name Manager button** in the Defined Names group
▶ Click the **name** of the range you want to rename
▶ Click **Edit**, enter the new range name in the Edit Name dialog box, click **OK**, then click **Close**

Shortcut Method

▶ Click the **Formulas tab**, then press **[Ctrl][F3]**
▶ Follow the steps in bullets 2–3 of the Rename a Named Range Ribbon Method

APPLY CELL RANGES IN FORMULAS

Enter a Cell Range Definition in the Formula Bar

Ribbon Method

▶ Click in the **cell** where the formula will appear
▶ Begin typing the formula; as you type the formula in the cell, type the first letter of the range name, then use **[↓]** to select the range name that appears in the list
▶ Press **[Tab]**, then type the rest of the formula and press **[Enter]**

Define a Cell Range

Ribbon Method

▶ Select a **range**
▶ Click the **Formulas tab**, then click the **Define Name button** in the Defined Names group
▶ In the New Name dialog box, type the **range name** in the Name text box, then click **OK**

OR

▶ Click the **Formulas tab**, then click the **Name Manager button** in the Defined Names group
▶ Click **New**
▶ In the New Name dialog box, type the **range name** in the Name text box, then click **OK**

Shortcut Method

▶ Select the **range** you want to name
▶ Click the **Name box** to the far left of the formula bar, type the **range name** using numbers and letters and without using spaces, then press **[Enter]**

OR

▶ Click the **Formulas tab**, then press **[Ctrl][F3]**
▶ Press **[Alt][N]** in the New Name dialog box, type the **range name** in the Name text box, press **[Enter]**, then click **Close**
OR
▶ Select a range you want to name
▶ Right-click the **range**, then click **Define Name**
▶ Enter the range name, then click **OK**

EXCEL CORE OBJECTIVE 6: PRESENTING DATA VISUALLY

CREATE CHARTS BASED ON WORKSHEET DATA

Ribbon Method
▶ Select the **data range** you want to use to create a chart
▶ Click the **Insert tab**, click a **chart type button** in the Charts group, using Table EX-15 as a guide, then click a **chart subtype** from the list

Table EX-15 Common Chart Types

Chart type	Used to
Column	Show relative amounts for one or multiple values at different points in time (displays vertically)
Line	Show growth trends over time
Pie	Show proportions or percentages of parts to a whole
Bar	Show relative amounts for one or multiple values at different points in time (displays horizontally)
Area	Show differences between several sets of data over time
Scatter	Show values that are not in categories and where each data point is a distinct measurement

APPLY AND MANIPULATE ILLUSTRATIONS

Insert

Ribbon Method
▶ Click the **Insert tab**, then click the **Picture**, **Clip Art**, **Shapes**, **SmartArt**, or **Screenshot button** in the Illustrations group
▶ Use the dialog box or task pane to select an illustration to insert

Excel

Position

Keyboard Method

▶ Click the **illustration**, then use the arrow keys to move it on the worksheet

Shortcut Method

▶ Click the **illustration**, then drag it to a new position on the worksheet

Size

Ribbon Method

▶ Select an **illustration**, then click the **Drawing Tools Format tab** or the **Picture Tools Format tab**
▶ In the Size group, type **new values** or use the arrows in the Shape Height and Shape Width text boxes

Shortcut Method

▶ Click the **illustration**, then position the pointer over a corner, side, top, or bottom sizing handle
▶ Drag the sizing handle to resize the chart

Rotate

Ribbon Method

▶ Select an **illustration**, then click the **Drawing Tools Format tab** or the **Picture Tools Format tab**
▶ In the Arrange group, click **Rotate**, then click one of the rotation options

Shortcut Method

▶ Right-click an **illustration**, click **Format Shape**, click **3-D Rotation**, then enter values in the Format Shape dialog box

Modify Clip Art SmartArt

Ribbon Method

▶ Select an existing **SmartArt graphic**, then click the **SmartArt Tools Format tab** or the **SmartArt Tools Design tab** to change options for the graphic

Modify Shape

Ribbon Method

▶ Select an existing **shape**, then click the **Drawing Tools Format tab**
▶ In the Insert Shapes group, click the **Edit Shape button arrow**, click **Change Shape**, then click the icon for the new shape

OR

▶ Select an existing **shape**, then click the **Drawing Tools Format tab**

▶ In the Insert Shapes group, click the **Edit Shape button arrow**, click **Edit Points**, then drag any of the existing points to modify the shape

Modify Screenshots

Ribbon Method

▶ Click a **screenshot object** in the worksheet, then click the **Picture Tools Format tab**

▶ In the Picture Styles group, click one of the **Picture Styles** to change the screenshot style

OR

▶ Click a **screenshot object** in the worksheet, then click the **Picture Tools Format tab**

▶ In the Picture Styles group, click the **Picture Border button** to change the screenshot border

OR

▶ Click a **screenshot object** in the worksheet, then click the **Picture Tools Format tab**

▶ In the Picture Styles group, click the **Picture Effects button**, then click a picture effect to apply a visual effect to the screenshot

OR

▶ Click a **screenshot object** in the worksheet, then click the **Picture Tools Format tab**

▶ In the Picture Styles group, click the **Picture Layout button** to convert the screenshot to a SmartArt Graphic

CREATE AND MODIFY IMAGES BY USING THE IMAGE EDITOR

Make Corrections to an Image

Sharpen or Soften an Image

Ribbon Method

▶ Click an **image** in the worksheet, then click the **Picture Tools Format tab**

▶ Click the **Corrections button** in the Adjust group, then click an image representing the appropriate Sharpen or Soften percentages

Change Brightness and Contrast

Ribbon Method

▶ Click an **image** in the worksheet, then click the **Picture Tools Format tab**
▶ Click the **Corrections button** in the Adjust group, then click an image representing the appropriate Brightness and Contrast percentages

Use Picture Color Tools

Ribbon Method

▶ Click a **picture**, then click the **Picture Tools Format tab**
▶ Click the **Color button** in the Adjust group, then select an image representing the appropriate Color Saturation, Color Tone, and Recolor settings

Shortcut Method

▶ Right-click a **picture**, then click **Format Picture**
▶ In the Format Picture dialog box, click **Picture Color**; click the **Presets buttons** for Color Saturation, Color Tone, and Recolor; click the image representing the desired color setting; then click **Close**

Change Artistic Effects on an Image

Ribbon Method

▶ Click an **image**, then click the **Picture Tools Format tab**
▶ Click the **Artistic Effects button** in the Adjust group, then select an artistic effect

Shortcut Method

▶ Right-click an **image**, then click **Format Picture**
▶ In the Format Picture dialog box, click **Artistic Effects**, click the **Artistic Effect button**, select the desired effect, then click **Close**

APPLY SPARKLINES

Use Line, Column, and Win/Loss Chart Types

Ribbon Method

▶ Select one or more cells where you want to insert sparklines, then click the **Insert tab**
▶ Click **Line** in the Sparklines group to display changes in data over time using a line chart

   OR

▶ Click **Column** in the Sparklines group to display changes in data over time using a column chart

OR

▶ Click **Win/Loss** in the Sparklines group if you want to show whether data was positive (win) or negative (loss) using different color bars

▶ In the Create Sparklines dialog box, enter the range of the cells that will be charted in the Data Range text box, then click **OK**

OR

▶ In the Create Sparklines dialog box, click the **Collapse button** ▦ for the Data Range text box, select the **data range** on the worksheet, click the **Expand button** ▦, then click **OK**

▶ Your sparklines will change as data changes and will print with your worksheet data

Create a Sparkline Chart

Ribbon Method

▶ Select a **cell** where you want to insert sparklines

▶ Click the **Insert tab**, then click the **Line**, **Column**, or **Win/Loss button** in the Sparklines group

▶ In the Create Sparklines dialog box, enter the range of the cells that will be charted in the Data Range text box, then click **OK**

OR

▶ In the Create Sparklines dialog box, click the **Collapse button** ▦ for the Data Range text box, select the **data range** on the worksheet, click the **Expand button** ▦, then click **OK**

Customize a Sparkline

Ribbon Method

▶ Click the **cell** displaying the sparkline, then click the **Sparkline Tools Design tab**

▶ Select from the options in the sparkline, Type, Show, Style, and Group groups to customize the sparkline

Format a Sparkline

Ribbon Method

▶ Click the **cell** displaying the sparkline, click the **Sparkline Tools Design tab**, then click a **style** in the Style group

▶ You can also click the **Sparkline Color button** or the **Marker Color button** in the Style group to adjust the sparkline and marker colors

Show or Hide Data Markers

Ribbon Method

▶ Click the **cell** displaying the sparkline, then click the **Sparkline Tools Design tab**

▶ Use the **Markers check box** in the Show group to display and hide all markers

EXCEL CORE OBJECTIVE 7: SHARING WORKSHEET DATA WITH OTHER USERS

SHARE SPREADSHEETS BY USING BACKSTAGE

Send a Worksheet via E-Mail

Ribbon Method

▶ Click the **File tab** to open Backstage view, then click **Save & Send**

▶ Click **Send Using E-mail**

▶ Click **Send as Attachment**, **Send a Link**, **Send as PDF**, **Send as Internet Fax**, or **Send as XPS**

▶ Enter the necessary information using your e-mail program

Send a Worksheet via SkyDrive

Ribbon Method

▶ Click the **File tab** to open Backstage view, then click **Save & Send**

▶ Click **Save to Web**

▶ Select a **folder** in Windows Live SkyDrive, then click **Save As**

▶ In the File name text box, type a name for your file, then click **Save**

Change the File Type to a Different Version of Excel

Ribbon Method

▶ Click the **File tab** to open Backstage view, then click **Save As**

▶ Click the **Save as type button** in the Save As dialog box, then click the desired version of Excel

▶ Click **Save**

Shortcut Method

▶ Press **[Ctrl][S]**

▶ Click the **Save as type button** in the Save As dialog box, then click the desired version of Excel

▶ Click **Save**

Save as PDF or XPS

Ribbon Method

▶ Click the **File tab** to open Backstage view, then click **Save As**
▶ Click the **Save as type button** in the Save As dialog box, then click **PDF (*.pdf)** or **XPS Document (*.xps)**
▶ Click **Save**

Shortcut Method

▶ Press **[Ctrl][S]**
▶ Click the **Save as type button** in the Save As dialog box, then click **PDF (*.pdf)** or **XPS Document (*.xps)**
▶ Click **Save**

OR

▶ Press **[F12]**
▶ Click the **Save as type button** in the Save As dialog box, then click **PDF (*.pdf)** or **XPS Document (*.xps)**
▶ Click **Save**

Excel

MANAGE COMMENTS

Insert

Ribbon Method

▶ Select the **cell** to which you want to attach a comment
▶ Click the **Review tab**, then click the **New Comment button** in the Comments group
▶ Type the appropriate text in the comment box
▶ Click outside the comment box

Shortcut Method

▶ Right-click the **cell** to which you want to attach a comment
▶ Click **Insert Comment**
▶ Follow the steps in bullets 3–4 of the Insert Ribbon Method

View

Ribbon Method

▶ Click the **Review tab**, then click a **cell** marked with a comment (a red triangle in the upper-right corner of the cell)
▶ Click the **Show/Hide Comment button** in the Comments group to view a single comment or click the **Show All Comments button** in the Comments group to view all workbook comments; the comments remain displayed when you click other cells

Shortcut Method
- ▶ Point to a **cell** containing the comment, then read the comment that appears

  OR
- ▶ Right-click a **cell** marked with a comment (a red triangle in the upper-right corner of the cell), then click **Show/Hide Comments**

Edit

Ribbon Method
- ▶ Click a **cell** marked with a comment (a red triangle in the upper-right corner of the cell)
- ▶ Click the **Review tab**, then click the **Edit Comment button** in the Comments group
- ▶ Modify the comment
- ▶ Click outside the comment box

Shortcut Method
- ▶ Right-click a **cell** marked with a comment (a red triangle in the upper-right corner of the cell), then click **Edit Comment**
- ▶ Follow the steps in bullets 3–4 of the Edit Ribbon Method

Delete

Ribbon Method
- ▶ Click the **cell** marked with a comment (a red triangle in the upper-right corner of the cell)
- ▶ Click the **Review tab**, then click the **Delete button** in the Comments group

Shortcut Method
- ▶ Right-click the **cell** marked with a comment (a red triangle in the upper-right corner of the cell), then click **Delete Comment**

EXCEL CORE OBJECTIVE 8: ANALYZING AND ORGANIZING DATA

FILTER DATA

Define a Filter

Ribbon Method
- ▶ Select a **range** of cells that you want to filter
- ▶ Click the **Data tab**, then click **Filter** in the Sort & Filter group
- ▶ Click the **column header arrow button** to filter the data

Excel

OR

▶ To define an advanced filter, create a criteria range on the worksheet with the column headers and criteria for filtering data
▶ Click any **cell** in the table, click the **Data tab**, then click the **Advanced button** in the Sort & Filter group
▶ Click the **Criteria range text box**, select the criteria range on the worksheet, then click **OK**

Shortcut Method

▶ Select a **range** of cells that you want to filter
▶ Right-click the selection, click **Filter**, then click the criteria on which to filter the data
▶ Click the **column header arrow button** to filter the data

Apply a Filter

Ribbon Method

▶ Click inside the range you want to filter
▶ Click the **Data tab**, then click the **Filter button** in the Sort & Filter group
▶ Click the **arrow button** at the top of the column on which you want to filter
▶ Click the **Select All check box** to remove all check marks
▶ Click the **check boxes** for the items you want to display
▶ Click **OK**

Shortcut Method

▶ Click inside the range, then press **[Ctrl][Shift][L]**
▶ Follow the steps in bullets 3–6 of the Apply a Filter Ribbon Method

OR

▶ Right-click in a cell that contains the value, color, font color, or icon on which you want to filter
▶ Point to **Filter**, then click **Filter by Selected Cell's Value** (or **Color**, **Font Color**, or **Icon**)

Remove a Filter

Ribbon Method

▶ Click in the filtered range
▶ Click the **Data tab**, then click the **Filter button** in the Sort & Filter group to deselect the button and remove the filter arrows

Shortcut Method

▶ Click the **column header arrow button** 🔽
▶ Click **Clear Filter From** to delete the filter

Filter Lists Using AutoFilter

Ribbon Method

▶ To filter a table, go to the last bullet; to filter a cell range, click a **cell** in the range, click the **Sort & Filter button** in the Editing group on the Home tab, then click **Filter**
  OR
▶ Click a **cell** in the range, click the **Data tab**, then click the **Filter button** in the Sort & Filter group
▶ Click a **column heading arrow button**, click the **(Select All) check box** to deselect it, click to select the **check box(es)** for the value(s) in the table you want to display, then click **OK**

SORT DATA

Use Sort Options: Values, Font Color, and Cell Color

Ribbon Method

▶ Click any cell in the range to be sorted
▶ Click the **Data tab**, then click the **Sort button** in the Sort & Filter group
▶ In the Sort dialog box, click the **Sort by arrow button**, then click the **column** on which to sort
▶ In the Sort dialog box, click the **Sort on arrow button**, then click **Values**, **Cell Color**, **Font Color**, or **Cell Icon**
▶ Select appropriate values in the Sort On and Order lists, then click **OK**
▶ To sort within the groupings you created, click **Add Level** in the Sort dialog box, then select another column on which to sort and specify Sort On and Order values
▶ Continue adding levels as necessary, then click **OK**

Shortcut Method

▶ Right-click a **cell value** on which you want to sort
▶ Point to **Sort**, then click the appropriate option

APPLY CONDITIONAL FORMATTING

Apply Conditional Formatting to Cells

Ribbon Method

▶ Select a **cell range** to format conditionally
▶ On the Home tab, click the **Conditional Formatting button** in the Styles group
▶ Point to a conditional formatting category, then click a category option, using Table EX-16 as a reference

Table EX-16 Conditional Formatting Options

Formatting category	Options	Available formatting
Highlight Cells Rules	Greater Than, Less Than, Between, Equal To, Text that Contains, A Date Occurring, Duplicate Values	Colored text and fills, or custom formats
Top/Bottom Rules	Top 10 Items, Top 10%, Bottom 10 Items, Bottom 10%, Above Average, Below Average	Colored text and fills, or custom formats
Data Bars	12 built-in types	Existing colors or click **More Rules** to create custom formats
Color Scales	12 built-in types	Existing scales or click **More Rules** to create custom formats
Icon Sets	20 built-in icon styles	Click **More Rules** to modify rules for icon display

Excel

Use the Rule Manager to Apply Conditional Formats

Ribbon Method

▶ Select a **data range**
▶ On the Home tab, click the **Conditional Formatting button** in the Styles group, then click **New Rule**
▶ In the New Formatting Rule dialog box, click a rule type in the Select a Rule Type section
▶ In the Edit the Rule Description section, specify the values that you want formatted
▶ Click the **Format button** in the Edit the Rule Description section, then specify a format in the Format Cells dialog box
▶ Click **OK**, then click **OK**

Use the IF Function to Apply Conditional Formatting

Ribbon Method

▶ On the Home tab, click the **Conditional Formatting button** in the Styles group, then click **Manage Rules**

▶ Select a rule, then click the **New Rule**, **Edit Rule**, **Delete Rule**, **Move Up**, or **Move Down button**
▶ Click the **Stop If True check box** to stop a rule from being applied if it is evaluated as True

Clear Rules

Ribbon Method

▶ Click any worksheet **cell**
▶ On the Home tab, click the **Conditional Formatting button** in the Styles group, point to **Clear Rules**, then click **Clear Rules from Selected Cells** or **Clear Rules from Entire Sheet**

OR

▶ Click any worksheet **cell**
▶ On the Home tab, click the **Conditional Formatting button** in the Styles group, then click **Manage Rules**
▶ In the Conditional Formatting Rules Manager dialog box, click the **Show formatting rules for arrow button**, then click **This Worksheet**
▶ Click the rule to delete, click **Delete Rule** or press **[Delete]**, then click **OK**

Use Icon Sets

Ribbon Method

▶ Select a **cell range** to format conditionally
▶ On the Home tab, click the **Conditional Formatting button** in the Styles group
▶ Point to **Icon Sets**, then click an option in the Directional, Shapes, Indicators, or Rating category to display relative cell values using icons

Use Data Bars

Ribbon Method

▶ Select a **cell range** to format conditionally
▶ On the Home tab, click the **Conditional Formatting button** in the Styles group
▶ Point to **Data Bars**, then click an option in the Gradient Fill or Solid Fill category to display relative cell values using data bar lengths

Excel Expert Objectives

Excel Expert Objective 1: Sharing and Maintaining Workbooks

Apply Workbook Settings, Properties, and Data Options

Set Advanced Properties

Ribbon Method

▶ Click the **File tab** to open Backstage view
▶ In the Info section, point to then click the **Properties button** on the right side of Backstage view
▶ Click **Advanced Properties**, then click the **Summary tab** to add properties to the workbook

Save a Workbook as a Template

Ribbon Method

▶ Open the workbook you want to save to another format, click the **File tab** to open Backstage view, then click **Save As**
▶ Enter a file location and file name, then click the **Save as type button**
▶ Click **Excel template (*.xltx)**, then click **Save**

Shortcut Method

▶ Press **[Ctrl][S]**
▶ Click the **Save as type button** in the Save As dialog box, then click **Excel template (*.xltx)**
▶ Click **Save**

OR

▶ Press **[F12]**
▶ Click the **Save as type button** in the Save As dialog box, then click **Excel template (*.xltx)**
▶ Click **Save**

Excel

Import and Export XML Data

Import XML

Ribbon Method

▶ Click the **Developer tab**, then click the **Import button** in the XML group
▶ In the Import XML dialog box, click the XML file that will be imported, then click **Import**
▶ If a schema hasn't been mapped to the workbook, click **OK** to have Excel create a schema based on the XML source data
▶ Enter the location for the data in the Import Data dialog box, then click **OK**

Export XML

Ribbon Method

▶ Click the **Developer tab**, then click the **Export button** in the XML group
▶ Enter a file location and file name in the Export XML dialog box, then click **Export**

APPLY PROTECTION AND SHARING PROPERTIES TO WORKBOOKS AND WORKSHEETS

Protect the Current Sheet

Ribbon Method

▶ Click the **Review tab**, then click the **Protect Sheet button** in the Changes group
▶ In the Protect Sheet dialog box, click to select the **Protect worksheet and contents of locked cells check box** if necessary, then type a **password** in the Password to unprotect sheet text box
▶ Click **OK**
▶ In the Confirm Password dialog box, retype the **password**, then click **OK**

    OR

▶ On the Home tab, click the **Format button** in the Cells group, then click **Protect Sheet**
▶ Follow the steps in bullets 2–4 of the Protect the Current Sheet Ribbon Method

Shortcut Method

▶ Right-click a **sheet tab**, then click **Protect Sheet**
▶ Follow the steps in bullets 2–4 of the Protect the Current Sheet Ribbon Method

Protect the Workbook Structure

Ribbon Method

▶ Click the **Review tab**, then click the **Protect Workbook button** in the Changes group
▶ In the Protect Structure and Windows dialog box, select the appropriate **check boxes**
▶ If desired, click the **Password text box**, type a **password**, then click **OK**
▶ Type the **password** to confirm it, then click **OK**

Restrict Permissions

Ribbon Method

▶ Save the workbook you want to restrict
▶ Click the **File tab** to open Backstage view, click **Info**, then click **Protect Workbook** under Permissions
▶ Select from the choices **Mark as Final**, **Encrypt with Password**, **Protect Current Sheet**, **Protect Workbook Structure**, and **Add a Digital Signature**

Require a Password to Open a Workbook

Ribbon Method

▶ Click the **File tab** to open Backstage view, click **Save As**, click the **Tools button** at the bottom of the Save As dialog box, then click **General Options**
▶ In the Password to open text box of the General Options dialog box, type the password
▶ Press **[Tab]**, in the Password to modify text box, type the password, then click **OK**
▶ Enter the password in the first Confirm Password dialog box, click **OK**, enter the password in the second Confirm Password dialog box, click **OK**, then click **Save**

MAINTAIN SHARED WORKBOOKS

Merge Workbooks

Ribbon Method

▶ Click the **File tab** to open Backstage view, click **Options**, click **Quick Access Toolbar**, click the **Choose commands from arrow**, then click **All Commands**
▶ Click **Compare and Merge Workbooks**, click **Add**, then click **OK**
▶ Open the master copy of the workbook, click **Compare and Merge Workbooks** on the Quick Access toolbar, then save the workbook if asked

Excel

▶ Click the workbooks that you want to merge in the Select Files to Merge into Current Workbook dialog box, then click **OK**

Set Track Changes Options

Ribbon Method

▶ Click the **Review tab**, click the **Track Changes button** in the Changes group, then click **Highlight Changes**
▶ In the Highlight Changes dialog box, click to select the **Track changes while editing check box**
▶ Make sure the Highlight changes on screen check box is selected, then click **OK**
▶ In the message box, click **OK**

EXCEL EXPERT OBJECTIVE 2: APPLYING FORMULAS AND FUNCTIONS

AUDIT FORMULAS

Trace Formula Precedents

Ribbon Method

▶ Click a **cell** that contains a formula
▶ Click the **Formulas tab**, then click the **Trace Precedents button** in the Formula Auditing group
▶ Double-click one of the **blue arrows** to navigate between the cell containing the formula and the precedent cells

Trace Dependents

Ribbon Method

▶ Click a **cell** that is referenced in a formula
▶ Click the **Formulas tab**, then click the **Trace Dependents button** in the Formula Auditing group
▶ Double-click the **blue arrow** to navigate between the cells

Trace Errors

Ribbon Method

▶ Click the **cell** that shows an error, using Table EX-17 as a reference
▶ Click the **Formulas tab**, click the **Error Checking button arrow** in the Formula Auditing group, then click **Trace Error**
▶ Use the formula bar to correct the formula

Table EX-17 Common Cell Errors

Error	Means
#DIV/0!	Value is divided by zero
#NAME?	Excel does not recognize text
#N/A	Value is not available for the formula
#NULL!	When a formula specifies an intersection of two areas that do not intersect
#NUM!	Invalid formula number(s)
#REF!	Invalid cell reference
#VALUE!	Operand or argument is incorrect

Locate Invalid Data

Ribbon Method

▶ Click the **Data tab**, click the **Data Validation button arrow**, then click **Circle Invalid Data** to display red circles around cells that are not consistent with data validation criteria

Locate Invalid Formulas

Ribbon Method

▶ Click the **Formulas tab**, then click the **Error Checking button** in the Formula Auditing group
▶ In the Error Checking dialog box, click the appropriate button using Table EX-18 as a reference, fix or view the error as prompted, then click **OK**
▶ Click the **Next** and **Previous buttons** to navigate through the errors

Table EX-18 Error Checking Dialog Box Options

Button	Action
Help on this error	Opens the Microsoft Excel Help Window with information about this type of function or formula
Show Calculation Steps	Opens the Evaluate Formula dialog box
Ignore Error	Moves to the next error without modifying the current error
Edit in Formula Bar	Activates the cell containing the error in the formula bar

Correct Errors in Formulas

Ribbon Method

▶ Click the **cell** that contains the formula
▶ Click the **Formulas tab**, then click **Evaluate Formula** in the Formula Auditing group
▶ In the Evaluate Formula dialog box, click the appropriate button, using Table EX-19 as a reference

Table EX-19 Evaluate Formula Dialog Box Options

Button	Action
Evaluate	Shows the result of the underlined value; click repeatedly to display additional levels of the formula
Step In	Views the formula that supports the highlighted argument; available when there is a formula within the formula you are evaluating
Step Out	Displays the previous cell and formula; available after you have clicked Step In

MANIPULATE FORMULA OPTIONS

Set Iterative Calculation Options

Ribbon Method

▶ Click the **File tab** to open Backstage view, click **Options**, then click **Formulas**
▶ Click the **Enable iterative calculation check box** in the Calculation options section, enter the maximum number of iterations in the Maximum Iterations text box, enter the maximum amount of change between recalculation results in the Maximum Change text box, then click **OK**

Shortcut Method

▶ Click the **Customize Quick Access Toolbar button** ⤓, click **More Commands**, then click **Formulas**
▶ Click the **Enable iterative calculation check box** in the Calculation options section, enter the maximum number of iterations in the Maximum Iterations text box, enter the maximum amount of change between recalculation results in the Maximum Change text box, then click **OK**

Enable or Disable Automatic Workbook Calculation

Ribbon Method

▶ Click the **File tab** to open Backstage view, click **Options**, then click **Formulas**
▶ Click the **Automatic option button** in the Calculation options section to enable or disable automatic workbook calculation

Shortcut Method

▶ Click the **Customize Quick Access Toolbar button** , click **More Commands**, then click **Formulas**
▶ Click the **Automatic option button** in the Calculation options section to enable or disable automatic workbook calculation

Perform Data Summary Tasks

Use an Array Formula

Keyboard Method

▶ Select the cells where the array formula results will appear
▶ Enter **=**, then enter the array ranges and the formula's mathematical operators
▶ Press **[Ctrl][Shift][Enter]** to display the results of the array formula

Use a SUMIFS Function

Keyboard Method

▶ Click the cell that will contain the conditional formula result, then enter **=**
▶ Enter the SUMIFS function using the syntax SUMIFS(*sum_range, criteria_range1, criteria1, criteria_range2, criteria2*...)

Ribbon Method

▶ Click the **Formulas tab**, then click the **Insert Function button** in the Function Library group
▶ Enter **Sumifs** in the Search for a function text box in the Insert Function dialog box, click **Go**, then click **OK**
▶ Enter the Sum_range, Criteria_range1, Criteria1,... in the Function Arguments dialog box, then click **OK**

Shortcut Method

▶ Click the **Insert Function button** f_x on the formula bar
▶ Enter **Sumifs** in the Search for a function text box in the Insert Function dialog box, click **Go**, then click **OK**
▶ Enter the Sum_range, Criteria_range1, Criteria1,... in the Function Arguments dialog box, then click **OK**

APPLY FUNCTIONS IN FORMULAS

Find and Correct Errors in Functions

Ribbon Method
- ▶ Click the **cell** that contains the formula
- ▶ Click the **Formulas tab**, then click **Evaluate Formula** in the Formula Auditing group
- ▶ In the Evaluate Formula dialog box, click the appropriate button, using Table EX-19 in the Correct Errors in Formulas section as a reference

Applying Arrays to Functions

Keyboard Method
- ▶ Select the cells where the array function results will appear, then enter the function using the syntax *function name(array range, array arguments* if required)
- ▶ Press **[Ctrl][Shift][Enter]** to display the results of the array formula

Use Statistical Functions

Ribbon Method
- ▶ Click the cell where you want the formula result to appear
- ▶ Click the **Formulas tab**, then click the **Insert Function button** in the Function Library group
- ▶ In the Insert Function dialog box, select the appropriate function, then click **OK**
- ▶ In the Function Argument dialog box, specify the appropriate settings or the appropriate cells if necessary, then click **OK**

  OR
- ▶ Click the **Formulas tab**, click the **More Functions button** in the Function Library group, point to **Statistical**, then click the function name in the list
- ▶ In the Function Argument dialog box, specify the appropriate settings or the appropriate cells if necessary, then click **OK**

Shortcut Method
- ▶ Click the appropriate cell
- ▶ Click the **Insert Function button** 🔣 on the formula bar
- ▶ In the Insert Function dialog box, select the appropriate function, then click **OK**
- ▶ In the Function Argument dialog box, specify the appropriate settings or the appropriate cells if necessary, then click **OK**

  OR
- ▶ Type **=**, start to type a function name, then observe the function list

- ▶ Press **[↓]** until the desired function name is highlighted, then press **[Tab]**
- ▶ Type or drag to enter the argument cell or range, then press **[Enter]**

Use Date, Time, Financial, and Text Functions

Ribbon Method

- ▶ Click the cell where you want the formula result to appear
- ▶ Click the **Formulas tab**; then click the **Insert Function button** in the Function Library group
- ▶ In the Insert Function dialog box, select the appropriate function, then click **OK**
- ▶ In the Function Argument dialog box, specify the appropriate settings or the appropriate cells if necessary, then click **OK**

  OR

- ▶ Click the **Formulas tab**; click the **Date & Time**, **Financial**, or **Text button** in the Function Library group; then click the function name in the list
- ▶ In the Function Argument dialog box, specify the appropriate settings or the appropriate cells if necessary, then click **OK**

Shortcut Method

- ▶ Click the appropriate cell
- ▶ Click the **Insert Function button** f_x on the formula bar
- ▶ In the Insert Function dialog box, select the appropriate function, then click **OK**
- ▶ In the Function Argument dialog box, specify the appropriate settings or the appropriate cells if necessary, then click **OK**

  OR

- ▶ Type **=**, start to type a function name, then observe the function list
- ▶ Press **[↓]** until the desired function name is highlighted, then press **[Tab]**
- ▶ Type or drag to enter the argument cell or range, then press **[Enter]**

Cube Functions

Ribbon Method

- ▶ Click the cell where you want the formula result to appear
- ▶ Click the **Formulas tab**, then click the **Insert Function button** in the Function Library group
- ▶ In the Insert Function dialog box, select the appropriate cube function, then click **OK**
- ▶ In the Function Argument dialog box, specify the appropriate settings or the appropriate cells if necessary, then click **OK**

Keyboard Method

▶ Click the appropriate cell
▶ Type **=**, start to type a function name, then observe the function list
▶ Press **[↓]** until the desired cube function name is highlighted, then press **[Tab]**
▶ Type or drag to enter the argument cell or range, then press **[Enter]**

Shortcut Method

▶ Click the cell where you want the formula result to appear
▶ Click the **Insert Function button** f_x on the formula bar
▶ In the Insert Function dialog box, select the appropriate cube function, then click **OK**
▶ In the Function Argument dialog box, specify the appropriate settings or the appropriate cells if necessary, then click **OK**

Excel Expert Objective 3: Presenting Data Visually

Apply Advanced Chart Features

Use Trendlines

Ribbon Method

▶ Select a data series in a chart, click the **Chart Tools Layout tab**, then click the **Trendline button** in the Analysis group
▶ Click **Linear Trendline**, **Exponential Trendline**, **Two Period Moving Average**, or **Linear Forecast Trendline**

Shortcut Method

▶ Right-click a data series, click **Add Trendline**, then select the Trendline type and options in the Format Trendline dialog box

Use Dual Axes

Ribbon Method

▶ Select the data you want to chart, click the **Insert tab**, then select the chart type and subtype
▶ Click the **Chart Tools Layout tab**
▶ Click the **Chart Elements button arrow** and select the data series that you want to move to a secondary axis, click **Format Selection** in the Current Selection group, click the **Secondary Axis option button**, then click **Close**

Use Chart Templates

Ribbon Method

▶ To create a chart template, click the **Chart Tools Design tab**, click **Save As Template** in the Type group, enter a file name in the Save Chart Template dialog box, then click **Save**

▶ To apply a chart template, select the **chart**, click the **Insert tab**, click a chart type in the Charts group, then click **All Chart Types**

▶ Click the **Templates folder** in the Change Chart Type dialog box, select a template in the My Templates area, then click **OK**

Use Sparklines

Ribbon Method

▶ Select an empty cell, click the **Insert tab**, then click **Line**, **Column**, or **Win/Loss** in the Sparklines group

▶ In the Create Sparklines dialog box, type the range of the cells to chart in the Data Range text box, then click **OK**

▶ Click the **Group button** in the Group group on the Sparkline Tools Design tab to add common formatting and scaling to sparklines

▶ Click the **Axis button** in the Group group on the Sparkline Tools Design tab to display an axis in the sparkline and change its scale

▶ Click the **Sparkline Color button** or the **Marker Color button** in the Style group on the Sparkline Tools Design tab to change the sparkline or marker color

▶ Click the **More button** in the Style group on the Sparkline Tools Design tab to change the sparkline style

▶ Click the **High Point**, **Low Point**, **Negative Points**, **First Point**, **Last Point**, or **Markers check box** in the Show group on the Sparkline Tools Design tab to display these indicators on the sparkline

▶ Click the **Line**, **Column**, or **Win/Loss button** in the Type group on the Sparkline Tools Design tab to change the sparkline type

▶ Click the **Edit Data button** in the Sparkline group on the Sparkline Tools Design tab to change the sparkline's location or data

APPLY DATA ANALYSIS

Use Automated Analysis Tools

Ribbon Method

▶ Click the **Developer tab**, then click the **Add-Ins button** in the Add-Ins group

▶ In the Add-Ins dialog box, click the **Analysis ToolPak check box** to select it, then click **OK**

Excel

▶ Click the **Data tab**, then click the **Data Analysis button** in the Analysis group
▶ Click an analysis tool in the Data Analysis dialog box, then click **OK**

Perform What-If Analysis

Ribbon Method

▶ Select the range of cells to analyze, click the **Data tab**, then click the **What-If Analysis button** in the Data Tools group
▶ Click **Scenario Manager** to set up scenarios to consider different variables
▶ Click **Add** in the Scenario Manager dialog box, enter a scenario name and changing cells in the Add Scenario dialog box, then click **OK**
▶ Enter values of the changing cells in the Scenario Values dialog box, click **OK**, then click **Close**

APPLY AND MANIPULATE PIVOTTABLES

Manipulate PivotTable Data

Ribbon Method

▶ Click a cell in the range of cells that contains the data for the PivotTable
▶ Click the **Insert tab**, then click the **PivotTable button** in the Tables group
▶ In the Create PivotTable dialog box, make sure that the Select a table or range option button is selected, then verify the range of cells in the Table/Range text box
▶ Specify the location of the PivotTable using the New Worksheet or Existing Worksheet option buttons and the Location text box, then click **OK**
▶ To add fields to the PivotTable, you can drag a field to the desired area, or right-click the field name in the field section, then select **Add to Report Filter**, **Add to Column Label**, **Add to Row Label**, or **Add to Values**
▶ To move the fields, click the **field name** in one of the areas at the bottom of the PivotTable Field List pane, and then select **Move Up** to move the field up, **Move Down** to move the field down, **Move to Beginning** to move the field to the beginning, or **Move to End** to move the field to the end

OR

▶ Move the field to a different location on the PivotTable by select-ing **Move to Report Filter**, **Move to Row Labels**, **Move to Column Labels**, or **Move to Values**

OR

▶ Click and hold a **field name**, then drag the field to the desired field area on the PivotTable Field List pane

Use the Slicer to Filter and Segment Your PivotTable Data in Multiple Layers

Ribbon Method

▶ Click any cell in the PivotTable, click the **Insert tab**, then click the **Insert Slicer button** in the Sort & Filter group
▶ Click the **check box** for each field you want to filter in the Insert Slicers dialog box to select it, then click **OK**

APPLY AND MANIPULATE PIVOTCHARTS

Create a PivotChart

Ribbon Method

▶ Click any cell in a PivotTable, click the **PivotTable Tools Options tab**, then click the **PivotChart button** in the Tools group
▶ Click a **chart type**, then click **OK**
▶ To move the PivotChart to a new location, click the **Move Chart button** in the Location group of the PivotChart Tools tab, click the **New sheet option button**, enter a name for the PivotChart in the text box, then click **OK**

OR

▶ Click a cell in the range of cells that contains the data, then click the **Insert tab**, click the **PivotTable button arrow** in the Tables group, then click **PivotChart**
▶ In the Create PivotTable with PivotChart dialog box, make sure that the Select a table or range option button is selected, then verify the range of cells in the Table/Range text box
▶ Specify the location of the PivotTable using the New Worksheet or Existing Worksheet option buttons and the Location text box, then click **OK**
▶ To add fields to the PivotChart, you can drag a field to the desired area, or right-click the field name in the field section, then select **Add to Report Filter**, **Add to Axis Fields**, **Add to Legend Fields**, or **Add to Values**

Manipulate PivotChart Data

Ribbon Method

▶ Click the **field name** in one of the areas at the bottom of the PivotTable Field List pane, and then select **Move Up** to move the field up, **Move Down** to move the field down, **Move to Beginning** to move the field to the beginning, or **Move to End** to move the field to the end

OR

▶ Move the field to a different location on the PivotTable by selecting **Move to Report Filter**, **Move to Values**, **Move to Axis Fields**, or **Move to Legend**

OR

▶ Click and hold a **field name**, then drag the field to the desired field area on the PivotTable Field List pane

Analyze PivotChart Data

Ribbon Method

▶ Click the **PivotTable**, click the **PivotTable Tools Options tab**, click the **What-If Analysis button** in the Tools group, then click **Enable What-If Analysis**
▶ Click the **What-If Analysis button** in the Tools group, click **Settings**, click the **Manually or Automatically option button** in the What-If Analysis Settings dialog box, then click **OK**
▶ Click the **What-If Analysis button** in the Tools group, then click **Publish Changes**

DEMONSTRATE HOW TO USE THE SLICER

Choose Data Sets from External Data Connections

Ribbon Method

▶ Click any cell outside the PivotTable, click the **Insert tab**, then click the **Slicer button** in the Filter group to open the Existing Connections dialog box
▶ Click the **Show arrow button**, select a connection, then click **Open**
▶ Click the **check box** for each field you want to filter in the Insert Slicers dialog box to select it, then click **OK**
▶ Click one or more of the buttons on the slicers to filter the PivotTable to display only data for the selected value(s)

EXCEL EXPERT OBJECTIVE 4: WORKING WITH MACROS AND FORMS

CREATE AND MANIPULATE MACROS

Run a Macro

Ribbon Method

▶ Click the **File tab** to open Backstage view, click **Options**, then click **Customize Ribbon** in the category list
▶ Click the **Developer check box** in the Main tabs area on the right of the screen to select it, then click **OK**
▶ Click the **Developer tab**, then click the **Macro Security button** in the Code group
▶ Click **Macro Settings** if necessary, click the **Enable all macros (not recommended; potentially dangerous code can run) option button** to select it, then click **OK**
▶ Click the **Developer tab**, then click the **Macros button** in the Code group
▶ Select the macro, then click **Run**

Run a Macro When a Workbook Is Opened

Ribbon Method

▶ Click the **Developer tab**, then click the **Record Macro button** in the Code group
▶ Enter **Auto_Open** in the Macro name text box of the Record Macro dialog box
▶ Click the **Store macro in arrow button**, select the workbook where you want to store the macro, then click **OK**
▶ Record the macro steps, click the **Developer tab**, then click the **Stop Recording button** in the Code group

Run a Macro When a Button Is Clicked

Ribbon Method

▶ Click the **Insert tab**, click the **Shapes button** in the Illustrations group, then click a shape for a button
▶ Click and drag the mouse pointer to create a button shape
▶ Type a name for the button
▶ Right-click the new button, then click **Assign Macro**
▶ Click the macro name that you want to assign to the button under Macro name, then click **OK**

Record an Action Macro

Ribbon Method

▶ Click the **File tab** to open Backstage view, click **Options**, then click **Customize Ribbon** in the category list
▶ Click the **Developer check box** in the Main tabs area on the right of the screen to select it, then click **OK**
▶ Click the **Developer tab**, then click the **Macro Security button** in the Code group
▶ Click **Macro Settings** if necessary, click the **Enable all macros (not recommended; potentially dangerous code can run) option button** to select it, then click **OK**
▶ Click the **Developer tab**, then click the **Record Macro button** in the Code group
▶ Enter the macro name in the Macro name text box of the Record Macro dialog box
▶ Click the **Store macro in arrow button**, select the workbook where you want to store the macro, then click **OK**
▶ Record the macro steps, click the **Developer tab**, then click the **Stop Recording button** in the Code group

Shortcut Method

▶ Click the **Record Macro button** 🖬 on the left side of the status bar
▶ Enter the macro name in the Macro name text box of the Record Macro dialog box
▶ Click the **Store macro in arrow button**, select the workbook where you want to store the macro, then click **OK**
▶ Record the macro steps, click the **Developer tab**, then click the **Stop Recording button** 🖬 on the left side of the status bar

Assign a Macro to a Command Button

Ribbon Method

▶ Click the **Developer tab**, click the **Insert button** in the Controls group, then click the **Command Button** in the ActiveX Controls section
▶ Click the cell in the worksheet where you want to place the upper-left corner of the button, then click the **View Code button** in the Controls group of the Developer tab to open the Visual Basic Editor
▶ Between the Private Sub and End Sub lines, type the name of the macro you want to assign to the button, then verify that Click appears in the upper-right list box

▶ Click the **View Microsoft Excel button** ▤ on the Visual Basic
Editor Standard toolbar to return to Excel, then click the **Design
Mode button** in the Controls group of the Developer tab

Create a Custom Macro Button on the Quick Access Toolbar

Ribbon Method

▶ Right-click the **Ribbon**, then click **Customize Quick Access
Toolbar**
▶ Click the **Choose commands from arrow button**, click
Macros, then select the macro to assign to a custom button in
the macro list on the left
▶ Click **Add** to move the macro to the list of buttons on the Quick
Access toolbar
▶ Click **OK** to close the Excel Options dialog box

Apply Modifications to a Macro

Ribbon Method

▶ Click the **Developer tab**, click the **Macros button** in the Code
group, click the macro that you want to change, then click **Edit**
▶ Edit the code in the Microsoft Visual Basic for Applications Code
window, click **File** on the menu bar, then click **Close and
Return to Microsoft Excel**

INSERT AND MANIPULATE FORM CONTROLS

Insert Form Controls

Ribbon Method

▶ Click the **Developer tab**, click the **Insert button** in the
Controls group, then click **Button (Form Control)** in the Form
Controls section
▶ Click the cell in the worksheet where you want to place the
upper-left corner of the button, click the macro name in the
Assign macro dialog box, then click **OK**

Set Form Properties

Shortcut Method

▶ Right-click a **form control**, then click **Format Control**
▶ Edit the properties in the Format Control dialog box, then click **OK**

MICROSOFT ACCESS 2010
EXAM REFERENCE
Getting Started with Access 2010

The Access Microsoft Office Specialist exam assumes a basic level of proficiency in Access. This section is intended to help you reference these basic skills while you are preparing to take the Access exam.

> ▶ Starting and exiting Access
> ▶ Using Backstage view
> ▶ Opening a database
> ▶ Viewing the database window
> ▶ Using the Navigation Pane
> ▶ Using the Ribbon
> ▶ Saving and closing objects and databases
> ▶ Using keyboard KeyTips
> ▶ Getting Help

START AND EXIT ACCESS

Start Access

Shortcut Method
- ▶ Click the **Start button** 🎯 on the Windows taskbar
- ▶ Point to **All Programs**
- ▶ Click **Microsoft Office**, then click **Microsoft Access 2010**

OR

- ▶ Double-click the **Microsoft Access program icon** on the desktop

Exit Access

Ribbon Method
- ▶ Click the **File tab** to open Backstage view, then click **Exit**

Shortcut Method
- ▶ Click the **Close button** ⊠ on the Access program window title bar

USE BACKSTAGE VIEW

Figure AC-1 Access Backstage View

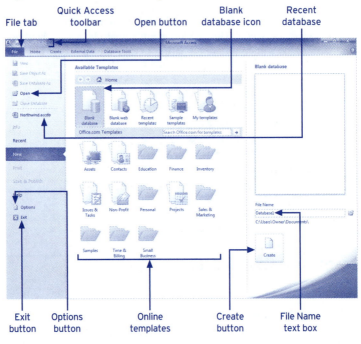

Exit button   Options button   Online templates   Create button   File Name text box

OPEN A DATABASE

Open an Existing Database

Ribbon Method

▶ Click the **File tab** to open Backstage view, then click **Open**

▶ In the Open dialog box, navigate to the appropriate drive and folder

▶ Click the file you want, then click **Open**

  OR

▶ Click the **File tab** to open Backstage view, then click the file you want in the Recent Documents list

  OR

▶ Click the **File tab** to open Backstage view, then click **Recent**

▶ Click the file you want to open

VIEW THE DATABASE WINDOW

Figure AC-2 Access Database Window

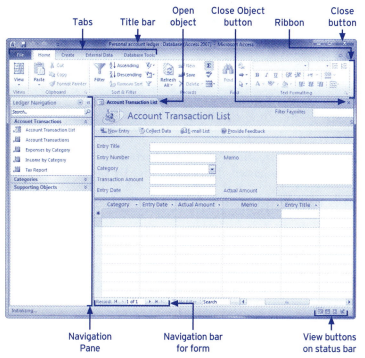

Navigation Pane   Navigation bar for form   View buttons on status bar

Access

USE THE NAVIGATION PANE

Open an Object

Shortcut Method

▶ Double-click the object in the Navigation Pane
  OR
▶ Right-click the object in the Navigation Pane, then click **Open**

Open an Object in Design View or Layout View

Ribbon Method

▶ Double-click the object in the Navigation Pane
▶ Click the **View button arrow** in the Views group on the Home tab, then click **Design View** or **Layout View**

Shortcut Method

▶ Right-click the object in the Navigation Pane, then click **Design View** or **Layout View**

Open and Close the Navigation Pane

Shortcut Method

▶ Click the **Shutter Bar Close button** ≪ to close the Navigation Pane or click the **Shutter Bar Open button** ≫ to open the Navigation Pane

Change the View of Objects in the Navigation Pane

Shortcut Method

▶ Click the **Navigation Pane arrow button** 🔽, click a **Navigate To Category option**, then click a **Filter By Group option**

USE THE RIBBON

Change Tabs

Ribbon Method

▶ Click the name of a tab, such as Home, Create, External Data, or Database Tools, or the name of a contextual tab, such as Table Tools Fields

Expand and Collapse the Ribbon

Ribbon Method

▶ Click the **Minimize the Ribbon button** ⌃ or the **Expand the Ribbon button** ⌄

OR

▶ Double-click a tab on the Ribbon

Shortcut Method

▶ Right-click a blank area of the Ribbon, then click **Minimize the Ribbon**

Open a Dialog Box or Task Pane

Ribbon Method

▶ Click the **dialog box launcher** 🔽 in a group on a tab, such as the Clipboard group on the Home tab

SAVE AND CLOSE OBJECTS AND DATABASES

Save an Object

Ribbon Method

▶ With the object open in the database window, click the **File tab** to open Backstage view, then click **Save**

Shortcut Method

▶ Click the **Save button** 🔲 on the Quick Access toolbar

Save a Database

Ribbon Method

▶ Click the **File tab** to open Backstage view, then click **Save Database As**
▶ In the Save As dialog box, navigate to the appropriate drive and folder, then click **Save**

Note: Access automatically saves changes you make to database settings, so you rarely need to save a database; however, you should save changes to a database object before you close it.

Save a Database with a Different Name, Location, or Format

Ribbon Method

▶ Click the **File tab** to open Backstage view, then click **Save Database As**
▶ In the Save As dialog box, enter a database name, navigate to the appropriate drive and folder, if necessary, then click **Save**

Close an Object

Shortcut Method

▶ Click the **Close object button** ☒
  OR
▶ Click the **Close button** ☒ on the object's title bar

Close a Database

Ribbon Method

▶ Save and close all database objects
▶ Click the **File tab** to open Backstage view, then click **Close Database**
  OR
▶ Click the **Close button** ☒ on the title bar

Access

USE KEYBOARD KEYTIPS

Display KeyTips

Shortcut Method

▶ Press and hold **[Alt]** to display the KeyTips for each command on the active tab of the Ribbon and on the Quick Access toolbar

▶ Press the letter or number for the specific command for the active tab on the Ribbon

▶ Press additional letters or numbers as needed to complete the command sequence

▶ If two letters appear, press each one in order; for some commands, you have to click an option from a gallery or menu to complete the command sequence

▶ The KeyTips are turned off automatically at the end of the command sequence

Hide KeyTips

Shortcut Method

▶ Press **[Alt]** to hide the KeyTips for the Ribbon commands

GET HELP

Ribbon Method

▶ Click the **Microsoft Access Help button** 🔵 on the Ribbon

▶ Use Table AC-1 as a reference to select the most appropriate way to get help using the Access Help window

Shortcut Method

▶ Press **[F1]**

▶ Use Table AC-1 as a reference to select the most appropriate way to get help using the Access Help window

Table AC-1 Access Help Window Options

Option	To use
Search help box	Type one or more keywords, press [Enter], then click a topic in the search results
Access Help window home page	Click a topic category such as Access basics, then click a topic
Table of Contents	Click the Show Table of Contents button 🟢 on the Help window toolbar, click a topic category in the Table of Contents pane, then click a topic

Access 2010 Exam Reference

Objectives:

1. Managing the Access environment
2. Building tables
3. Building forms
4. Creating and managing queries
5. Designing reports

Access Objective 1: Managing the Access Environment

Create and Manage a Database

Use Save Object As

Ribbon Method

▶ With the object open in the database window, click the **File tab** to open Backstage view, then click **Save Object As**
▶ In the Save As dialog box, enter a name for the object, then click **Save**

Use Open

Ribbon Method

▶ To open a database, click the **File tab** to open Backstage view, then click **Open**
▶ In the Open dialog box, navigate to the appropriate drive and folder
▶ Click the file you want, then click **Open**

Shortcut Method

▶ To open an object, double-click the object in the Navigation Pane
OR
▶ Right-click the object in the Navigation Pane, then click **Open**

Use Save & Publish

Ribbon Method

▶ Click the **File tab** to open Backstage view, then click **Save & Publish**
▶ Select the type of file you want to save
  • To save the database using the Access 2007 format, click **Save Database As**, then click the **Save As button**
  • To save the current object, click **Save Object As**

- To save the database using a format other than Access 2007, click the database format, then click the **Save As button**
▶ In the Save As dialog box, enter a database name, navigate to the appropriate drive and folder, if necessary, then click **Save**

  OR

▶ Click the **File tab** to open Backstage view, then click **Save & Publish**
▶ Click **Publish to Access Services**, select options in the right pane, then click the **Publish to Access Services button**

Use the Compact & Repair Database

Ribbon Method

▶ Save and close all objects in the database
▶ Click the **File tab** to open Backstage view, click **Info**, then click the **Compact & Repair Database button**

  OR

▶ Click the **File tab** to open Backstage view, click **Options**, click **Current Database**, click the **Compact on Close check box**, click **OK**, then close the database

Use the Encrypt with Password Command

Ribbon Method

▶ Open the database in exclusive mode
▶ Save and close all objects in the database
▶ Click the **File tab** to open Backstage view, click **Info**, if necessary, then click the **Encrypt with Password button**
▶ In the Set Database Password dialog box, type the password, type it again to verify the password, then click **OK**

Create a Database from a Template

Ribbon Method

▶ Click the **File tab** to open Backstage view, then click **New**
▶ Click the template you want to use
▶ Change the database name in the File Name text box, if necessary, then specify where you want to save the database
▶ Click **Create** if you selected a local template; click **Download** if you selected an online template

Set Access Options

Ribbon Method

▶ Click the **File tab** to open Backstage view, then click **Options**
▶ In the Access Options dialog box, select a category in the left pane
▶ Change the options you want to set, then click **OK**

CONFIGURE THE NAVIGATION PANE
Rename Objects
Shortcut Method
▶ In the Navigation Pane, right-click the object you want to rename, then click **Rename**
▶ Type a name for the object and press **[Enter]**

Delete Objects
Ribbon Method
▶ In the Navigation Pane, click the object you want to delete
▶ On the Home tab, click the **Delete button** in the Records group
▶ Click **Yes** to confirm the deletion

Shortcut Method
▶ In the Navigation Pane, right-click the object you want to delete, then click **Delete**
▶ Click **Yes** to confirm the deletion

Set Navigation Options
Shortcut Method
▶ Right-click the **Navigation Pane title bar**, then click **Navigation Options**
▶ In the Navigation Options dialog box, select options, then click **OK**

APPLY APPLICATION PARTS
Use Blank Forms
Ribbon Method
▶ Click the **Create tab**
▶ Click the **Application Parts button** in the Templates group, then click a blank form

Use Quick Start
Ribbon Method
▶ Click the **Create tab**
▶ Click the **Application Parts button** in the Templates group, then click an icon in the Quick Start area

Use User Templates
Ribbon Method
▶ Click the **File tab** to open Backstage view, then click **New**

Access

▶ Click the **My templates icon,** then click the template you want to use
▶ Change the database name in the File Name text box, if necessary, then specify where you want to save the database
▶ Click **Create** to create a database based on the template

ACCESS OBJECTIVE 2: BUILDING TABLES

CREATE TABLES

Create Tables in Design View

Ribbon Method

▶ Click the **Create tab**, then click the **Table Design button** in the Tables group
▶ For each field you want in the table, type the field name in the Field Name column, then press **[Enter]**
▶ To specify the type of data for a field, click the **Data Type list arrow**, then using Table AC-2 as a reference, click the appropriate data type for the field
▶ To set properties for data that is entered in a field, click the appropriate property text box in the Field Properties pane, then using Table AC-3 as a reference, specify and modify the property for that field
▶ Click the field you want to define as the primary key, then click the **Primary Key button** in the Tools group on the Table Tools Design tab

Table AC-2 Basic Data Types

Data type	Description
Text	Text, combinations of text and numbers, or formatted numbers such as phone numbers
Memo	Text longer than 255 characters
Number	Numeric data to be used in calculations
Date/Time	Dates and times
Currency	Monetary values
AutoNumber	Integers that Access assigns to sequentially order each record added to a table
Yes/No	Only two values (Yes or No, On or Off, True or False) can be chosen for this type of field
Attachment	External files of any supported type, including .jpg, .xlsx, and .docx
Hyperlink	Web and e-mail addresses

Table AC-3 Selected Field Properties

Field property	Purpose	Data types
Field Size	Set the maximum size for data stored in a field	Text, Number, and AutoNumber
Format	Customize the way numbers, dates, times, and text are displayed and printed, or use special symbols to create custom formats, such as to display information in all uppercase	Text, Memo, Date/Time, AutoNumber, Yes/No, Hyperlink, and Number
Decimal Places	Specify the number of decimal places that are displayed (not the number of decimal places stored)	Number and Currency
New Values	Specify whether an AutoNumber field is incremented or assigned a random value	AutoNumber
Input Mask	Make data entry easier and control the values users can enter in a text box control, such as (___) ___-____ for a phone number	Text and Date
Caption	Provide helpful information to the user through captions on objects in various views	All
Default Value	Specify a value that is entered in a field automatically when a new record is added	All except AutoNumber and OLE Object
Validation Rule	Specify requirements for data entered into a record, field, or control	All except AutoNumber and OLE Object
Validation Text	Specify a message to be displayed when the user enters data that violates the Validation Rule property	All when a Validation Rule property is set
Required	Specify whether a value is required in a field	All except AutoNumber

Access

(continued)

Table AC-3 Selected Field Properties (continued)

Field property	Purpose	Data types
Allow Zero Length	Allow users to enter a zero-length string ("")	Text and Memo
Indexed	Set a single-field index to speed up queries, sorting, and grouping on the indexed fields	Text, Currency, Number, Date/Time, AutoNumber, Yes/No, Memo, and Hyperlink
Smart Tags	Specify that certain data be marked as a Smart Tag	Text, Currency, Number, Date/Time, AutoNumber, and Hyperlink

CREATE AND MODIFY FIELDS

Insert a Field

Ribbon Method

▶ Open a table in Design View
▶ Enter a field name in the first blank row of the Field Name column or click a field and then click the **Insert Rows button** in the Tools group

Shortcut Method

▶ Open a table in Design View
▶ Right-click a row selector, then click **Insert Rows**

Delete a Field

Ribbon Method

▶ Open a table in Design View
▶ Click a field, then click the **Delete Rows button** in the Tools group

Shortcut Method

▶ Open a table in Design View
▶ Right-click a row selector, then click **Delete Rows** or press **[Delete]**

Rename a Field

Shortcut Method

▶ Open a table in Design View
▶ Select the text in the Field Name column, then type a new name

Hide or Unhide Fields

Ribbon Method

▶ Open a table in Datasheet View
▶ Click a column heading to select a field
▶ Click the **More button** in the Records group, then click **Hide Fields** or click **Unhide Fields**

Shortcut Method

▶ Open a table in Datasheet View
▶ Right-click a column heading, then click **Hide Fields** or click **Unhide Fields**

Freeze or Unfreeze Fields

Ribbon Method

▶ Open a table in Datasheet View
▶ Click a column heading to select a field
▶ Click the **More button** in the Records group, then click **Freeze Fields** or click **Unfreeze All Fields**

Shortcut Method

▶ Open a table in Datasheet View
▶ Right-click a column heading, then click **Freeze Fields** or click **Unfreeze All Fields**

Modify Data Types

Shortcut Method

▶ Open a table in Design View
▶ Click in the Data Type column for the field, then click the **Data Type arrow**
▶ Click a data type using Table AC-2 as a guide

Modify the Field Description

Shortcut Method

▶ Open a table in Design View
▶ Select the text in the Description column (if any), then type a field description

Modify Field Properties

Shortcut Method

▶ Open a table in Design View
▶ Click the field for which you want to modify field properties
▶ In the Field Properties pane, set or change the properties for the field using Table AC-3 as a guide

Access

SORT AND FILTER RECORDS

Use Find

Ribbon Method

▸ Open a table in Datasheet View or a form in Form View
▸ On the Home tab, click the **Find button** in the Find group
▸ In the Find and Replace dialog box, enter the value you want to find in the Find What text box
▸ To search using wildcards, enter the value using * (asterisk) to stand for any number of characters and ? (question mark) to stand for a single character
▸ To specify additional criteria, click the **Look In list arrow**, then select a field name; click the **Match list arrow**, then select which part of the field you want to search; click the **Search list arrow**, then select the direction in which you want to search
▸ Click **Find Next**

Shortcut Method

▸ Open a table in Datasheet View or a form in Form View
▸ Press **[Ctrl][F]**
▸ Follow the steps in bullets 3–6 of the Use Find Ribbon Method above

Use Sort

Ribbon Method

▸ Open the table in Datasheet View
▸ Click any value in the field you want to sort
▸ On the Home tab, click the **Ascending button** or the **Descending button** in the Sort & Filter group
▸ To remove the sort, click the **Clear All Sorts button** in the Sort & Filter group on the Home tab

Shortcut Method

▸ Open the table in Datasheet View
▸ Click the **column heading list arrow** for the field you want to sort
▸ Click a sort option, such as Sort Smallest to Largest or Sort Newest to Oldest, then click **OK**
▸ To remove the sort, click **Clear filter from *field***, where *field* is the name of the field, then click **OK**

Use Filter Commands

Ribbon Method

▸ Open the table in Datasheet View
▸ Click a value in the field you want to filter

▶ On the Home tab, click the **Filter button** in the Sort & Filter group to display the AutoFilter menu
▶ Click a field value for which you want to filter, then click **OK**
   OR
▶ On the AutoFilter menu, click a field value for which you want to filter, point to **Data type Filters**, where *Data type* is the data type for the field, click a filter option, such as Equals, enter a value in the Custom Filter dialog box, then click **OK**
▶ To remove the filter, click the **column heading list arrow** for the field, click **Clear filter from *field***, where *field* is the name of the field, then click **OK**

Shortcut Method
▶ Open the table or query in Datasheet View
▶ Click the **column heading list arrow** for the field you want to filter to display the AutoFilter menu
▶ Click a field value for which you want to filter, then click **OK**
   OR
▶ On the AutoFilter menu, click a field value for which you want to filter, point to **Data type Filters**, where *Data type* is the data type for the field, click a filter option, such as Equals, enter a value in the Custom Filter dialog box, then click **OK**
▶ To remove the filter, right-click the field, then click **Clear Filter from *field***, where *field* is the name of the field

SET RELATIONSHIPS

Define Primary Keys
Ribbon Method
▶ Open a table in Design View
▶ Click the field you want to set as the primary key
▶ On the Table Tools Design tab, click the **Primary Key button** in the Tools group

Shortcut Method
▶ Open a table in Design View
▶ Right-click the field you want to set as the primary key, then click **Primary Key**

Note: When you create a table in Datasheet View, Access automatically creates a primary key for you and assigns it the AutoNumber data type.

Use Primary Keys to Create Relationships

Ribbon Method

▶ Open a database that contains two tables for which you want to establish a one-to-many relationship
▶ Click the **Database Tools tab**, then click the **Relationships button** in the Relationships group
▶ On the Relationship Tools Design tab, click the **Show Table button** in the Relationships group, if necessary
▶ In the Show Table dialog box, double-click the object(s) you want to relate, then click **Close**
▶ To create a one-to-many relationship, drag the "one" field (usually the primary key) from its field list to the "many" field (usually the foreign key) in another field list
▶ In the Edit Relationships dialog box, click **Create**
▶ Close and save the Relationships window

Shortcut Method

▶ In a database that contains two tables for which you want to establish a one-to-many relationship, open one of the tables in Design View
▶ If necessary, click the **Restore Window button** to resize the table window so it is not maximized
▶ Right-click the **title bar** of the table window, then click **Relationships**
▶ Follow the steps in bullets 3–7 of the Use Primary Keys to Create Relationships Ribbon Method above

Edit Relationships

Ribbon Method

▶ Click the **Database Tools tab**, then click the **Relationships button** in the Relationships group
▶ In the Relationships window, click the **join line** for the relationship you want to modify, then on the Relationship Tools Design tab, click the **Edit Relationships button** in the Tools group
OR
▶ Double-click the **join line** for the relationship you want to modify
▶ In the Edit Relationships dialog box, make the appropriate modifications, then click **OK**

Shortcut Method

▶ Open a related table in Design View, restore its window, if necessary, right-click the **title bar**, then click **Relationships**
▶ Follow the steps in bullets 2–3 of the Edit Relationships Ribbon Method above

IMPORT DATA FROM A SINGLE DATA FILE

Import Source Data into a New Table

Ribbon Method

▶ Click the **External Data tab**, then click a button in the Import & Link group; for example, to import from an Excel spreadsheet, click the **Excel button**
▶ In the Get External Data dialog box, click **Browse** to navigate to the appropriate drive and folder, click the file you want to import, then click **Open**
▶ Click the **Import the source data into a new table in the current database option button**
▶ Click **OK**
▶ Follow the instructions in the wizard dialog boxes, then click **Finish**
▶ Click **Close**

Append Records to an Existing Table

Ribbon Method

▶ Click the **External Data tab**, then click a button in the Import & Link group; for example, to import from an Excel spreadsheet, click the **Excel button**
▶ In the Get External Data dialog box, click **Browse** to navigate to the appropriate drive and folder, click the file you want to import, then click **Open**
▶ Click the **Append a copy of the records to the table option button**, click the **list arrow**, then select a table
▶ Click **OK**
▶ Follow the instructions in the wizard dialog boxes, then click **Finish**
▶ Click **Close**

Import Data as a Linked Table

Ribbon Method

▶ Click the **External Data tab**, then click a button in the Import & Link group; for example, to link to an Excel spreadsheet, click the **Excel button**
▶ In the Get External Data dialog box, click **Browse** to navigate to the appropriate drive and folder, click the file you want to import, then click **Open**
▶ Click the **Link to the data source by creating a linked table option button**
▶ Click **OK**

Access

▶ Follow the instructions in the wizard dialog boxes, then click **Finish**

▶ Click **Close**

ACCESS OBJECTIVE 3: BUILDING FORMS

CREATE FORMS

Use the Form Wizard

Ribbon Method

▶ Click the **Create tab**, then click the **Form Wizard button** in the Forms group

▶ Follow the instructions in the Form Wizard dialog boxes, then click **Finish**

Create a Blank Form

Ribbon Method

▶ Click the **Create tab**, then click the **Blank Form button** in the Forms group

▶ On the Form Layout Tools Design tab, click the **Add Existing Fields button** in the Tools group if necessary, to open the Field List

▶ Drag one or more fields from the Field List to the appropriate location on the form

▶ Click the **Save button** 🖫 on the Quick Access toolbar, type an appropriate name for the form in the Save As dialog box, then click **OK**

Use Form Design Tools

Ribbon Method

▶ To create a new form using form design tools, click the **Create tab**, then click the **Form Design button** in the Forms group

▶ Click the **Add Existing Fields button** in the Tools group to open the Field List, if necessary

▶ Drag a field from the Field List to the form

▶ To add other types of controls, click a button in the Controls group on the Form Design Tools tab, then click where you want to place the control

Create Navigation Forms

Ribbon Method

▶ Click the **Create tab**, click the **Navigation button** in the Forms group, then select the style of navigation form you want to create

▶ To add a form or report to the Navigation form, drag the object from the Navigation Pane to the **[Add New] button**

APPLY FORM DESIGN OPTIONS

Apply a Theme

Ribbon Method

▶ In an open form, click the **View button arrow** on the Home tab, then click **Layout View** or **Design View**
▶ On the Design tab, click the **Themes button** in the Themes group, then click a theme

Shortcut Method

▶ Right-click a form in the Navigation Pane, then click **Layout View** or **Design View**
▶ On the Design tab, click the **Themes button** in the Themes group, then click a theme

Add Bound Controls

Text Box

Ribbon Method

▶ In an open form, click the **View button arrow** on the Home tab, then click **Layout View** or **Design View**
▶ On the Design tab, click the **Text Box button** in the Controls group, then click where you want to insert a text box

Shortcut Method

▶ Right-click a form in the Navigation Pane, then click **Layout View** or **Design View**
▶ Click the **Text Box button** in the Controls group, then click where you want to insert a text box

Drop Down

Ribbon Method

▶ In an open form, click the **View button arrow** on the Home tab, then click **Layout View** or **Design View**
▶ On the Design tab, click the **Combo Box button** in the Controls group, then click where you want to insert a combo box

Shortcut Method

▶ Right-click a form in the Navigation Pane, then click **Layout View** or **Design View**
▶ On the Design tab, click the **Combo Box button** in the Controls group, then click where you want to insert a combo box

Access

Format a Header/Footer

Ribbon Method

▶ In an open form, click the **View button arrow** on the Home tab, then click **Design View**

▶ Click the **Form Header** or **Form Footer bar**, then on the Form Design Tools Design tab, click the **Property Sheet button** in the Tools group to use the Property Sheet to format the header or footer

OR

▶ Click the **Form Design Tools Format tab**, then use tools such as the Background Color button

Shortcut Method

▶ Right-click a form in the Navigation Pane, then click **Design View**

▶ To use the Property Sheet to format the header or footer, right-click the **Form Header** or **Form Footer bar** then click **Properties** or double-click the **Form Header** or **Form Footer bar**

View Code

Ribbon Method

▶ To view code for an entire form, click the form in the Navigation Pane, click the **Database Tools tab**, then click the **Visual Basic button** in the Macro group

Shortcut Method

▶ To view code for a form control, right-click a form in the Navigation Pane, click **Design View**, then double-click the control to display its Property Sheet

▶ Click the **Event tab** in the Property Sheet, then click an event property

▶ Click the **Build button** [...] to open the Choose Builder dialog box, click **Code Builder**, then click **OK**

Convert Macros to Visual Basic

Shortcut Method

▶ Display the macro in Macro Design View
  • Right-click a macro in the Navigation Pane, then click **Design View**

    OR

  • To convert a macro included in a form, right-click the form in the Navigation Pane, then click **Design View**
  • Display the Property Sheet for the form or control to which the macro is assigned (see View Property Sheet for steps on displaying the Property Sheet)

- Click the **Event tab** in the Property Sheet, then click the **Build button** ... for the event associated with a macro
- ▶ Click the **Convert Macros to Visual Basic button** in the Tools group, click **Yes** to save the macro, then click **Convert**
- ▶ If necessary, click **OK** in the Convert macros to Visual Basic dialog box to complete the conversion

View the Property Sheet

Ribbon Method

- ▶ In an open form, click the **View button arrow** on the Home tab, then click **Design View** or **Layout View**
- ▶ On the Design tab, click the **Property Sheet button** in the Tools group

Shortcut Method

- ▶ Right-click a form in the Navigation Pane, then click **Design View** or **Layout View**
- ▶ On the Design tab, click the **Property Sheet button** in the Tools group

  OR

- ▶ In Design View, double-click the **Form Selector button** ☐ to open the Property Sheet

Add Existing Fields

Ribbon Method

- ▶ In an open form, click the **View button arrow** on the Home tab, then click **Design View** or **Layout View**
- ▶ Click the **Add Existing Fields button** in the Tools group on the Design tab

Shortcut Method

- ▶ Right-click a form in the Navigation Pane, then click **Design View** or **Layout View**
- ▶ On the Design tab, click the **Add Existing Fields button** in the Tools group

Access

APPLY FORM ARRANGE OPTIONS

Use the Table Functions

Insert

Ribbon Method

- ▶ In an open form, click the **View button arrow** on the Home tab, then click **Design View** or **Layout View**
- ▶ Select the controls to group together in a layout

▶ Click the **Arrange tab**

▶ Click the **Stacked button** or the **Tabular button** in the Table group to apply a layout to the controls

Shortcut Method

▶ In Layout View or Design View of an open form, select the controls to group together in a layout

▶ Right-click the selected controls, point to **Layout**, then click **Stacked** or **Tabular**

Merge

Ribbon Method

▶ In an open form, click the **View button arrow** on the Home tab, then click **Design View** or **Layout View**

▶ In a layout, select the empty cells you want to merge

▶ Click the **Arrange tab**

▶ Click the **Merge button** in the Merge/Split group

Shortcut Method

▶ In Layout View or Design View of an open form, select the empty cells you want to merge

▶ Right-click the selected controls, point to **Merge/Split**, then click **Merge Split**

Ribbon Method

▶ In an open form, click the **View button arrow** on the Home tab, then click **Design View** or **Layout View**

▶ In a layout, select the cells you want to split

▶ Click the **Arrange tab**

▶ Click the **Split Vertically button** or the **Split Horizontally button** in the Merge/Split group

Shortcut Method

▶ In Layout View or Design View of an open form, select the cells you want to split

▶ Right-click the selected controls, point to **Merge/Split**, then click **Split Vertically** or **Split Horizontally**

Move Table

Ribbon Method

▶ In an open form, click the **View button arrow** on the Home tab, then click **Design View** or **Layout View**

▶ Click the **layout selector** ⊞ to select the entire layout

▶ Drag the layout to a new location

Reposition/Format Controls

Anchor

Ribbon Method

- ▶ In an open form, click the **View button arrow** on the Home tab, then click **Layout View**
- ▶ Select any control in a layout
- ▶ Click the **Arrange tab**
- ▶ Click the **Anchoring button** in the Position group, then click an anchoring option

Shortcut Method

- ▶ In Form Layout View, select the controls you want to anchor in a layout
- ▶ Right-click the selected controls, point to **Anchoring**, then click an anchoring option

Padding

Ribbon Method

- ▶ In an open form, click the **View button arrow** on the Home tab, then click **Layout View**
- ▶ Select any control in a layout
- ▶ Click the **Arrange tab**
- ▶ Click the **Control Padding button** in the Position group, then click a padding option

Margins

Ribbon Method

- ▶ In an open form, click the **View button arrow** on the Home tab, then click **Layout View**
- ▶ Select any control in a layout
- ▶ Click the **Arrange tab**
- ▶ Click the **Control Margins button** in the Position group, then click a margin option

APPLY FORM FORMAT OPTIONS

Reformat a Font in a Form

Ribbon Method

- ▶ In an open form, click the **View button arrow** on the Home tab, then click **Design View** or **Layout View**
- ▶ Select the controls using the font you want to change
- ▶ Click the **Font arrow button** in the Text Formatting group on the Home tab, then click a font

Apply a Background Image to a Form

Ribbon Method

▶ In an open form, click the **View button arrow** on the Home tab, then click **Design View** or **Layout View**
▶ Click the **Format tab**
▶ Click the **Background Image button** in the Background group, then click the image to use or click **Browse** to navigate to the drive and folder of the background image file, then double-click the image file to select it

Shortcut Method

▶ In Layout View or Design View for a form, right-click the background of the form, then click **Form Properties** to display the Property Sheet for the form
▶ Click the **Format tab** in the Property Sheet
▶ Click the **Picture property**, then click **Build button** ⬚
▶ Navigate to the drive and folder of the background image file, then double-click the image file to select it

Apply Quick Styles to Controls in a Form

Ribbon Method

▶ In an open form, click the **View button arrow** on the Home tab, then click **Design View** or **Layout View**
▶ Click a **command button** to select it
▶ Click the **Format tab**
▶ Click the **Quick Styles button** in the Control Formatting group, then click a Quick Style

Apply Conditional Formatting in a Form

Ribbon Method

▶ In an open form, click the **View button arrow** on the Home tab, then click **Design View** or **Layout View**
▶ Click a field to which you want to apply conditional formatting
▶ Click the **Format tab**
▶ Click the **Conditional Formatting button** in the Control Formatting group
▶ In the Conditional Formatting Rules Manager dialog box, click the formatting rule you want to apply, then click **OK**
▶ To create a formatting rule, click the **New Rule** button, select the rule type, edit the rule description, then click **OK**

Shortcut Method

▶ Open a form in Design View

▶ Right-click a field to which you want to apply conditional formatting, then click **Conditional Formatting**

▶ In the Conditional Formatting Rules Manager dialog box, click the formatting rule you want to apply, then click **OK**

▶ To create a formatting rule, click the **New Rule** button, select the rule type, edit the rule description, then click **OK**

ACCESS OBJECTIVE 4: CREATING AND MANAGING QUERIES

CONSTRUCT QUERIES

Create a Select Query

Ribbon Method

▶ Click the **Create tab**, then click the **Query Design button** in the Queries group

▶ In the Show Table dialog box, double-click each object you want to query, then click **Close**

▶ Move the fields into the query design grid by dragging the fields from the field list to the appropriate column in the query design grid

OR

▶ To add all fields from a table to a query, double-click the title bar of the field list, then drag the selected fields to the query design grid

▶ To specify a sort order for a field, click the **Sort cell list arrow**, then click the sort order

▶ On the Query Tools Design tab, click the **Run button** in the Results group

▶ Click the **Save button** 🖫 on the Quick Access toolbar, type an appropriate name for the query in the Save As dialog box, then click **OK**

OR

▶ Click the **Create tab**, then click the **Query Wizard button** in the Queries group

▶ In the New Query dialog box, click **Simple Query Wizard**, then click **OK**

▶ Navigate through the Query Wizard, making changes or accepting the defaults as appropriate to create the query, then click **Finish**

Note: When two related tables have fields with the same name, use the field from the "one" (or parent) table in the query.

Create a Make Table Query

Ribbon Method

▶ Follow the steps under Create a Select Query to create a query
▶ Switch to Design View, if necessary
▶ To preview the new table before you create it, on the Query Tools Design tab, click the **View button arrow** in the Results group, then click **Datasheet View**
▶ Return to Design View, make any necessary changes, then on the Query Tools Design tab, click the **Make Table button** in the Query Type group
▶ In the Make Table dialog box, enter or select the name of the table you want to make
▶ To create the table in the current database, click the **Current Database option button**; to create a table in a different database, click the **Another Database option button**, type the path of the database where you want to make the new table or click **Browse** to locate the database, then click **OK**
▶ On the Query Tools Design tab, click the **Run button** in the Results group
▶ Click **Yes**

Create an Append Query

Ribbon Method

▶ Follow the steps under Create a Select Query to create a query
▶ Switch to Design View, if necessary
▶ To preview the records before you append them, on the Query Tools Design tab, click the **View button arrow** in the Results group, then click **Datasheet View**
▶ Return to Design View, make any necessary changes, then on the Query Tools Design tab, click the **Append button** in the Query Type group
▶ In the Append dialog box, enter or select the name of the table to which you want to append records
▶ To add records to the table in the current database, click the **Current Database option button**; to add records to a table in a different database, click the **Another Database option button**, type the path of the database where you want to append records or click **Browse** to locate the database, then click **OK**
▶ On the Query Tools Design tab, click the **Run button** in the Results group
▶ Click **Yes**

Create a Crosstab Query

Ribbon Method

▶ Click the **Create tab**, then click the **Query Wizard button** in the Queries group
▶ In the New Query dialog box, click **Crosstab Query Wizard**, then click **OK**
▶ Follow the instructions in the Crosstab Query Wizard dialog boxes, then click **Finish**

MANAGE SOURCE TABLES AND RELATIONSHIPS

Use the Show Table Command

Ribbon Method

▶ Open a query in Design View
▶ On the Query Tools Design tab, click the **Show Table button** in the Query Setup group
▶ In the Show Table dialog box, click the table or query to display, then click the **Add button**
▶ Click the **Close button**

Shortcut Method

▶ Open a query in Design View
▶ Right-click the background of Query Design View, then click **Show Table**
▶ In the Show Table dialog box, click the table or query to display, then click the **Add button**
▶ Click the **Close button**

Use the Remove Table Command

Shortcut Method

▶ Open a query in Design View
▶ Right-click the title bar of the field list you want to remove, then click **Remove Table**

Create Ad-Hoc Relationships

Shortcut Method

▶ Open a query in Design View
▶ Use the Show Table command to display the tables you want to relate
▶ To create a one-to-many relationship, drag the primary key field of one table to the foreign key field of another table, as appropriate

Access

MANIPULATE FIELDS

Add Fields

Shortcut Method

▶ Open a query in Design View
▶ Use the Show Table command to display the tables containing the fields you want to add to the query
▶ Move the fields into the query design grid by dragging the fields from the field list to the appropriate column in the query design grid

OR

▶ Double-click a field to add it to the next available column in the query design grid

OR

▶ To add all fields from a table to a query, double-click the title bar of the field list, then drag the selected fields to the query design grid

Remove Fields

Ribbon Method

▶ Open a query in Design View
▶ Click the field you want to remove
▶ Click the **Delete Columns button** in the Query Setup group

Shortcut Method

▶ Open a query in Design View
▶ Click a field selector to select the field you want to remove, then press **[Delete]**

Rearrange Fields

Shortcut Method

▶ Open a query in Design View
▶ Click a field selector to select the field you want to move
▶ Drag the field to a new location in the query design grid

Use Sort and Show Options

Shortcut Method

▶ Open a query in Design View
▶ To specify a sort order for a field, click the **Sort cell list arrow**, then click the sort order
▶ To show a field in the query results, make sure the Show check box is selected; to hide a field in the query results, click the **Show check box** to remove the check mark

CALCULATE TOTALS

Use the Total Row

Ribbon Method

▶ Display a query in Datasheet View
▶ On the Home tab, click the **Totals button** in the Records group
▶ In the Total row, click the field for which you want to display a total, click the list arrow, then click a calculation, such as **Sum** or **Count**

Shortcut Method

▶ Display a query in Design View
▶ On the Query Tools Design tab, click the **Totals button** in the Show/Hide group
▶ In the Total row, click the field for which you want to display a total, click the list arrow, then click a calculation, such as **Sum** or **Count**

Use Group By

Shortcut Method

▶ Display a query in Design View
▶ On the Query Tools Design tab, click the **Totals button** in the Show/Hide group
▶ In the Total row, click the field you want to group by, click the list arrow, then click **Group By**

GENERATE CALCULATED FIELDS

Perform Calculations

Shortcut Method

▶ Open a query in Design View
▶ Click the first blank field in the query design grid, type the heading for the calculated field, then type **:** (colon)
▶ Type the expression enclosing field names in brackets and using arithmetic operators (+, -, /, *), comparison operators (=, <, >, <=, >=, < >), and logical operators (And, Or, Not, Like) as necessary to create the calculation

Use the Zoom Box

Shortcut Method

▶ Open a query in Design View
▶ Right-click the first blank field, click **Zoom**, type the heading for the calculated field, then type **:** (colon), type the expression, enclosing field names in brackets, then click **OK**

Use Expression Builder

Ribbon Method

▶ Open a query in Design View
▶ Click the first blank field in the query design grid, type the heading for the calculated field, then type **:** (colon)
▶ On the Query Tools Design tab, click the **Builder button** in the Query Setup group
▶ In the Expression Builder dialog box, use the expression elements and common operators to build the expression, then click **OK**, or type the exact expression
▶ In the expression, use arithmetic operators (+, -, /, *), comparison operators (=, <, >, <=, >=, < >), and logical operators (And, Or, Not, Like) as necessary to create the calculation

Shortcut Method

▶ Open a query in Design View
▶ Right-click the first blank field in the query design grid, click **Build**, use the Expression Builder dialog box to create an expression, then click **OK**
▶ In the expression, use arithmetic operators (+, -, /, *), comparison operators (=, <, >, <=, >=, < >), and logical operators (And, Or, Not, Like) as necessary to create the calculation

ACCESS OBJECTIVE 5: DESIGNING REPORTS

CREATE REPORTS

Create a Blank Report

Ribbon Method

▶ Click the **Create tab**, then click the **Blank Report button** in the Reports group

Use Report Design Tools

Ribbon Method

▶ To create a new report using report design tools, click the **Create tab**, then click the **Report Design button** in the Reports group
▶ Click the **Add Existing Fields button** in the Tools group to open the Field List, if necessary
▶ Drag a field from the Field List to the report
▶ To add other types of controls, on the Report Design Tools tab, click a button in the Controls group, then click where you want to place the control

Use the Report Wizard

Ribbon Method

▶ Click the **Create tab**, then click the **Report Wizard button** in the Reports group
▶ Follow the instructions in the Report Wizard dialog boxes, then click **Finish**

APPLY REPORT DESIGN OPTIONS

Apply a Theme

Ribbon Method

▶ Open a report in Layout View or Design View
▶ On the Design tab, click the **Themes button** in the Themes group, then click a theme

Add Calculated Controls

Total Report Records

Ribbon Method

▶ Open a report in Design View
▶ On the Report Design Tools Design tab, click the **Text Box button** in the Controls group
▶ To calculate a total or average for a group of records, click in the Group Header or Group Footer section to insert the text box
   OR
▶ To calculate a grand total or average for all records in the report, click in the Report Header or Report Footer section to insert the text box
▶ Click the text box, then type an expression, such as =Sum ([Price])

Shortcut Method

▶ Open a report in Layout View
▶ Right-click a field for which you want to display a calculation, then click a function, such as **Sum** or **Count**

Add Bound/Unbound Controls

Text Box

Ribbon Method

▶ Open a report in Layout View or Design View
▶ On the Design tab, click the **Text Box button** in the Controls group, then click where you want to insert a text box

Hyperlink

Ribbon Method

▶ Open a report in Layout View or Design View
▶ On the Design tab, click the **Hyperlink button** 🔍 in the
Controls group, then click where you want to insert a hyperlink
▶ Select and enter settings in the Insert Hyperlink dialog box, then
click **OK**

Drop Down

Ribbon Method

▶ Open a report in Layout View or Design View
▶ On the Design tab, click the **Combo Box button** 🔲 in the
Controls group, click where you want to insert a combo box, then
complete the Combo Box Wizard

Graph

Ribbon Method

▶ Open a report in Design View
▶ On the Report Design Tools Design tab, click the **More button** ⊡
in the Controls group, if necessary, click **Chart** 📊, then click
where you want to insert a chart

Insert Page Break

Ribbon Method

▶ Open a report in Design View
▶ On the Report Design Tools Design tab, click the **Insert Page
Break button** 📄 in the Controls group, then click where you
want to insert a page break

Add a Header/Footer

Insert Page Number

Ribbon Method

▶ Open a report in Layout View or Design View
▶ On the Design tab, click the **Page Numbers button** in the
Header/Footer group
▶ In the Page Numbers dialog box, select Format, Position,
Alignment, and First Page options, then click **OK**

Insert Logo

Ribbon Method

▶ Open a report in Layout View or Design View
▶ On the Design tab, click the **Logo button** in the
Header/Footer group

▶ In the Insert Pictures dialog box, navigate to the drive and folder containing the logo, click the file, then click **Open**

Reorder Tab Function

Ribbon Method

▶ Open a report in Design View
▶ On the Design tab, click the **Tab Order button** in the Tools group
▶ In the Tab Order dialog box, click **Auto Order** or set a custom order, then click **OK**

Shortcut Method

▶ Open a report in Design View
▶ Right-click a control, then click **Tab Order**
▶ In the Tab Order dialog box, click **Auto Order** or set a custom order, then click **OK**

APPLY REPORT ARRANGE OPTIONS

Use the Table Functions

Insert

Ribbon Method

▶ Open a report in Layout View or Design View
▶ Select the controls to group together in a layout
▶ Click the **Arrange tab**
▶ Click the **Stacked button** or the **Tabular button** in the Table group to apply a layout to the controls

Shortcut Method

▶ Open a report in Layout View or Design View
▶ Right-click the selected controls, then click **Stacked** or **Tabular**

Merge

Ribbon Method

▶ Open a report in Layout View or Design View
▶ In a layout, select the empty cells you want to merge
▶ Click the **Arrange tab**
▶ Click the **Merge button** in the Merge/Split group

Shortcut Method

▶ Open a report in Layout View or Design View
▶ Right-click the selected controls, point to **Merge/Split**, then click **Merge**

Split

Ribbon Method

▶ Open a report in Layout View or Design View
▶ In a layout, select the cells you want to split
▶ Click the **Arrange tab**
▶ Click the **Split Vertically button** or the **Split Horizontally button** in the Merge/Split group

Shortcut Method

▶ Open a report in Layout View or Design View
▶ In a layout, select the cells you want to split
▶ Right-click the selected controls, point to **Merge/Split**, then click **Split Vertically** or **Split Horizontally**

Move Table

Ribbon Method

▶ Open a report in Layout View or Design View
▶ Click the **layout selector** ⊞ to select the entire layout
▶ Drag the layout to a new location

Reposition/Format Controls

Padding

Ribbon Method

▶ Open a report in Layout View
▶ Select any control in a layout
▶ Click the **Report Layout Tools Arrange tab**
▶ Click the **Control Padding button** in the Position group, then click a padding option

Margins

Ribbon Method

▶ Open a report in Layout View
▶ Select any control in a layout
▶ Click the **Report Layout Tools Arrange tab**
▶ Click the **Control Margins button** in the Position group, then click a margin option

Align Report Outputs to Grid

Ribbon Method

▶ Open a report in Design View
▶ Select the controls you want to align to the grid
▶ Click the **Report Design Tools Arrange tab**
▶ Click the **Align button** in the Size & Ordering group, then click **To Grid**

Shortcut Method

▶ Open a report in Design View
▶ Select the controls you want to align to the grid
▶ Right-click the selected controls, point to **Align**, then click **To Grid**

APPLY REPORT FORMAT OPTIONS

Rename a Label in a Report

Shortcut Method

▶ Open a report in Layout View or Design View
▶ Click a label control to select it
▶ Click the label control again to edit it, then type the new text

Apply a Background Image to a Report

Ribbon Method

▶ Open a report in Layout View or Design View
▶ Click the **Format tab**
▶ Click the **Background Image button** in the Background group, then click the image to use or click **Browse** to navigate to the drive and folder of the background image file and double-click the image file to select it

Shortcut Method

▶ Open a report in Layout View or Design View
▶ Click the **Format tab** in the Property Sheet
▶ Click the **Picture property**, then click the **Build button** [...]
▶ In the Insert Picture dialog box, navigate to the drive and folder of the background image file, then double-click the image file to select it

Change a Shape in a Report

Ribbon Method

▶ Open a report in Design View
▶ Click a command button to select it
▶ Click the **Report Design Tools Format tab**
▶ Click the **Change Shape button** in the Control Formatting group, then click a shape

Apply Conditional Formatting in a Report

Ribbon Method

▶ Open a report in Layout View or Design View
▶ Click a field to which you want to apply conditional formatting
▶ Click the **Format tab**

▶ Click the **Conditional Formatting button** in the Control Formatting group

▶ In the Conditional Formatting Rules Manager dialog box, click the formatting rule you want to apply, then click **OK**

▶ To create a formatting rule, click the **New Rule** button, select the rule type, edit the rule description, then click **OK**

Shortcut Method

▶ Open a report in Design View

▶ Right-click a field to which you want to apply conditional formatting, then click **Conditional Formatting**

▶ In the Conditional Formatting Rules Manager dialog box, click the formatting rule you want to apply, then click **OK**

▶ To create a formatting rule, click the **New Rule** button, select the rule type, edit the rule description, then click **OK**

APPLY REPORT PAGE SETUP OPTIONS

Change the Page Size

Ribbon Method

▶ Open a report in Layout View or Design View

▶ Click the **Page Setup tab**

▶ Click the **Size button** in the Page Size group, then click a size

Change the Page Orientation

Ribbon Method

▶ Open a report in Layout View or Design View

▶ Click the **Page Setup tab**

▶ Click the **Portrait button** or the **Landscape button** in the Page Layout group

SORT AND FILTER RECORDS FOR REPORTING

Use the Find Command

Ribbon Method

▶ Open a report in Report View or Layout View

▶ Click the field you want to search, click the **Home tab**, then click the **Find button** in the Find group

▶ In the Find dialog box, enter the value you want to find in the Find What text box

• To search using wildcards, enter the value using * (asterisk) to stand for any number of characters and ? (question mark) to stand for a single character

- To specify additional criteria, click the **Look In list arrow**, then select a field name; click the **Match list arrow**, then select which part of the field you want to search; click the **Search list arrow**, then select the direction you want to search
▶ Click **Find Next**

Shortcut Method

▶ Open a report in Report View or Layout View
▶ Click the field you want to search, then press **[Ctrl][F]**
▶ Follow the steps in bullets 3–6 of the Use the Find Command Ribbon Method

Use Sort

Ribbon Method

▶ Open a report in Report View or Layout View
▶ Click any value in the field you want to sort
▶ In the Sort & Filter group on the Home tab, click the **Ascending button** or the **Descending button**
▶ To remove the sort, click the **Clear All Sorts button** in the Sort & Filter group on the Home tab

Shortcut Method

▶ Open a report in Report View or Layout View
▶ Click the **column heading list arrow** for the field you want to sort
▶ Click a sort option, such as Sort Smallest to Largest or Sort Newest to Oldest, then click **OK**
▶ To remove the sort, click **Clear filter from *field***, where *field* is the name of the field, then click **OK**

Use Filter Commands

Ribbon Method

▶ Open a report in Report View or Layout View
▶ Click a value in the field you want to filter
▶ Click the **Filter button** in the Sort & Filter group on the Home tab to display the AutoFilter menu
▶ Click a field value for which you want to filter, then click **OK**
  OR
▶ On the AutoFilter menu, click a field value for which you want to filter, point to ***Data type* Filters**, where *Data type* is the data type for the field, click a filter option, such as Equals, enter a value, then click **OK**
▶ To remove the filter, click the **column heading list arrow** for the field, click **Clear filter from *field***, where *field* is the name of the field, then click **OK**

Shortcut Method

▶ Open a report in Report View or Layout View

▶ Click the **column heading list arrow** for the field you want to filter to display the AutoFilter menu

▶ Click a field value for which you want to filter, then click **OK**

OR

▶ On the AutoFilter menu, click a field value for which you want to filter, point to **Data type Filters**, where *Data type* is the data type for the field, click a filter option, such as Equals, enter a value, then click **OK**

▶ To remove the filter, right-click the field, then click **Clear Filter from field**, where *field* is the name of the field

Use View Types

Ribbon Method

▶ On the Home tab, click the **View button arrow** in the Views group, then click a view, using Table AC-4 as a reference

Shortcut Method

▶ Right-click the object in the Navigation Pane, then using Table AC-4 as a reference, click a view type

OR

▶ Click a View icon in the status bar, using Table AC-4 as a reference

Table AC-4 Report Views

View	Purpose
Report	To quickly review the first page of a report as it will appear if printed
Print Preview	To review each page of an entire report as it will appear if printed
Layout	To modify the size, position, or formatting of controls; shows live data as you modify the report, making it the tool of choice when you want to change the appearance and positioning of controls on a report while also reviewing live data
Design	To work with report sections or to access the complete range of controls and report properties; Design View does not display data

MICROSOFT POWERPOINT 2010
EXAM REFERENCE

Getting Started with PowerPoint 2010

The PowerPoint Microsoft Office Specialist exam assumes a basic level of proficiency in PowerPoint. This section is intended to help you reference these basic skills while you are preparing to take the PowerPoint exam.

> ▶ Starting and exiting PowerPoint
> ▶ Viewing the PowerPoint window
> ▶ Using the Ribbon
> ▶ Changing views
> ▶ Using task panes
> ▶ Using keyboard KeyTips
> ▶ Using Backstage view
> ▶ Creating, opening, and closing presentations
> ▶ Navigating in the PowerPoint window
> ▶ Saving presentations
> ▶ Getting Help

START AND EXIT POWERPOINT

Start PowerPoint

Mouse Method
▶ Click the **Start button** 🏁 on the Windows taskbar
▶ Point to **All Programs**
▶ Click **Microsoft Office**, then click **Microsoft PowerPoint 2010**
  OR
▶ Double-click the **Microsoft PowerPoint program icon** 🅿 on the desktop

Exit PowerPoint

Ribbon Method
▶ Click the **File tab** to open Backstage view, then click **Exit**
  OR
▶ Click the **Close button** ⊠ on the program window title bar

Shortcut Method

▶ Press **[Alt][F4]**, then click **Exit**

VIEW THE POWERPOINT WINDOW

Figure PPT-1 PowerPoint Window

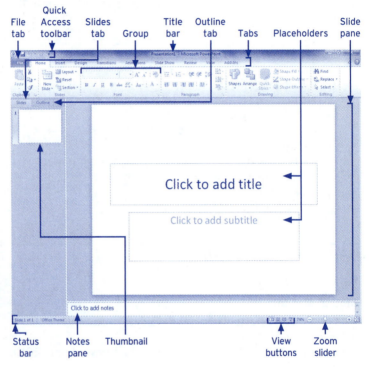

USE THE RIBBON

Display the Ribbon

Ribbon Method

▶ Double-click any tab

OR

▶ Click the **Expand the Ribbon button** ♡

OR

▶ Right-click any tab, then click **Minimize the Ribbon** to deselect it

Shortcut Method

▶ Press **[Ctrl][F1]**

Hide the Ribbon

Ribbon Method

▶ Double-click the active tab

OR

▶ Click the **Minimize the Ribbon button** 🔼

OR

▶ Right-click any tab, then click **Minimize the Ribbon**

Shortcut Method

▶ Press **[Ctrl][F1]**

CHANGE VIEWS

Ribbon Method

▶ Click the **View tab**, then click the **Normal, Slide Sorter, Notes Page**, or **Reading View button** in the Presentation Views group to switch to the presentation view that meets your needs or click the **Slide Master, Handout Master**, or **Notes Master button** in the Master Views group to switch to the master view that meets your needs

Note: You can click the Fit to Window button in the Zoom group to adjust the size of the slide to fit in the current view window.

Shortcut Method

▶ Click the **Normal button** 🔲, **Slide Sorter button** 🔡, **Reading View button** 📖, or **Slide Show button** 🖵 on the status bar to switch to Normal, Slide Sorter, Reading, or Slide Show view, respectively

OR

▶ From Normal view, press and hold **[Shift]**, then click the **Normal button** 🔲 on the status bar to switch to Slide Master view

▶ From Slide Sorter view, press and hold **[Shift]**, then click the **Slide Sorter button** 🔡 on the status bar to switch to Handout Master view

Note: To adjust the size of the slide to fit in the current view window, you click the Fit slide to current window button 🔲.

PowerPoint

USE TASK PANES

Display Task Panes

Ribbon Method

▶ See Table PPT-1 for a list of task panes and the Ribbon commands that open them

Mouse Method

▶ To open the Clip Art task pane, click the **Clip Art button** 🖼 in a content placeholder

Close Task Panes

Ribbon Method

▶ See Table PPT-1 for a list of task panes and the Ribbon commands that close them

Shortcut Method

▶ Click the **Close button** ✖ on the task pane title bar

OR

▶ Click the **Task Pane Options button** ▼ on the task pane title bar, then click **Close**

Table PPT-1 Task Panes

Task pane	Click to open or close the task pane
Animation	**Animation Pane button** in the Advanced Animation group on the Animations tab
Clip Art	**Clip Art button** in the Images group on the Insert tab OR **Video list arrow** in the Media group on the Insert tab, then click **Clip Art Video** OR **Audio list arrow** in the Media group on the Insert tab, then click **Clip Art Audio**
Home	**Arrange list arrow** in the Drawing group on the Home tab, then click the **Selection pane button**
Research	**Research button** in the Proofing group on the Review tab
Reuse Slides	**New Slide list arrow** in the Slides group on the Home tab, then click **Reuse Slides**

(continued)

Table PPT-1 Task Panes (continued)

Task pane	Click to open or close the task pane
Selection and Visibility	**Select arrow** in the Editing group on the Home tab, then click **Selection pane** OR **Selection Pane button** in the Arrange group on the Drawing Tools Format tab or the Picture Tools Format tab

USE KEYBOARD KEYTIPS

Display KeyTips

▶ Press **[Alt]** to display the KeyTips for each command on the active tab on the Ribbon and on the Quick Access toolbar

▶ Press the letter or number shown in a command's KeyTip to perform that command

▶ Press additional letters or numbers as needed to complete the command sequence

▶ If two letters appear, press each one in order

▶ For some commands, you have to click an option from a gallery or menu to complete the command sequence

▶ The KeyTips turn off automatically at the end of the command sequence

Hide KeyTips

▶ Press **[Alt]**

PowerPoint

USE BACKSTAGE VIEW

Figure PPT-2 PowerPoint Backstage View

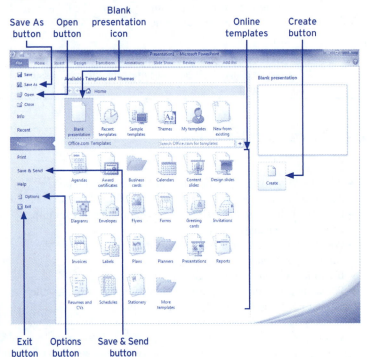

CREATE, OPEN, AND CLOSE PRESENTATIONS

Create a New Presentation

Ribbon Method

▶ Click the **File tab** to open Backstage view, then click **New**
▶ Verify that Blank presentation is selected under the Available
Templates and Themes section, then click **Create** in the right pane

Shortcut Method

▶ Press **[Ctrl][N]**

Open an Existing Presentation

Ribbon Method

▶ Click the **File tab** to open Backstage view, then click **Open**
▶ In the Open dialog box, navigate to the drive and folder that con-
tains the presentation you want to open
▶ Click the presentation file you want, then click **Open**

Shortcut Method

▶ Press **[Ctrl][O]**
▶ In the Open dialog box, navigate to the drive and folder that con-
 tain the presentation you want to open
▶ Click the presentation file you want, then click **Open**

Close a Presentation

Ribbon Method

▶ Click the **File tab** to open Backstage view, then click **Close**
▶ If prompted to save the presentation, click **Save** or **Don't Save**,
 whichever best meets your needs

 OR

▶ Click the **Close button** 🗙 on the PowerPoint title bar
▶ If prompted to save the presentation, click **Save** or **Don't Save**,
 whichever best meets your needs

Shortcut Method

▶ Press **[Ctrl][W]** or **[Alt][F4]**
▶ If prompted to save the presentation, click **Save** or **Don't Save**,
 whichever meets your needs

NAVIGATE IN THE POWERPOINT WINDOW

Use Table PPT-2 as a reference to navigate in the PowerPoint window.

Table PPT-2 Keyboard Navigation Techniques

Press these keys	To move the insertion point
[Ctrl][Home] or **[Ctrl][End]**	To the beginning or end of the selected text box
	OR
	To the first or last slide on the Outline or Slides tab in the task pane or in Slide Sorter view (if no object is selected on the slide)
[Home] or **[End]**	To the beginning or end of the line of text in a selected text box or text placeholder
	OR
	To the first or last slide on the Outline or Slides tab in the task pane or in Slide Sorter view (if no object is selected on the slide)
[PgDn] or **[PgUp]**	Down or up one slide at a time

PowerPoint

(continued)

Table PPT-2 Keyboard Navigation Techniques (continued)

Press these keys	To move the insertion point
[Tab] or **[Shift][Tab]**	Between objects on a slide
[Ctrl][Right Arrow] or **[Ctrl][Left Arrow]**	One word to the right or left
[Ctrl][Enter]	To the next title or body text placeholder; if it is the last placeholder on a slide, a new slide with the same layout will be inserted

SAVE PRESENTATIONS

Save an Existing Presentation with the Same File Name

Ribbon Method
▶ Click the **File tab** to open Backstage view, then click **Save**
   OR
▶ Click the **Save button** 🔲 on the Quick Access toolbar

Shortcut Method
▶ Press **[Ctrl][S]**

Use Save As

Ribbon Method
▶ Click the **File tab** to open Backstage view, then click **Save As**
▶ In the Save As dialog box, navigate to the drive and folder where you want to store the presentation
▶ Type a file name in the File name text box, then click **Save**

Shortcut Method
▶ Press **[F12]**
▶ Follow the steps in bullets 2–3 in the Use Save As Ribbon Method

GET HELP

Ribbon Method
▶ Click the **Microsoft Office PowerPoint Help button** 🔘 on the Ribbon

▶ Use Table PPT-3 as a reference to select the most appropriate way to search for help in the PowerPoint Help window

Shortcut Method

▶ Press **[F1]**
▶ Use Table PPT-3 as a reference to select the most appropriate way to search for help in the PowerPoint Help window

Table PPT-3 PowerPoint Help Window Options

Option	To use
Search	If you are connected to the Internet:
	Type a keyword in the Search text box beneath the toolbar in the PowerPoint Help window, then click the **Search button** or press **[Enter]**
	OR
	Type a keyword in the Search help text box at the top of the Help window between "Office" and "Bing," then click the **Click to search button** 🔍 or press **[Enter]**
	If you are not connected to the Internet:
	Follow the search process using the Search text box above
Table of Contents	Click the **Show/Hide Table of Contents button** 📗 or 📙 on the PowerPoint Help toolbar to show the table of contents, then click a topic in the left pane of the window to display the information in the right pane
	OR
	Click the topic links in the PowerPoint Help window to find the information

POWERPOINT 2010 EXAM REFERENCE

Objectives:

1. Managing the PowerPoint environment
2. Creating a slide presentation
3. Working with graphical and multimedia elements
4. Creating charts and tables
5. Applying transitions and animations
6. Collaborating on presentations
7. Preparing presentations for delivery
8. Delivering presentations

POWERPOINT OBJECTIVE 1: MANAGING THE POWERPOINT ENVIRONMENT

ADJUST VIEWS

Adjust Views by Using the Ribbon

Ribbon Method

▶ Click the **View tab**, then click the **Normal**, **Slide Sorter**, **Notes Page**, or **Reading View button** in the Presentation Views group to switch to the presentation view that meets your needs

OR

▶ Click the **View tab**, then click the **Slide Master**, **Handout Master**, or **Notes Master button** in the Master Views group to switch to the master view that meets your needs

Note: To fit the slide in the current view window, you click the Fit to Window button in the Zoom group to adjust the size of the slide.

Adjust Views by Using Status Bar Commands

Shortcut Method

▶ Click the **Normal button** ⊞, **Slide Sorter button** ⊞, **Reading View button** ⊞, or **Slide Show button** ⊒ on the status bar to switch to Normal, Slide Sorter, Reading, or Slide Show view, respectively

OR

▶ From Normal view, press and hold **[Shift]**, then click the **Normal button** ⊞ on the status bar to switch to Slide Master view
▶ From Slide Sorter view, press and hold **[Shift]**, then click the **Slide Sorter button** ⊞ on the status bar to switch to Handout Master view

Note: To adjust the size of the slide to fit in the current view window, you click the Fit slide to current window button 🔳.

MANIPULATE THE POWERPOINT WINDOW

Work with Multiple Presentation Windows Simultaneously

Ribbon Method

▶ Open two or more presentations, then click the **View tab**
▶ Click **Arrange All** in the Window group to show each PowerPoint window side by side on the screen

  OR

▶ Click **Cascade** in the Window group to show each PowerPoint window overlapped in Restore Down view

  OR

▶ Open a presentation, click the **New Window button** in the Window group, then click **Arrange All** or **Cascade** in the Window group to work with multiple versions of the same presentation

Note: PowerPoint assigns the number "1" to the original presentation name in the title bar, and numbers each presentation in a new window "2," "3," and so on.

  OR

▶ Click the **Switch Windows button** in the Window group, then click the presentation you want to view

CONFIGURE THE QUICK ACCESS TOOLBAR

Show the Quick Access Toolbar (QAT) Below the Ribbon

Shortcut Method

▶ Right-click any tab or Quick Access toolbar button
▶ Click **Show Quick Access Toolbar Below the Ribbon**

CONFIGURE POWERPOINT FILE OPTIONS

Use PowerPoint Proofing

Ribbon Method

▶ Click the **File tab** to open Backstage view, then click the **Options button** to display the PowerPoint Options dialog box
▶ Click **Proofing** in the left pane

PowerPoint

- ▶ In the When correcting spelling in PowerPoint section of the right pane, click the **Check spelling as you type check box**, **Use contextual spelling check box**, or **Hide spelling errors check box** to insert a check mark to turn on those features
- ▶ Click **OK** to close the PowerPoint Options dialog box

  OR
- ▶ Click the **Review tab**, then click the **Spelling button** in the Proofing group to open the Spelling dialog box
- ▶ Click the **Options button** to open the PowerPoint Options dialog box, then follow the steps in bullets 2–4 in the Use PowerPoint Proofing Ribbon Method

Shortcut Method

- ▶ Press **[Alt][F4]**, click the **Options button** to open the PowerPoint Options dialog box, then follow the steps in bullets 2–4 in the Use PowerPoint Proofing Ribbon Method

Use PowerPoint Save Options

Ribbon Method

- ▶ Click the **File tab** to open Backstage view, then click **Options** to display the PowerPoint Options dialog box
- ▶ Click **Save** in the left pane
- ▶ In the Save presentations section, click the **Save AutoRecover information every check box** to turn the feature on or off, then type or use the up and down arrows to select the number of minutes that PowerPoint automatically saves the presentation, choose whether to keep the last autosaved version of a file if you close without saving, or change the location where the AutoRecover files are saved
- ▶ In the Offline editing options for document management server files section, choose where to save checked-out files and the server drafts location on your computer
- ▶ In the File merge options section, choose whether or not to show detailed merged changes when a merge occurs
- ▶ In the Preserve fidelity section, click the **Embed fonts in the file check box** to turn the feature on or off, then choose whether to embed some or all characters used in the presentation

POWERPOINT OBJECTIVE 2: CREATING A SLIDE PRESENTATION

CONSTRUCT AND EDIT PHOTO ALBUMS

Add Captions to a Picture

Ribbon Method

▶ For a new photo album, click the **Insert tab**, click the **Photo Album list arrow** in the Images group, then click **New Photo Album**

▶ In the Photo Album dialog box, insert pictures, click the **Picture layout list arrow** in the Album Layout section, then click a layout

OR

▶ For an existing photo album, click the **Insert tab**, click the **Photo Album list arrow** in the Images group, then click **Edit Photo Album**

▶ In the Album Content section, click the **Caption below ALL picture check box** to select it

▶ For a new album, click **Create**, or for an existing album, click **Update**

Insert Text

Ribbon Method

▶ For a new photo album, click the **Insert tab**, click the **Photo Album list arrow** in the Images group, then click **New Photo Album**

▶ For an existing photo album, click the **Insert tab**, click the **Photo Album list arrow** in the Images group, then click **Edit Photo Album**

▶ In the Photo Album dialog box or the Edit Photo Album dialog box, insert pictures, then click the **New Text Box button**

▶ For a new album, click **Create**, or for an existing album, click **Update**

▶ Click the slide containing the text box, click the **text box**, select the text, then type the text that meets your needs

Insert Images in Black and White

Ribbon Method

▶ For a new photo album, click the **Insert tab**, click the **Photo Album list arrow** in the Images group, click **New Photo Album**, then insert pictures

▶ For an existing photo album, click the **Insert tab**, click the **Photo Album list arrow** in the Images group, then click **Edit Photo Album**

▶ Click the **ALL pictures black and white check box**

▶ For a new album, click **Create**, or for an existing album, click **Update**

Reorder Pictures in an Album

Ribbon Method

▶ For a new photo album, click the **Insert tab**, then click the **Photo Album list arrow** in the Images group

▶ Click **New Photo Album**, then insert pictures

▶ For an existing photo album, click the **Insert tab**, click the **Photo Album list arrow** in the Images group, then click **Edit Photo Album**

▶ Click a picture in the Pictures in album section, then click the **Move up button** ⬆ or the **Move down button** ⬇ to change its slide order

▶ For a new album, click **Create**, or for an existing album, click **Update**

Adjust Image: Rotation

Ribbon Method

▶ For a new photo album, click the **Insert tab**, then click the **Photo Album list arrow** in the Images group

▶ Click **New Photo Album**, then insert pictures

▶ For an existing photo album, click the **Insert tab**, click the **Photo Album list arrow** in the Images group, then click **Edit Photo Album**

▶ Click a picture in the Pictures in album section, then click the **Rotate left button** ⟲ or the **Rotate right button** ⟳ to rotate the picture

▶ For a new album, click **Create**, or for an existing album, click **Update**

Adjust Image: Brightness

Ribbon Method

▶ For a new photo album, click the **Insert tab**, then click the **Photo Album list arrow** in the Images group

▶ Click **New Photo Album**, then insert pictures

▶ For an existing photo album, click the **Insert tab**, click the **Photo Album list arrow** in the Images group, then click **Edit Photo Album**

▶ Click a picture in the Pictures in album section, then click the
Increase brightness button [icon] or the **Decrease brightness
button** [icon] to adjust the brightness of the picture

▶ For a new album, click **Create**, or for an existing album,
click **Update**

Adjust Image: Contrast

Ribbon Method

▶ For a new photo album, click the **Insert tab**, then click the
Photo Album list arrow in the Images group

▶ Click **New Photo Album**, then insert pictures

▶ For an existing photo album, click the **Insert tab**, click the
Photo Album list arrow in the Images group, then click **Edit
Photo Album**

▶ Click a picture in the Pictures in album section, then click the
Increase contrast button [icon] or the **Decrease contrast
button** [icon] to adjust the lightest and darkest parts of the picture

▶ For a new album, click **Create**, or for an existing album,
click **Update**

APPLY SLIDE SIZE AND ORIENTATION SETTINGS

Set Up a Custom Size

Ribbon Method

▶ Click the **Design tab**, then click the **Page Setup arrow** in the
Page Setup group

▶ In the Page Setup dialog box, click the **Slides sized for list
arrow**, then click **Custom**

Note: To see all the choices in the list box, you scroll to the bottom
of the list.

▶ Type a number or use the up and down arrows to select a width
and height and the number of slides to include, then click **OK**

Change the Orientation

Ribbon Method

▶ Click the **Design tab**, then click the **Page Setup button** in the
Page Setup group

▶ In the Page Setup dialog box, click the **Portrait option button**
or the **Landscape option button** in the Slides or Notes, handouts & outline section to change the orientation of those elements

▶ Click **OK**

PowerPoint

Add and Remove Slides

Insert an Outline

Ribbon Method

▶ Click the **New Slide list arrow** in the Slides group on the Home tab, then click **Slides from Outline**

▶ In the Insert Outline dialog box, navigate to and select the file that meets your needs, then click **Insert**

Reuse Slides from a Saved Presentation

Ribbon Method

▶ Click the **New Slide list arrow** in the Slides group on the Home tab, then click **Reuse Slides**

▶ In the Reuse Slides pane, click the **Browse button**, then click **Browse File**

OR

▶ In the Reuse Slides pane, click **Open a PowerPoint File**

▶ In the Browse dialog box, navigate to and select the presentation that meets your needs, then click **Open**

▶ To add a single slide, click the slide in the Reuse Slides pane

Shortcut Method

▶ To add all of the slides, right-click any slide, then select **Insert All Slides** in the Reuse Slides pane

Note: To retain the formatting from the presentation you want to reuse, you select the Keep source formatting check box at the bottom of the Reuse Slides pane.

Reuse Slides from a Slide Library

Ribbon Method

▶ Click the **New Slide list arrow** in the Slides group on the Home tab, then click **Reuse Slides**

▶ In the Reuse Slides pane, click the **Browse button**, then click **Browse Slide Library**

OR

▶ In the Reuse Slides pane, click **Open a Slide Library**

▶ In the Select a Slide Library dialog box, navigate to and select a slide library that meets your needs, then click **Select**

▶ In the All Slides list, click the slide that you want to add

Note: To access slides from a Microsoft Office SharePoint Library, your computer must be running Microsoft Office PowerPoint 2007 or PowerPoint 2010, and it must be connected to a server running Office SharePoint Server 2007 or Microsoft SharePoint Server 2010.

Duplicate Selected Slides

Ribbon Method

▶ In Normal view, with the Slides tab in the task pane selected, or in Slide Sorter view, press **[Ctrl]**, then click the slides you want to duplicate
▶ Click the **New Slide list arrow** in the Slides group on the Home tab, then click **Duplicate Selected Slides**

OR

▶ Click the **Copy list arrow** in the Clipboard group on the Home tab, then click **Duplicate**

Shortcut Method

▶ Follow the steps in bullet 1 in the Duplicate Selected Slides Ribbon Method
▶ Right-click any slide in the Slides tab in the task pane or in Slide Sorter view, then click **Duplicate Slide** on the shortcut menu

Delete Multiple Slides Simultaneously

Shortcut Method

▶ In Normal view, with the Slides tab selected in the task pane, or in Slide Sorter view, press **[Ctrl]**, then click the slides you want to delete
▶ Press **[Delete]**

OR

▶ Follow the steps in bullet 1 in the Delete Multiple Slides Simultaneously Ribbon Method
▶ Press **[Ctrl][X]**

OR

▶ Right-click any slide in the Slides tab in the task pane or in Slide Sorter view, then click **Delete Slide** on the shortcut menu

Include Non-Contiguous Slides in a Presentation

Ribbon Method

▶ Open the presentation containing the slides you want to include in another presentation
▶ In Normal view, with the Slides tab selected in the task pane, or in Slide Sorter view, press and hold **[Ctrl]**, then click the slides you want to select
▶ Click **Copy** in the Clipboard group on the Home tab
▶ Open the presentation where you want to use the copied slides; or click the **View tab**, click the **Switch Windows list arrow**, then click the name of the presentation
▶ Click the **Home tab**, then click **Paste** in the Clipboard group

PowerPoint

FORMAT SLIDES

Format Sections

Ribbon Method

▶ Open a presentation with sections inserted, then in Normal view with the Slides tab selected in the task pane, or in Slide Show view, click a section to select all the slides in that section
▶ Click the **Design tab**, then select a new theme, theme color, font, effect, or background style to apply it only to the slides in the selected section

Modify Themes

Ribbon Method

▶ Click the **Design tab**, click the **More button** ⬇ in the Themes group, then click a theme in the gallery

Switch to a Different Slide Layout

Ribbon Method

▶ In Normal view or Slide Sorter view, select the slide whose layout you want to change, click the **Layout list arrow** in the Slides group on the Home tab, then click the layout that meets your needs

Shortcut Method

▶ In Normal view or Slide Sorter view, right-click the slide whose layout you want to change, point to **Layout**, then click the layout that meets your needs

Apply Formatting to a Slide: Fill Color

Ribbon Method

▶ In Normal view or Slide Sorter view, click the slide whose fill you want to change, then click the **launcher** 🔲 in the Background group
▶ In the Format Background dialog box, click the **Solid fill option button**, click the **Color button** 🖌 ▾, click a color, then click **Close**

Shortcut Method

▶ In Normal view or Slide Sorter view, right-click the slide whose fill you want to change, then click **Format Background** on the shortcut menu
▶ Follow the steps in bullet 2 in the Apply Formatting to a Slide: Fill Color Ribbon Method

Note: To adjust how much color appears, you drag the Transparency slider.

Apply Formatting to a Slide: Gradient

Ribbon Method

▶ In Normal view or Slide Sorter view, click the slide whose fill you want to change, then click the **launcher** in the Background group

▶ In the Format Background dialog box, click the **Gradient fill option button**; select preset colors, type, direction, and gradient color options; then click **Close**

Shortcut Method

▶ In Normal view or Slide Sorter view, right-click the slide to which you want to apply a gradient, then click **Format Background** on the shortcut menu

▶ Follow the steps in bullet 2 in the Apply Formatting to a Slide: Gradient Ribbon Method

Apply Formatting to a Slide: Picture

Ribbon Method

▶ In Normal view or Slide Sorter view, click the slide whose fill you want to change, then click the **launcher** in the Background group

▶ In the Format Background dialog box, click the **Picture or texture fill option button**

▶ Click the **File button** to open the Insert Picture dialog box, then navigate to and click a file that meets your needs

▶ Click **Open**

OR

▶ Click the **Clip Art button** to open the Select Picture dialog box, type keywords in the Search text text box, click a thumbnail that meets your needs, then click **OK**

▶ Click **Close**

Shortcut Method

▶ In Normal view or Slide Sorter view, right-click the slide to which you want to add a picture, then click **Format Background** on the shortcut menu

▶ Follow the steps in bullets 2-6 in the Apply Formatting to a Slide: Picture Ribbon Method

Apply Formatting to a Slide: Texture

Ribbon Method

▶ In Normal view or Slide Sorter view, click the slide whose fill you want to change, then click the **launcher** ⌷ in the Background group
▶ In the Format Background dialog box, click the **Picture or texture fill option button**
▶ Click the **Texture list arrow**, click a texture, then select tiling and transparency options
▶ Click **Close**

Shortcut Method

▶ In Normal view or Slide Sorter view, right-click the slide to which you want to add a texture, then click **Format Background** on the shortcut menu
▶ Follow the steps in bullets 2–4 in the Apply Formatting to a Slide: Texture Ribbon Method

Apply Formatting to a Slide: Pattern

Ribbon Method

▶ In Normal view or Slide Sorter view, click the slide whose fill you want to change, then click the **launcher** ⌷ in the Background group
▶ In the Format Background dialog box, click the **Pattern fill option button**, then click a pattern
▶ Click **Close**

Shortcut Method

▶ In Normal view or Slide Sorter view, right-click the slide to which you want to add a pattern, then click **Format Background** on the shortcut menu
▶ Follow the steps in bullets 2–3 in the Apply Formatting to a Slide: Pattern Ribbon Method

Note: To change a pattern's foreground or background color, you click the Foreground Color list arrow 🖉▾ or the Background Color list arrow 🖉▾, then click a color.

Set Up Slide Footers

Ribbon Method

▶ Click the **Insert tab**, then click the **Header & Footer button** in the Text group
▶ In the Header and Footer dialog box, click options for date and time, slide number, and text that will appear in the footer
▶ Click **Apply** or **Apply All**

Shortcut Method

▶ Press **[Alt][V][H]** to open the Header and Footer dialog box

▶ Follow the steps in bullets 2–3 in the Set Up Slide Footers Ribbon Method

Note: To prevent the footer from appearing on the title slide, you click the Don't show on title slide check box.

ENTER AND FORMAT TEXT

Use Text Effects

Ribbon Method

▶ Enter and select text, click the **Drawing Tools Format tab**, click **Text Effects** in the WordArt Styles group, point to an effect, click an effect style, or click the **WordArt Styles More button** ▾ in the WordArt Styles group, then click a style from the gallery

OR

▶ Enter and select text, click the **Drawing Tools Format tab**, then click the **launcher** ▫ in the WordArt Styles group to open the Format Text Effects dialog box

▶ Click an effect (Shadow, Reflections, Glow and Soft Edges, 3-D Format, or 3-D Rotation) in the left pane, then set options associated with the selected style

▶ Click **Close**

Shortcut Method

▶ Enter and select text, right-click the text, then click **Format Text Effects** on the shortcut menu

▶ In the Format Text Effects dialog box, follow the steps in bullets 2–3 in the Use Text Effects Ribbon Method

Change Text Format: Indentation

Ribbon Method

▶ Select the text

▶ Click the **View tab**, then click the **Ruler check box** in the Show group to display the Ruler if it is not already displayed

▶ Drag the **indent markers** on the Ruler to adjust the position of the text on the line

Shortcut Method

▶ Select the text

▶ Right-click the text in the text box, then click **Paragraph** on the shortcut menu

PowerPoint

▶ In the Paragraph dialog box, type a value in the Before text text box or use the up and down arrows to adjust the amount of indentation in the Indentation section
▶ Click the **Special list arrow**, click an option (First line or Hanging), then adjust the number in the **By text box** as necessary
▶ Click **OK**

Change Text Format: Alignment

Ribbon Method

▶ Select the text
▶ Use the appropriate button or keyboard shortcut listed in Table PPT-4 to align text to meet your needs

Shortcut Method

▶ Select the text
▶ Right-click the text box, then click **Paragraph** on the shortcut menu
▶ In the Paragraph dialog box, click the **Alignment arrow** in the General section
▶ Click **OK**

Table PPT-4 Text Alignment Buttons and Keyboard Shortcuts

Alignment	Button (in Paragraph group on Home tab or on Mini toolbar)	Keyboard shortcut
Align Text Left	≣	[Ctrl][L]
Center	≣	[Ctrl][E]
Align Text Right	≣	[Ctrl][R]
Justify*	≣	

* not included on the Mini toolbar

Change Text Format: Line Spacing

Ribbon Method

▶ Select the text
▶ Click the **Line Spacing button** ‡≣▾ in the Paragraph group on the Home tab, then click a line spacing option in the list
OR
▶ Select the text

- ► Click the **Line Spacing button** [icon] in the Paragraph group on the Home tab, then click **Line Spacing Options**
- ► In the Paragraph dialog box, type a value in the Before and After text boxes or use the up and down arrows to adjust the amount of spacing in the Spacing section
- ► Click the **Line Spacing list arrow**, select the spacing option (Exactly or Multiple), then adjust the number in the At text box to meet your needs
- ► Click **OK**

Shortcut Method
- ► Right-click the text, then click **Paragraph** on the shortcut menu

OR
- ► Select the text, then click the **launcher** [icon] in the Paragraph group on the Home tab
- ► Follow the steps in bullets 3–5 in the second Change Text Format: Line Spacing Ribbon Method

Change Text Format: Direction
Ribbon Method
- ► Select the text
- ► Click the **Text Direction button** [icon] in the Paragraph group on the Home tab, then click a direction option in the list

OR
- ► Select the text
- ► Click the **Text Direction button** [icon] in the Paragraph group on the Home tab, then click **More Options**
- ► In the Format Text Effects dialog box, click the **Text direction list arrow**, then click a direction option in the list
- ► Click **Close**

Change the Formatting of Bulleted and Numbered Lists
Ribbon Method
- ► Select the bulleted or numbered list, then click the **Bullets list arrow** [icon] or **Numbering list arrow** [icon] in the Paragraph group on the Home tab
- ► Click **Bullets and Numbering** at the bottom of the gallery to open the Bullets and Numbering dialog box
- ► For a bulleted list, click a bullet style on the Bulleted tab to change the bullet style
- ► Adjust the value in the Size text box to change the bullet size

PowerPoint

▶ Click the **Color button** [icon], then click a color to change the bullet color

▶ Click the **Picture button**, select a picture in the Picture Bullet dialog box, then click **OK** to create a picture bullet

▶ For a numbered list, click the **Numbered tab**, then click a number style

▶ Adjust the value in the Size text box to change the number size

▶ Click the **Color button** [icon], then click a color to change the number color

▶ Click **OK**

Shortcut Method

▶ Select and right-click the bulleted or numbered list, point to **Bullets** or **Numbering**, respectively, on the shortcut menu, then click **Bullets and Numbering**

▶ Follow the steps in bullets 3–6 in the Change the Formatting of Bulleted and Numbered Lists Ribbon Method

Enter Text in a Placeholder Text Box

Ribbon Method

▶ Click the **Layout button** in the Slides group on the Home tab, then select any slide layout except Blank

▶ Click the placeholder text box, then type the text that meets your needs

Shortcut Method

▶ Right-click a slide in the Slides tab in the task pane, point to **Layout**, then click any slide layout except Blank

▶ Follow the steps in bullet 2 in the Enter Text in a Placeholder Text Box Ribbon Method

Convert Text to SmartArt

Ribbon Method

▶ Click anywhere in the text object, then click the **Convert to SmartArt button** in the Paragraph group on the Home tab

▶ Click a graphic style in the gallery or click **More SmartArt Graphics** to open the Choose a SmartArt Graphic dialog box

▶ Click a graphic style, then click **OK**

Shortcut Method

▶ Right-click anywhere in the text object, then click **Convert to SmartArt** on the shortcut menu

▶ Follow the steps in bullets 2–3 in the Convert Text to SmartArt Ribbon Method

Copy and Paste Text

Ribbon Method

▶ Select the text you want to copy, then click the **Copy button** 🖹 in the Clipboard group on the Home tab

▶ Position the insertion point where you want to paste the text, then click the **Paste button** 🖺 in the Clipboard group on the Home tab

Shortcut Method

▶ Select and right-click the text you want to copy, then click **Copy** on the shortcut menu

▶ Position the insertion point where you want to paste the text, right-click, then click **Paste** on the shortcut menu

OR

▶ Select the text you want to copy, then press **[Ctrl][C]**

▶ Position the insertion point where you want to paste the text, then press **[Ctrl][V]**

Use Paste Special

Ribbon Method

▶ Select the text or object you want to copy, then click the **Copy button** 🖹 or the **Cut button** ✂ in the Clipboard group on the Home tab

▶ Click in the new location in the presentation where you want to paste the text or object

▶ Click the **Paste list arrow** 🖺 in the Clipboard group on the Home tab

▶ Click **Paste Special**

▶ In the Paste Special dialog box, select the Paste Special option that meets your needs

▶ Click **OK**

Shortcut Method

▶ Select and right-click the text or object you want to copy, then click **Cut** or **Copy** on the shortcut menu

▶ Follow the steps in bullets 2–6 in the Use Paste Special Ribbon Method

OR

▶ Select the text or object you want to copy, then press **[Ctrl][X]** to cut or **[Ctrl][C]** to copy the selected text or object

▶ Press **[Ctrl][Alt][V]** to open the Paste Special dialog box

▶ Select the Paste Special options in the Paste Special dialog box that meet your needs

▶ Click **OK**

PowerPoint

Use the Format Painter

Ribbon Method

▶ Select the text or object whose attributes you want to copy, then click the **Format Painter button** ✐ in the Clipboard group on the Home tab
▶ Locate the destination text or object, then click the text or object to apply the formatting

Shortcut Method

▶ Select the text or object whose attributes you want to copy
▶ Right-click the text or object, then click the **Format Painter button** ✐ on the Mini toolbar
▶ Locate the destination text or object, then click the text or object to apply the formatting

FORMAT TEXT BOXES

Apply Formatting to a Text Box: Fill Color

Ribbon Method

▶ Select the text box
▶ Click the **Drawing Tools Format tab**, click the **Shape Fill list arrow** in the Shape Styles group, then click a color

OR

▶ Select the text box
▶ Click the **Drawing Tools Format tab**, then click the **launcher** 🗔 in the Shape Styles group to open the Format Shape dialog box
▶ Click **Fill** in the left pane if it is not already selected, then select color and transparency options to meet your needs
▶ Click **Close**

Shortcut Method

▶ Select the text box
▶ Right-click the text box, then click **Format Shape** on the shortcut menu to open the Format Shape dialog box
▶ Follow the steps in bullets 3–4 in the second Apply Formatting to a Text Box: Fill Color Ribbon Method

Apply Formatting to a Text Box: Gradient

Ribbon Method

▶ Select the text box

▶ Click the **Drawing Tools Format tab**, click the **Shape Fill list arrow** in the Shape Styles group, point to **Gradient**, then select a variation or click **More Gradients** to open the Format Shape dialog box

▶ In the Format Shape dialog box, click **Fill** in the left pane if it is not selected, click the **Gradient Fill option button**, then click preset colors, type, direction, and gradient color options

▶ Click **Close**

OR

▶ Select the text box

▶ Click the **Drawing Tools Format tab**, then click the **launcher** in the Shape Styles group to open the Format Shape dialog box

▶ Follow the steps in bullets 3–4 in the Apply Formatting to a Text Box: Gradient Ribbon Method

Shortcut Method

▶ Select the text box

▶ Right-click the text box, then click **Format Shape** on the shortcut menu to open the Format Shape dialog box

▶ Follow the steps in bullets 3–4 in the Apply Formatting to a Text Box: Gradient Ribbon Method

Apply Formatting to a Text Box: Picture

Ribbon Method

▶ Select the text box

▶ Click the **Drawing Tools Format tab**, click the **Shape Fill list arrow** in the Shape Styles group, then click **Picture** on the menu

▶ In the Insert Picture dialog box, navigate to the file that meets your needs, then click the file

▶ Click **Insert**

Apply Formatting to a Text Box: Texture

Ribbon Method

▶ Select the text box

▶ Click the **Drawing Tools Format tab**, click the **Shape Fill list arrow** in the Shape Styles group, point to **Texture**, then select a texture or click **More Textures** to open the Format Shape dialog box

▶ In the Format Shape dialog box, click **Fill** in the left pane if it is not already selected, click the **Picture or texture fill option button**, click the **Texture list arrow**, click a texture, then select tiling and transparency options

► Click **Close**

OR

► Select the text box
► Click the **Drawing Tools Format tab**, then click the **launcher** ⬚ in the Shape Styles group to open the Format Shape dialog box
► Follow the steps in bullets 3–4 in the Apply Formatting to a Text Box: Texture Ribbon Method

Apply Formatting to a Text Box: Pattern

Ribbon Method

► Select the text box
► Click the **Drawing Tools Format tab**, click the **Shape Fill list arrow** in the Shape Styles group, point to **Texture**, then click **More Textures** to open the Format Shape dialog box
► In the Format Shape dialog box, click **Fill** in the left pane if it is not already selected, click the **Pattern fill option button**, click a pattern, then select foreground and background colors
► Click **Close**

OR

► Select the text box
► Click the **Drawing Tools Format tab**, then click the **launcher** ⬚ in the Shape Styles group to open the Format Shape dialog box
► Follow the steps in bullets 3–4 in the Apply Formatting to a Text Box: Pattern Ribbon Method

Shortcut Method

► Select the text box
► Right-click the text box, then click **Format Shape** on the shortcut menu to open the Format Shape dialog box
► Follow the steps in bullets 3–4 in the Apply Formatting to a Text Box: Pattern Ribbon Method

Change the Outline of a Text Box: Color

Ribbon Method

► Select the text box
► Click the **Drawing Tools Format tab**, click the **Shape Outline list arrow** in the Shape Styles group, then click a color

OR

► Select the text box

▶ Click the **Drawing Tools Format tab**, then click the **launcher**
🔲 in the Shape Styles group to open the Format Shape
dialog box

▶ Click **Line Color** in the left pane if it is not selected, then click
the **No line option button**, **Solid line option button**, or
Gradient line option button to meet your needs

▶ For solid or gradient lines, select colors and options to meet
your needs

▶ Click **Close**

Shortcut Method

▶ Select the text box

▶ Right-click the text box, then click **Format Shape** on the shortcut menu to open the Format Shape dialog box

▶ Follow the steps in bullets 3–5 in the second Change the Outline
of a Text Box: Color Ribbon Method

Change the Outline of a Text Box: Weight

Ribbon Method

▶ Select the text box

▶ Click the **Drawing Tools Format tab**, click the **Shape Outline
list arrow** in the Shape Styles group, point to **Weight**, then click
a line weight to meet your needs

OR

▶ Select the text box

▶ Click the **Drawing Tools Format tab**, then click the **launcher**
🔲 in the Shape Styles group to open the Format Shape
dialog box

▶ Click **Line Style** in the left pane if it is not already selected, then
select line style options to meet your needs

▶ Click **Close**

Shortcut Method

▶ Select the text box

▶ Right-click the text box, then click **Format Shape** on the shortcut menu to open the Format Shape dialog box

▶ Follow the steps in bullets 3–4 in the second Change the Outline
of a Text Box: Weight Ribbon Method

Change the Outline of a Text Box: Style

Ribbon Method

▶ Select the text box

▶ Click the **Drawing Tools Format tab**, click the **More button** ⊡ in the Shape Styles group, then click a style in the gallery

Change the Shape of a Text Box

Ribbon Method
▶ Select the text box
▶ Click the **Drawing Tools Format tab**, click the **Edit Shape list arrow** in the Insert Shapes group, point to **Change Shapes**, then click a shape

Apply Effects

Ribbon Method

▶ Select the text box
▶ Click the **Drawing Tools Format tab**, click the **Shape Effects list arrow** in the Shape Styles group, point to an effect, then click the effect style
OR
▶ Click the **Drawing Tools Format tab**, then click the **launcher** ⊡ in the Shape Styles group to open the Format Shape dialog box
▶ In the Format Shape dialog box, click an effect (Shadow, Reflections, Glow and Soft Edges, 3-D Format, or 3-D Rotation) in the left pane, then set options associated with that effect
▶ Click **Close**

Shortcut Method

▶ Right-click the text box, then click **Format Shape** on the shortcut menu
▶ In the Format Text Effects dialog box, click an effect (Shadow, Reflections, Glow and Soft Edges, 3-D Format, or 3-D Rotation) in the left pane, then set options associated with that effect
▶ Click **Close**

Set the Alignment

Ribbon Method

▶ Select the text box
▶ Click the **Drawing Tools Format tab**, click the **Align button** in the Arrange group, then click an alignment option

Create Columns in a Text Box

Ribbon Method

▶ Select the text box

▶ Click the **Drawing Tools Format tab**, then click the **launcher** in the Shape Styles group to open the Format Shape dialog box

▶ In the Format Shape dialog box, click **Text Box** in the left pane, then click the **Columns button**

▶ In the Columns dialog box, enter a value in the Number text box or use the up and down arrows to set the number of columns

▶ Enter a value in the Spacing text box or use the up and down arrows to set the space between columns

▶ Click **OK**

▶ Click **Close**

Shortcut Method

▶ Right-click the text box, then click **Format Shape** on the short-cut menu

▶ Follow the steps in bullets 2–7 in the Create Columns in a Text Box Ribbon Method

Set Internal Margins

Ribbon Method

▶ Select the text box

▶ Click the **Drawing Tools Format tab**, then click the **launcher** in the Shape Styles group to open the Format Shape dialog box

▶ In the Format Shape dialog box, click **Text Box** in the left pane, then enter values in the Left, Right, Top, and Bottom text boxes or use the up and down arrows to set the internal margins

▶ Click **Close**

Shortcut Method

▶ Right-click the text box, then click **Format Shape** on the short-cut menu

▶ Follow the steps in bullets 2–4 in the Set Internal Margins Ribbon Method

Set the Current Text Box Formatting as the Default for New Text Boxes

Shortcut Method

▶ Right-click the text box, then click **Set as Default Text Box** on the shortcut menu

Adjust Text in a Text Box: Wrap

Ribbon Method

▶ Select the text box

PowerPoint

▶ Click the **Drawing Tools Format tab**, then click the **launcher** ⬚ in the Shape Styles group to open the Format Shape dialog box

▶ In the Format Shape dialog box, click **Text Box** in the left pane, then click the **Wrap text in shape check box** to select it if it is not already selected

▶ Click **Close**

Shortcut Method

▶ Right-click the text box, then click **Format Shape** on the short-cut menu

▶ Follow the steps in bullets 3–4 in the Adjust Text in a Text Box: Wrap Ribbon Method

Adjust Text in a Text Box: Size

Ribbon Method

▶ Select the text box

▶ Click the **Drawing Tools Format tab**, then click the **launcher** ⬚ in the Shape Styles group to open the Format Shape dialog box

▶ In the Format Shape dialog box, click **Size** in the left pane, then enter values in the Height, Width, and Rotation text boxes in the Size and rotate section, or use the up and down arrows to set the size and rotation values

OR

▶ Enter values in the Height and Width text boxes in the Scale section or use the up and down arrows to set the scale

▶ Click **Close**

Note: To maintain the same relationship between the height and width settings, you click the Lock aspect ratio check box.

Adjust Text in a Text Box: Position

Ribbon Method

▶ Select the text box

▶ Click the **Drawing Tools Format tab**, then click the **launcher** ⬚ in the Shape Styles group to open the Format Shape dialog box

▶ In the Format Shape dialog box, click **Position** in the left pane, then enter values in the Horizontal and Vertical text boxes, or use the up and down arrows to set the value, then click each From list arrow and identify if the position is set from Top Left Center or Center

Use Autofit

Ribbon Method

▶ Select the text box
▶ Click the **Drawing Tools Format tab**, then click the **launcher**
    in the Shape Styles group to open the Format Shape
dialog box
▶ In the Format Shape dialog box, click **Text Box** in the left pane,
then select an option in the Autofit section described in
Table PPT-5
▶ Click **Close**

Shortcut Method

▶ Right-click the text box, then click **Format Shape** on the shortcut menu
▶ Follow the steps in bullets 3–4 in the Use Autofit Ribbon Method

Table PPT-5   Text Box Autofit Options

Option	Description	Keyboard shortcut
Do not Autofit	Turns off automatic resizing; text can spill out of shape border	[Alt][D]
Shrink text on overflow	Automatically reduces text size to fit within shape	[Alt][S]
Resize shape to fit text	Maintains the maximum vertical size of the shape to the amount of text	[Alt][F]

PowerPoint

PowerPoint Objective 3: Working with Graphical and Multimedia Elements

Manipulate Graphical Elements

Arrange Graphical Elements

Ribbon Method

▶ Select a slide that contains two or more objects (shapes, pictures,
SmartArt diagrams, charts, illustrations, videos, and so on)
▶ Click the object you want to arrange, then click the **Picture
Tools Format tab** or the **Drawing Tools Format tab**, based on
the selected object

▶ Click the **Bring Forward button** in the Arrange group, or click the **Bring Forward list arrow**, then click **Bring to Front**; or click the **Send Backward button** in the Arrange group, or click the **Send Backward list arrow**, then click **Send to Back**

Shortcut Method

▶ Right-click the object you want to arrange
▶ Point to **Bring to Front** on the shortcut menu, then click **Bring to Front** or **Bring Forward**; or point to **Send to Back** on the shortcut menu, then click **Send to Back** or **Send Backward** to meet your needs

Note: You can also access Arrange options by clicking the Arrange list arrow in the Drawing group on the Home tab, then clicking an arrange option in the Order Objects section on the menu.

Position Graphical Elements

Ribbon Method

▶ Press and hold **[Ctrl]**, then click the objects to be positioned
▶ Click the **Picture Tools Format tab** or the **Drawing Tools Format tab**, based on the selected objects
▶ Click the **Align button** in the Arrange group, then click **View Gridlines**, or click the **View tab**, then click the **Gridlines check box** in the Show group to select it
▶ Drag the objects to position them, using the grid as needed

OR

▶ Click the **Align button** in the Arrange group on the Picture Tools or Drawing Tools Format tab, then click **Grid Settings** to open the Grids and Guides dialog box
▶ In the Grids and Guides dialog box, click the **Display grid on screen check box**
▶ Click the **Display drawing guides on screen check box** to select it
▶ Click the **Snap objects to grid check box** or **Snap objects to other objects check box** to meet your needs
▶ Click **OK**
▶ Drag the objects to position them on the grid, guides, and snap to feature as needed

OR

▶ Select several objects you want to align, click the **Align button** in the Arrange group on the Picture Tools Format or Drawing Tools Format tab, then select an option (such as Align Center) to align the selected objects according to that specification

Shortcut Method

▶ Press and hold **[Ctrl]**, then click the objects to be positioned
▶ Right-click a blank area of any slide, then click **Grids and Guides** on the shortcut menu to open the Grids and Guides dialog box
▶ Follow the steps in bullets 2–6 in the second Position Graphical Elements Ribbon Method

OR

▶ Press **[Shift][F9]** to show or hide the grid
▶ Press **[Alt][F9]** to show or hide the drawing guide
▶ Drag the objects to position them on the grid or guides as needed

Resize Graphical Elements

Ribbon Method

▶ Select the object
▶ Click the **Drawing Tools Format tab**
▶ Click the **Shape Height text box** in the Size group, enter a value, or use the up and down arrows to adjust the height
▶ Click the **Shape Width text box** in the Size group, enter a value, or use the up and down arrows to adjust the width

OR

▶ Select the object
▶ Click the **Drawing Tools Format tab**
▶ Click the **launcher** 🔲 in the Size group to open the Format Shape dialog box
▶ In the Format Shape dialog box, click **Size** in the left pane, then enter values in the Height, Width, and Rotation text boxes in the Size and rotate section, or use the up and down arrows to set the size and rotation values
▶ Enter values in the Height and Width text boxes in the Scale section or use the up and down arrows to set the scale
▶ Click **Close**

Note: To maintain the same relationship between the height and width settings, you click the Lock aspect ratio check box.

Shortcut Method

▶ Select the object, then drag any of the sizing handles to resize the object as needed

OR

PowerPoint

▶ Right-click the object, then click **Size and Position** on the shortcut menu

▶ Follow the steps in bullets 4–6 in the second Resize Graphical Elements Ribbon Method

Apply Effects to Graphical Elements

Ribbon Method

▶ Select the object

▶ Click the **Drawing Tools Format tab**

▶ Click the **Shape Effects list arrow** in the Shape Styles group, point to an effect, then click that effect style

OR

▶ Click the **Drawing Tools Format tab**, then click the **launcher** 🔲 in the Shape Styles group to open the Format Shape dialog box

▶ In the Format Shape dialog box, click an effect (Shadow, Reflections, Glow and Soft Edges, 3-D Format, or 3-D Rotation) in the left pane, then click an effect style

▶ Click **Close**

Shortcut Method

▶ Right-click the object, then click **Format Shape** on the shortcut menu

▶ Follow the steps in bullets 2–3 in the second Apply Effects to Graphical Elements Ribbon Method

Apply Styles to Graphical Elements

Ribbon Method

▶ Select the object

▶ Click the **Drawing Tools Format tab** or **Picture Tools Format tab** as appropriate, then click a style in the Shape Styles gallery in the Shape Styles group or in the Picture Styles gallery in the Picture Styles group

OR

▶ Click the **Shape Styles More button** 🔻 or the **Picture Styles More button** 🔻 in the Shape Styles group or Picture Styles group, then click a shape or picture style, respectively

Apply Borders to Graphical Elements

Ribbon Method

▶ Select the object

▶ Click the **Drawing Tools Format tab** or **Picture Tools Format tab** as appropriate, click the **Shape Outline list arrow** in the Shape Styles group, or click the **Picture Border list arrow** in the Picture Styles group, then click a border color, weight, and line style

OR

▶ Click the **Drawing Tools Format tab** or **Picture Tools Format tab** as appropriate, then click the **launcher** in the Shape Styles group or Picture Styles group to open the Format Shape dialog box

▶ In the Format Shape dialog box, click **Line Color** in the left pane, select options for a solid or gradient line in the right pane, click **Line Style** in the left pane, then select line style options in the right pane

▶ Click **Close**

Shortcut Method

▶ Right-click the object, then click **Format Shape** on the shortcut menu

▶ Follow the steps in bullets 2–3 in the second Apply Borders to Graphical Elements Ribbon Method

Add Hyperlinks to Graphical Elements

Ribbon Method

▶ Select the object to which you want to add a hyperlink

▶ Click the **Insert tab**, then click the **Hyperlink button** in the Links group

▶ In the Insert Hyperlink dialog box, make the appropriate selections using Table PPT-6 as a reference, then click **OK**

Shortcut Method

▶ Select the object in which you want to insert a hyperlink

▶ Right-click the object, then click **Hyperlink** on the shortcut menu, or press **[Ctrl][K]**

▶ In the Insert Hyperlink dialog box, make the appropriate selections using Table PPT-6 as a reference, then click **OK**

PowerPoint

Table PPT-6 Inserting Hyperlinks Using the Insert Hyperlink Dialog Box

To link to	Do this
Another document or Web page	Click **Existing File or Web Page**, navigate to the drive and folder that meet your needs, click the file name in the list, then click **OK** OR Click the **Address text box**, type the URL, then click **OK** *Note:* Make sure you are connected to the Internet to successfully follow this link.
Another place in the document	Click **Place in This Document**, select a location in the Select a place in this document list, then click **OK**
A new document	Click **Create New Document**, name the document, verify the drive and folder, choose to edit it now or later, then click **OK**
An e-mail address	Click **E-mail Address**, type the address and any other text to display, then click **OK**

MANIPULATE IMAGES

Apply Color Adjustments

Ribbon Method
▶ Click the picture whose color you want to adjust
▶ Click the **Color list arrow** in the Adjust group on the Picture Tools Format tab, then make the appropriate selections using Table PPT-7 as a reference

Table PPT-7 Color Adjustment Options

Option	Description
More Variations	Opens a menu of theme and standard colors, and a link to the Colors dialog box
Set Transparent Color	Removes pixels based on a single color you select in the image

(continued)

Table PPT-7 Color Adjustment Options (continued)

Option	Description
Picture Color Options:	Opens Picture Color options in the Format Picture dialog box, where you can fine-tune the color
• Color Saturation	Adjusts the intensity of the color
• Color Tone	Adjusts the color temperature by increasing or decreasing the coolness (blue) or warmness (orange)
• Recolor	Converts the color to grayscale, black and white, sepia, and color hues

Apply Image Corrections: Sharpen

Ribbon Method

▶ Click the picture whose image you want to sharpen

Note: You can sharpen a picture but not a clip art image.

▶ Click the **Corrections list arrow** in the Adjust group on the Picture Tools Format tab
▶ Click the **Sharpen: 25% thumbnail** or the **Sharpen: 50% thumbnail** in the Sharpen and Soften section to sharpen edges of pixels in the picture

OR

▶ Click **Picture Corrections Options** beneath the thumbnails to open the Format Picture dialog box, click the **Presets list arrow** in the Sharpen and Soften section, click the **Sharpen: 25% thumbnail** or the **Sharpen: 50% thumbnail**, then drag the **Soften Sharpen slider** to a positive percentage to the right
▶ Click **Close**

Apply Image Corrections: Soften

Ribbon Method

▶ Click the picture whose image you want to soften

Note: You can soften a picture but not a clip art image.

▶ Click the **Corrections list arrow** in the Adjust group on the Picture Tools Format tab

▶ Click the **Soften: 50% thumbnail** or the **Soften: 25%
thumbnail** in the Sharpen and Soften section to blur edges of
pixels in the picture

OR

▶ Click **Picture Corrections Options** beneath the thumbnails to
open the Format Picture dialog box, click the **Sharpen and
Soften Presets list arrow** in the Sharpen and Soften section,
click the **Soften: 50% thumbnail** or the **Soften: 25%
thumbnail**, then drag the **Soften Sharpen slider** to a negative
percentage to the left

▶ Click **Close**

Apply Image Corrections: Brightness

Ribbon Method

▶ Click the picture or clip art image whose brightness you want
to adjust

▶ Click the **Corrections list arrow** in the Adjust group on the
Picture Tools Format tab

▶ Click a thumbnail in the Brightness and Contrast section to adjust
the brightness of pixels in the picture

OR

▶ Click **Picture Corrections Options** beneath the thumbnails to
open the Format Picture dialog box, click the **Brightness and
Contrast Presets list arrow** in the Brightness and Contrast
section, click a thumbnail, then drag the **Brightness slider** to
the percentage that meets your needs

▶ Click **Close**

Apply Image Corrections: Contrast

Ribbon Method

▶ Click the picture or clip art image whose contrast you want
to adjust

▶ Click the **Corrections list arrow** in the Adjust group on the
Picture Tools Format tab

▶ Click a thumbnail in the Brightness and Contrast section to adjust
the contrast of pixels in the picture

OR

▶ Click **Picture Corrections Options** beneath the thumbnails to
open the Format Picture dialog box, click the **Brightness and
Contrast Presets list arrow**, click a thumbnail, then drag the
Contrast slider to the percentage that meets your needs

▶ Click **Close**

Add Artistic Effects to an Image

Ribbon Method

▶ Click the picture to which you want to apply an artistic effect

Note: You can add artistic effects to a picture but not to a clip art image.

▶ Click the **Artistic Effects list arrow** in the Adjust group on the Picture Tools Format tab
▶ Click a thumbnail to apply that artistic effect

OR

▶ Follow the steps in bullets 1–3 in the Add Artistic Effects to an Image Ribbon Method to apply an artistic effect, click the **Artistic Effects list arrow** in the Adjust group on the Picture Tools Format tab, then click **Artistic Effects Options** to open the Format Picture dialog box
▶ Be sure Artistic Effects is selected in the left pane, click the **Artistic Effects list arrow**, click a thumbnail, then drag each slider to the setting that meets your needs
▶ Click **Close**

Remove a Background

Ribbon Method

▶ Click the picture or clip art image whose background you want to remove
▶ Click the **Remove Background button** in the Adjust group on the Picture Tools Format tab
▶ Resize the selection marquee as needed
▶ Click the **Mark Areas to Keep button**, **Mark Areas to Remove button**, or **Delete Mark button** in the Refine group to adjust the selection to meet your needs
▶ Click the **Discard All Changes button** to cancel the background removal or click the **Keep Changes button** in the Close group to accept changes to the selected areas

Crop a Picture

Ribbon Method

▶ Click the picture you want to crop
▶ Click the **Picture Tools Format tab**, then click the **Crop button** in the Size group
▶ Place the pointer over a corner or side cropping handle, resize the picture to meet your needs, then press **[Esc]** or click a blank part of the slide

PowerPoint

Shortcut Method

▶ Click the picture you want to crop
▶ Right-click the picture, then click **Format Picture** on the short-cut menu
▶ In the Format Picture dialog box, click **Crop** in the left pane, then enter values in the Width, Height, Offset X, and Offset Y text boxes in the Picture position section, or use the up and down arrows to set the size and offset values
▶ Enter values in the Width, Height, Left, and Top text boxes in the Crop position section, or use the up and down arrows to set the crop position
▶ Click **Close**

Compress Selected Pictures or All Pictures

Ribbon Method

▶ Click the picture that you want to compress, click the **Picture Tools Format tab**, then click the **Compress Pictures button** 🖼 in the Adjust group
▶ Click the **Apply only to this picture check box** to select it to compress only the selected picture in the Compression options section of the Compress Pictures dialog box; leave the check box unselected to compress all the pictures in the presentation
▶ Click the **Delete cropped areas of pictures check box** to delete the cropped portions of the picture from the presentation file
▶ Select an option in the Target output section to set picture resolution
▶ Click **OK**

Change a Picture

Ribbon Method

▶ Click the picture that you want to change, click the **Picture Tools Format tab,** then click the **Change Picture button** 🖼 in the Adjust group
▶ Navigate to the folder containing the picture you want to insert, click the file, then click **Insert**

Shortcut Method

▶ Right-click the picture that you want to change, then click the **Change Picture button** 🖼 on the shortcut menu
▶ Navigate to the folder containing the picture you want to insert, click the file, then click **Insert**

Reset a Picture

Ribbon Method

▶ Click the picture that you want to reset, click the **Picture Tools Format tab**, then click the **Reset Picture list arrow** 🖾 in the Adjust group

▶ Click **Reset Picture** to reset removed background, color, corrections, and artistic effects changes, or click **Reset Picture and Size** to reset size in addition to the other adjustment changes

MODIFY WORDART AND SHAPES

Set the Formatting of the Current Shape as the Default for Future Shapes

Shortcut Method

▶ Select the current WordArt or shape to which you have applied attributes you want to set as the default

▶ Right-click the border, then click **Set as Default Shape** on the shortcut menu

Change the Fill Color or Texture

Ribbon Method

▶ Click the WordArt or shape whose fill or texture you want to change

▶ Click the **Shape Fill list arrow** in the Drawing group on the Home tab or in the Shape Styles group on the Drawing Tools Format tab

▶ Click a color, or point to **Texture**, then click a texture

OR

▶ Click the **launcher** 🖾 in the Drawing group on the Home tab or the Shape Styles group on the Drawing Tools Format tab to open the Format Shape dialog box

▶ In the Format Shape dialog box, click the **Solid fill option button**, click the **Color button** 🖾 ▾, click a color or click **More Colors** to open the Colors dialog box and set color options, then click **OK** to close the More Colors dialog box

Note: To adjust how much color appears, you drag the Transparency slider.

▶ Click the **Picture or texture fill option button**, click the **Texture list arrow**, click a texture, then select tiling and transparency options

▶ Click **Close**

OR

▶ Click the **launcher** 🔲 in the Drawing group on the Home tab or the Shape Styles group on the Drawing Tools Format tab to open the Format Shape dialog box

▶ Follow the steps in bullets 2–4 in the second Change the Fill Color or Texture Ribbon Method

Shortcut Method

▶ Right-click the WordArt or shape, then click **Format Shape** on the shortcut menu

▶ Follow the steps in bullets 2–4 in the second Change the Fill Color or Texture Ribbon Method

Change the WordArt

Ribbon Method

▶ Click the WordArt you want to change, then click the **Drawing Tools Format tab**

▶ Click the **More button** 🔽 in the WordArt Styles group, then click a new WordArt style in the gallery

Convert WordArt to SmartArt

Ribbon Method

▶ Click the WordArt you want to convert

▶ Click the **Convert to SmartArt Graphic button** 📊▼ in the Paragraph group on the Home tab, then click a SmartArt graphic or click **More SmartArt Graphics**, click a SmartArt graphic in the Choose a SmartArt graphic dialog box, then click **OK**

Manipulate SmartArt

Add and Remove Shapes

Ribbon Method

▶ Click the **SmartArt Tools Design tab**, then click a shape or object in the SmartArt graphic where you want to add or remove a shape

▶ To add a shape, click the **Add Shape list arrow** in the Create Graphic group, then click an option to select the type of SmartArt graphic and location for the new shape that meets your needs

▶ To delete a shape, select the SmartArt graphic shape in the SmartArt graphic, then press **[Delete]**

OR

▶ To add a shape from the Text pane, click **Text Pane** in the Create Graphic group on the SmartArt Tools Design tab to open the text pane if it is not open, move the pointer to the end of the text where you want to add the shape, then press **[Enter]**; to delete a shape, select the text you want to delete, then press **[Delete]**

Shortcut Method

▶ To add a shape, right-click the SmartArt graphic shape in the SmartArt graphic, then point to **Add Shape** on the shortcut menu

▶ Click an option to select the type of SmartArt graphic and location for the new shape that meets your needs

▶ To delete a shape, right-click the SmartArt graphic shape in the SmartArt graphic, then click **Cut** on the shortcut menu

Note: You can also select a shape and press [Delete].

Change SmartArt Styles

Ribbon Method

▶ Select the SmartArt graphic whose style you want to change

▶ Click the **SmartArt Tools Design tab**, click the **SmartArt Styles More button** ⊽ in the SmartArt Styles group, then click a style from the gallery

Note: To change theme colors, you click the Change Colors button in the SmartArt Styles group.

Change the SmartArt Layout

Ribbon Method

▶ Select the SmartArt graphic whose layout you want to change

▶ Click the **SmartArt Tools Design tab**, click the **Layouts More button** ⊽ in the Layouts group, then click a layout from the gallery; or click **More Layouts**, click a SmartArt layout in the Choose a SmartArt graphic dialog box, then click **OK**

Shortcut Method

▶ Right-click the SmartArt graphic, click **Change Layout** on the shortcut menu, click a SmartArt layout in the Choose a SmartArt graphic dialog box, then click **OK**

Reorder Shapes

Ribbon Method

▶ Select the SmartArt graphic shape you want to reorder

PowerPoint

▶ Click the **SmartArt Tools Design tab**, then click the **Move Up button** or the **Move Down button** in the Create Graphic group as needed to meet your needs

Convert a SmartArt Graphic to Text

Ribbon Method

▶ Select the SmartArt graphic you want to convert to text
▶ Click the **SmartArt Tools Design tab**, click the **Convert list arrow** in the Reset group, then click **Convert to Text**

Shortcut Method

▶ Right-click the SmartArt graphic, then click **Convert to Text** on the shortcut menu

Convert A SmartArt Graphic to Shapes

Ribbon Method

▶ Select the SmartArt graphic you want to convert to shapes
▶ Click the **SmartArt Tools Design tab**, click the **Convert list arrow** in the Reset group, then click **Convert to Shapes**

Shortcut Method

▶ Right-click the SmartArt graphic, then click **Convert to Shapes** on the shortcut menu

Make Shapes Smaller or Larger

Ribbon Method

▶ Select the SmartArt shape you want to resize
▶ Click the **SmartArt Tools Format tab**
▶ Click the **Shape Height text box** in the Size group, then enter a value or use the up and down arrows to adjust the height
▶ Click the **Shape Width text box** in the Size group, then enter a value or use the up and down arrows to adjust the width

OR

▶ Select the SmartArt shape
▶ Click the **SmartArt Tools Format tab**
▶ Click the **launcher** 🔲 in the Size group to open the Format Shape dialog box
▶ In the Format Shape dialog box, click **Size** in the left pane, then enter values in the Height, Width, and Rotation text boxes in the Size and rotate section, or use the up and down arrows to set the size and rotation values
▶ Enter values in the Height and Width text boxes in the Scale section or use the up and down arrows to set the scale
▶ Click **Close**

Note: To maintain the same relationship between the height and width settings, you click the Lock aspect ratio check box.

Shortcut Method

▶ Select the shape, then drag any of the sizing handles to resize the object as needed

OR

▶ Right-click the object, then click **Size and Position** on the shortcut menu

▶ Follow the steps in bullets 4–6 in the second Make Shapes Smaller or Larger Ribbon Method

Promote Bullet Levels

Ribbon Method

▶ Click the **SmartArt Tools Design tab**

▶ Click the sub-bullet you want to promote in the SmartArt graphic Text pane, then click the **Promote button** in the Create Graphic group

OR

▶ Click the bulleted text you want to promote in the shape, then click the **Promote button** in the Create Graphic group

Demote Bullet Levels

Ribbon Method

▶ Click the **SmartArt Tools Design tab**

▶ Click the sub-bullet you want to demote in the SmartArt graphic Text pane, then click the **Demote button** in the Create Graphic group

OR

▶ Click the bulleted text you want to demote in the shape, then click the **Demote button** in the Create Graphic group

EDIT VIDEO AND AUDIO CONTENT

Apply a Style to Video and Audio Content

Ribbon Method

▶ Select the video or audio icon to which you want to apply a style

▶ For video, click the **Video Tools Format tab**, click the **More button** ⯆ in the Video Styles group, then click a style in the gallery

▶ For audio, click the **Audio Tools Format tab**, click the **More button** ⯆ in the Picture Styles group, then click a style in the gallery

PowerPoint

Adjust Video or Audio Content

Ribbon Method

▸ Select the video or audio icon you want to adjust
▸ For video, click the **Video Tools Format tab**, click the **Corrections list arrow**, **Color list arrow**, **Poster Frame list arrow**, or **Reset Design list arrow** in the Adjust group, then click an option to meet your needs
▸ For audio, click the **Audio Tools Format tab**, click the **Corrections list arrow**, **Color list arrow**, **Artistic Effects list arrow**, **Compress Pictures button**, **Change Picture button**, or **Reset Picture list arrow** in the Adjust group, then click an option to meet your needs

Arrange Video or Audio Content

Ribbon Method

▸ Select the video or audio icon whose content you want to arrange
▸ For video, click the **Video Tools Format tab**, click the **Bring Forward list arrow**, **Send Backward list arrow**, **Selection Pane button**, **Align list arrow**, or **Group list arrow** in the Arrange group, then click an option to meet your needs
▸ For audio, click the **Audio Tools Format tab**, click the **Bring Forward list arrow**, **Send Backward list arrow**, **Selection Pane button**, **Align list arrow**, or **Group list arrow** in the Arrange group, then click an option to meet your needs

Shortcut Method

▸ Right-click the video or audio icon
▸ Point to **Bring to Front** on the shortcut menu, then click **Bring to Front** or **Bring Forward**; or point to **Send to Back** on the shortcut menu, then click **Send to Back** or **Send Backward** to whichever meets your needs

Size Video or Audio Content

Ribbon Method

▸ Select the video or audio icon you want to resize, then click the **Video Tools Format tab** or the **Audio Tools Format tab**, respectively
▸ For video, click the **Video Height text box** in the Size group, then enter a value or use the up and down arrows to adjust the height
▸ Click the **Video Width text box** in the Size group, then enter a value or use the up and down arrows to adjust the width
OR

- ▶ Select the video or audio icon
- ▶ Click the **Video Tools Format tab** or **Audio Tools Format tab**, respectively
- ▶ Click the **launcher** 🔲 in the Size group to open the Format Video dialog box or Format Audio dialog box, respectively
- ▶ In the Format Video dialog box or Format Audio dialog box, click **Size** in the left pane, then enter values in the Height, Width, and Rotation text boxes in the Size and rotate section, or use the up and down arrows to set the size and rotation values
- ▶ Enter values in the Height and Width text boxes in the Scale section or use the up and down arrows to set the scale
- ▶ Click **Close**

Note: To maintain the same relationship between the height and width settings, you click the Lock aspect ratio check box.

Shortcut Method

- ▶ Select the video or audio icon, then drag any of the sizing handles to resize the object as needed

  OR

- ▶ Right-click the video or audio icon, then click **Size and Position** on the shortcut menu
- ▶ Follow the steps in bullets 4–6 in the second Size Video or Audio Content Ribbon Method

Adjust Playback Options

Ribbon Method

- ▶ Select the video or audio icon whose playback you want to adjust
- ▶ For video, click the **Video Tools Playback tab**, then select the playback options to meet your needs in the Bookmarks, Editing, or Video Options groups
- ▶ For audio, click the **Audio Tools Playback tab**, then select the playback options to meet your needs in the Bookmarks, Editing, or Video Options groups

POWERPOINT OBJECTIVE 4: CREATING CHARTS AND TABLES

CONSTRUCT AND MODIFY TABLES

Draw a Table

Ribbon Method

- ▶ Click the **Insert tab**, click the **Table list arrow** in the Tables group, then click **Draw Table**

▶ Drag on the slide to draw the lines for the columns and rows in the table

OR

▶ Click the **Insert tab**, click the **Table list arrow** in the Tables group, then drag across the grid on the menu that opens to draw a table with the selected rows and columns

Insert a Microsoft Excel Spreadsheet

Ribbon Method

▶ Click the **Insert tab**, then click the **Object button** in the Text group
▶ In the Insert Object dialog box, click the **Create from file option button**
▶ Click the **Browse button**, navigate to the drive and folder that meet your needs, click the Excel file you want, then click **Open**
▶ Click the **Link check box** in the Insert Object dialog box so data in the PowerPoint table will be updated when changes are made in Excel

Set Table Style Options

Ribbon Method

▶ Select the table whose table style options you want to set, then click the **Table Tools Design tab**
▶ Click the **Header Row check box**, **Total Row check box**, **Banded Rows check box**, **First Column check box**, **Last Column check box**, and/or **Banded Columns check box** in the Table Style Options group

Add Shading

Ribbon Method

▶ Select the table or cells to which you want to apply shading
▶ Click the **Table Tools Design tab**, click the **Shading list arrow** in the Table Styles group, then click a color

Shortcut Method

▶ Right-click the cells to which you want to apply shading
▶ Click the **Shape Fill list arrow** on the Mini toolbar, then click a color

Add Borders

Ribbon Method

▶ Select the table or cells to which you want to apply a border
▶ Click the **Table Tools Design tab**, click the **Borders list arrow** in the Table Styles group, then click a border

Shortcut Method

▶ Right-click the cells to which you want to apply a border
▶ Click the **No Borders list arrow** ⊞ on the Mini toolbar, then click a border

Add Effects

Ribbon Method

▶ Select the table or cells to which you want to apply an effect
▶ Click the **Table Tools Design tab**, then click the **Effects list arrow** 🔲 in the Table Styles group
▶ Point to **Cell Bevel**, **Shadow**, or **Reflections**, then click an effect

Columns and Rows: Change the Alignment

Ribbon Method

▶ Select the cells whose alignment you want to change
▶ Click the **Table Tools Layout tab**, then click an alignment button in the Alignment group
▶ Click the **Text Direction list arrow** in the Alignment group, then click an option on the menu to change the text orientation; or click **More Options** to open the Format Text Effects dialog box and change the Text box layout and features

Columns and Rows: Resize

Ribbon Method

▶ Select the column or row you want to resize, then click **Table Tools Layout tab**
▶ For a column, enter a value in the Table Column Width text box in the Cell Size group or use the up and down arrows to set the size
▶ For a row, enter a value in the Table Row Height text box in the Cell Size group or use the up and down arrows to set the size

OR

▶ Select the column or row you want to resize
▶ For a column, position the pointer on the inside border, then when the pointer changes to ◀┃▶, drag the **border** left or right to the column width that meets your needs
▶ For a row, position the pointer on the inside border, then when the pointer changes to ⬍, drag the **border** up or down to the row height that meets your needs

PowerPoint

Columns and Rows: Merge

Ribbon Method

▶ Select the columns or rows you want to merge, then click the **Table Tools Layout tab**

▶ Click the **Merge Cells button** in the Merge group

Shortcut Method

▶ Select the columns or rows you want to merge

▶ Right-click the cells, then click **Merge Cells** on the shortcut menu

Columns and Rows: Split

Ribbon Method

▶ Select the columns or rows you want to split, then click the **Table Tools Layout tab**

▶ Click the **Split Cells button** in the Merge group

Shortcut Method

▶ Select the columns or rows you want to split

▶ Right-click the cells, then click **Split Cells** on the shortcut menu

Columns and Rows: Distribute

Ribbon Method

▶ Select the tables whose columns or rows you want to distribute, then click the **Table Tools Layout tab**

▶ Click the **Distribute Rows button** or the **Distribute Columns button** in the Cell Size group

Columns and Rows: Arrange

Ribbon Method

▶ Click the table you want to arrange, then click the **Table Tools Layout tab**

▶ Click the **Bring Forward button** in the Arrange group, or click the **Bring Forward list arrow**, then click **Bring to Front**; click the **Send Backward button** in the Arrange group, or click the **Send Backward list arrow**, then click **Send to Back**

Shortcut Method

▶ Right-click the table you want to arrange

▶ Point to **Bring to Front** on the shortcut menu, then click **Bring to Front** or **Bring Forward**; or point to **Send to Back** on the shortcut menu, then click **Send to Back** or **Send Backward** to meet your needs

Note: You can also access Arrange options by clicking the Arrange list arrow in the Drawing group on the Home tab, then clicking an Arrange option in the Order Objects section on the menu.

INSERT AND MODIFY CHARTS

Select a Chart Type

Ribbon Method

▶ Click the **Insert tab**, then click the **Insert Chart button** in the Illustrations group
▶ Click a chart type in the left pane of the Insert Chart dialog box, then click the thumbnail for the chart in the right pane that meets your needs
▶ Click **OK**

Shortcut Method

▶ Select the slide containing a content placeholder
▶ Click the **Insert Chart button** in the content placeholder
▶ Follow the steps in bullets 2–3 in the Select a Chart Type Ribbon Method

Enter Chart Data

Ribbon Method

▶ Follow the steps in bullets 1–3 in the Select a Chart Type Ribbon Method

Note: The screen splits into two windows: a PowerPoint window on the left with the sample chart on the slide, and an Excel window on the right with sample data in the worksheet.

▶ Replace the sample data in the Excel worksheet with the labels and values for your chart
▶ Close the chart in the Microsoft Office PowerPoint – Microsoft Excel window in Excel
   OR
▶ Click an existing chart, then click the **Edit Data button** in the Data group on the Chart Tools Design tab
▶ Enter data in Excel to meet your needs, then close the chart in the Microsoft Office PowerPoint – Microsoft Excel window

Change the Chart Type

Ribbon Method

▶ Select the chart
▶ Click the **Chart Tools Design tab**, then click the **Change Chart Type button** in the Type group
▶ In the left pane of the Change Chart Type dialog box, click the new chart type, click the thumbnail for the new chart in the right pane, then click **OK**

Shortcut Method
▶ Right-click the chart
▶ Click **Change Chart Type** on the shortcut menu
▶ In the left pane of the Change Chart Type dialog box, click the new chart type, click the thumbnail for the new chart type in the right pane, then click **OK**

Change the Chart Layout

Ribbon Method
▶ Select the chart
▶ Click the **Chart Tools Design tab**, click the **More button** ⌄ in the Chart Layouts group, then click a layout in the gallery

Switch Rows and Columns

Ribbon Method
▶ Select the chart
▶ Click the **Chart Tools Design tab**, then click the **Edit Data button** in the Data group
▶ Click the chart, click the **Switch Row/Column button** in the Data group, then close Excel
   OR
▶ Select the chart
▶ Click the **Chart Tools Design tab**, then click the **Select Data button** in the Data group
▶ In the Select Data Source dialog box, click the **Switch Row/Column button**, click **OK**, then close Excel

Select Data

Ribbon Method
▶ Select the chart
▶ Click the **Chart Tools Design tab**, click the **Select Data button** in the Data group, adjust data in the Select Data Source dialog box to meet your needs, then close the Select Data dialog box and Excel

Edit Data

Ribbon Method
▶ Select the chart
▶ Click the **Chart Tools Design tab**, click the **Edit Data button** in the Data group, adjust data in Excel to meet your needs, then close Excel

Shortcut Method
▶ Right-click the chart
▶ Click **Edit Data** on the shortcut menu, adjust data in Excel to meet your needs, then close Excel

Apply Chart Elements

Use Chart Labels

Ribbon Method
▶ Select a chart
▶ Click the **Chart Tools Layout tab**; click the **Chart Title list arrow**, **Axis Titles list arrow**, **Legend list arrow**, **Data Labels list arrow**, or **Data Table list arrow** in the Labels group; then click the label option that meets your needs
  OR
▶ On each menu that opens, click **More Title Options**, **More Legend Options**, **More Data Label Options**, or **More Data Table Options**, then set options in the appropriate dialog box
  OR
▶ Select a label, click the **Chart Tools Format tab**, then format the shape or text to meet your needs
  OR
▶ Select the text in a Chart Title or Axis Title, then type new text

Use Axes

Ribbon Method
▶ Select a chart
▶ Click the **Chart Tools Layout tab**, click the **Axes list arrow** in the Axes group, point to **Primary Horizontal Axis** or **Primary Vertical Axis**, then click the axis option that meets your needs; or on each menu that opens, click **More Primary Horizontal Axis Options** or **More Vertical Horizontal Axis Options**, then set axis options in the appropriate dialog box

Use Gridlines

Ribbon Method
▶ Select a chart

PowerPoint

▶ Click the **Chart Tools Layout tab**, click the **Gridlines list arrow** in the Axes group, point to **Primary Horizontal Gridlines** or **Primary Vertical Gridlines**, then click the gridline option that meets your needs; or on each menu that opens, click **More Primary Horizontal Gridlines Options** or **More Vertical Horizontal Gridlines Options**, then set gridline options in the appropriate dialog box

Use Backgrounds

Ribbon Method

▶ Select a chart
▶ Click the **Chart Tools Layout tab**, then depending on the chart type, click the **Plot Area list arrow**, **Chart Wall list arrow**, **Chart Floor list arrow**, or **3-D Rotation button**
▶ On the menu that opens, set options to meet your needs

   OR

▶ On each menu that opens, click **More Plot Area Options**, **More Chart Wall Options**, **More Chart Floor Options**, or **3-D Rotation Options**, then set background options in the appropriate dialog box

MANIPULATE CHART LAYOUTS

Select Chart Elements

Ribbon Method

▶ Click the **Chart Tools Format tab**, click the **Chart Elements list arrow** in the Current Selection group, then click the element you want from the list

Note: You can also select a chart, then click the element you want to select or click the specific element again to separate it from the series or group.

Format Selections

Ribbon Method

▶ Select the chart element you want to format
▶ Click the **Chart Tools Format tab**, then click the **Format Selection button** in the Current Selection group to open the Format dialog box for that element
▶ Click a format you want in the left pane, then set options in the right pane

Manipulate Chart Elements

Arrange Chart Elements

Mouse Method

▶ Click the chart element you want to arrange
▶ Click a chart label you want to position, position the pointer over the label, then drag the label to the position that meets your needs

Specify a Precise Position

Ribbon Method

▶ Click the chart; click the **Chart Tools Layout tab**; click the **Chart Title list arrow, Axis Titles list arrow, Legend button list arrow, Data Labels list arrow**, or **Data Table list arrow** in the Labels group; then click the specific position on the menu that meets your needs

Apply Effects

Ribbon Method

▶ Click a chart element to which you want to apply an effect
▶ Click the **Chart Tools Format tab**, click the **Shape Effects button** in the Shape Styles group, point to an effect, then click an option

Resize Chart Elements

Ribbon Method

▶ Click a 3-D chart whose elements you want to resize
▶ Click the **Chart Tools Layout tab**, click the **Chart Elements list arrow** in the Current Selection group, then click a data series
▶ Click **Format Selection** in the Current Selection group to open the Format Data Series dialog box
▶ In the Series Options section, select options to meet your needs and resize the elements

Apply Quick Styles

Ribbon Method

▶ Click the chart to which you want to apply a Quick Style
▶ Click the **Chart Tools Design tab**, click a style in the Chart Styles group or click the **More button** in the Chart Styles group, then click a style in the gallery

Apply a Border

Ribbon Method

▶ Click the chart to which you want to apply a border
▶ Click the **Chart Tools Format tab**, click the **Shape Outline button** in the Shape Styles group, then click a color and set border options

Add Hyperlinks

Ribbon Method

▶ Click the chart to which you want to add a hyperlink
▶ Click the **Insert tab**, then click the **Hyperlink button** in the Links group
▶ In the Insert Hyperlink dialog box, use the options listed in Table PPT-6 (page 286) to create the hyperlink, then click **OK**

POWERPOINT OBJECTIVE 5: APPLYING TRANSITIONS AND ANIMATIONS

APPLY BUILT-IN AND CUSTOM ANIMATIONS

Use More Entrance

Ribbon Method

▶ Click the object to which you want to apply an entrance effect
▶ Click the **Animations tab**, click the **More button** ⊡ in the Animation group, then click **More Entrance Effects** in the gallery
▶ In the Change Entrance Effect dialog box, click an entrance effect, then click **OK**

Use More Emphasis

Ribbon Method

▶ Click the object to which you want to apply an emphasis effect
▶ Click the **Animations tab**, click the **More button** ⊡ in the Animation group, then click **More Emphasis Effects** in the gallery
▶ In the Change Emphasis Effect dialog box, click an emphasis effect, then click **OK**

Use More Exit Effects

Ribbon Method

▶ Click the object to which you want to apply an exit effect

▶ Click the **Animations tab**, click the **More button** 🔽 in the Animation group, then click **More Exit Effects** in the gallery

▶ In the Change Exit Effect dialog box, click an exit effect, then click **OK**

Use More Motion Effects

Ribbon Method

▶ Click the object to which you want to apply a motion path effect

▶ Click the **Animations tab**, click the **More button** 🔽 in the Animation group, then click **More Motion Paths** in the gallery

▶ In the Change Motion Path dialog box, click a motion path, then click **OK**

APPLY EFFECT AND PATH OPTIONS

Set Timing

Ribbon Method

▶ Click the animated object whose timing you want to set

▶ Click the **Animations tab**

▶ Enter a value in the Duration text box in the Timing group or use the up and down arrows to set the length of the animation

▶ Enter a value in the Delay text box in the Timing group or use the up and down arrows to set how long of a pause before the animation plays

OR

▶ Click the animated object whose timing you want to set

▶ Click the **Animations tab**, then click the **Animation Pane button** in the Advanced Animation group to open the Animation Pane

▶ Click the **Animated object list arrow**, click **Timing** in the list, set timing options on the Timing tab of the animation dialog box for the selected animation, then click **OK**

OR

▶ Click the animated object whose timing you want to set

▶ Click the **Animations tab**, then click the **launcher** 🔲 in the Animation group to open the animation dialog box for the selected animation

▶ Follow the steps in bullet 3 in the second Set Timing Ribbon Method

PowerPoint

Set Start Options

Ribbon Method

▶ Click the animated object whose options you want to set
▶ Click the **Animations tab**, click the **Start list arrow** in the Timing group, then click **On Click**, **With Previous**, or **After Previous** to set when the animation starts to play

OR

▶ Click the animated object whose timing you want to set
▶ Click the **Animations tab**, then click the **Animation Pane button** in the Advanced Animation group to open the Animation Pane
▶ Click the **Animated object list arrow**, click **Timing**, then click **Start on Click**, **Start With Previous**, or **Start After Previous** on the menu

OR

▶ Click the animated object whose timing you want to set
▶ Click the **Animations tab**, then click the **Animation Pane button** in the Advanced Animation group to open the Animation Pane
▶ Click the **Animated object list arrow**, click **Timing**, click the **Start list arrow** on the Timing tab of the animation dialog box for the selected animation, select an option, then click **OK**

OR

▶ Click the animated object whose timing you want to set
▶ Click the **Animations tab**, then click the **launcher** 🔲 in the Animation group to open the animation dialog box for the selected animation
▶ Follow the steps in bullet 3 in the third Set Timing Ribbon Method

---

MANIPULATE ANIMATIONS

Change the Direction of the Animation

Ribbon Method

▶ Click the animated object whose direction you want to change
▶ Click the **Animations tab**
▶ Click the **Effect Options button** in the Animation group, then click a direction option

OR

▶ Click the animated object whose direction you want to change
▶ Click the **Animations tab**, then click the **Animation Pane button** in the Advanced Animation group to open the Animation Pane

▶ Click the **Animated object list arrow**, click **Effect Options**, click the **Direction list arrow** on the Timing tab of the animation text box, select an option, then click **OK**

Note: Depending on the selected animation, you can also adjust the direction on the Effects tab in the animation dialog box for the selected animation.

Attach a Sound to an Animation

Ribbon Method

▶ Click the animated object to which you want to attach a sound
▶ Click the **Animations tab**, then click the **Animation Pane button** in the Advanced Animation group to open the Animation Pane
▶ Click the **Animated object list arrow**, click **Effect Options**, click the **Sound list arrow** on the Effect tab of the animation text box, click a sound, then click **OK**

Note: To add a sound from a file, scroll down the Sound list, click Other Sound, navigate to the drive and folder in the Add Audio dialog box that meet your needs, click the sound file you want to use, then click Open.

Use the Animation Painter

Ribbon Method

▶ Click the animated object whose animation you want to apply to another object
▶ Click the **Animations tab**, then click the **Animation Painter button** in the Advanced Animation group
▶ Click the slide containing the object you want to animate, position the **Animation Painter pointer** ⌖ over the object, then click the mouse

Reorder Animation

Ribbon Method

▶ Click the slide containing two or more animated objects you want to reorder
▶ Click the **Animations tab**, select the animated object you want to reorder, then click the **Move Earlier button** or **Move Later button** in the Timing group

OR

▶ Click the slide containing two or more animated objects you want to reorder

▸ Click the **Animations tab**, then click the **Animation Pane button** in the Advanced Animation group
▸ In the Animation Pane, click an animation in the pane
▸ Click the **Re-Order Up button** ⬆ or **Re-Order Down button** ⬇ at the bottom of the Animation Pane

Select Text Options

Ribbon Method

▸ Click the animated text object whose options you want to select
▸ Click the **Animations tab**, then click the **Animation Pane button** in the Advanced Animation group to open the Animation Pane
▸ Click the **Animated object list arrow**, click **Effect Options**, then click the **Text Animation tab** in the animation text box
▸ Click the **Group text list arrow**, click an option, then click **Close**

APPLY AND MODIFY TRANSITIONS BETWEEN SLIDES

Modify a Transition Effect

Ribbon Method

▸ Click the slide with a transition you want to modify
▸ Click the **Transitions tab**
▸ Click the **Effect Options button** in the Transition to This Slide group, then click a direction option

Add a Sound to a Transition

Ribbon Method

▸ Click the slide with a transition to which you want to add a sound
▸ Click the **Transitions tab**
▸ Click the **Sound list arrow** in the Timing group, then click a sound

Note: To add a sound from a file, scroll down the Sound list, click Other Sound, navigate to the drive and folder in the Add Audio dialog box that meet your needs, click the sound file you want to use, then click Open.

Modify Transition Duration

Ribbon Method

▸ Click the slide with a transition whose duration you want to modify
▸ Click the **Transitions tab**
▸ Enter a value in the Duration text box in the Timing group or use the up and down arrows to set the length of the transition

PowerPoint

Set Up Manual or Automatically Timed Advance Options

Ribbon Method

▶ Click the slide with a transition whose timing you want to advance
▶ Click the **Transitions tab**
▶ Click the **On Mouse Click check box** to set the slide to move manually by mouse click
▶ Click the **After check box**, then use the up and down arrows to set the amount of time before the presentation moves automatically to the next slide

POWERPOINT OBJECTIVE 6: COLLABORATING ON PRESENTATIONS

MANAGE COMMENTS IN PRESENTATIONS

Insert and Edit Comments

Ribbon Method

▶ Click the slide or object to which the comment applies
▶ Click the **Review tab**, click the **New Comment button** in the Comments group, then type in the comment balloon that opens
▶ Click the **Edit Comments button** in the Comments group to move to and open a comment, then edit its contents to meet your needs

Shortcut Method

▶ Right-click an existing comment thumbnail, then click **Insert Comment** on the shortcut menu
▶ Type in the comment balloon that opens
▶ Double-click a comment balloon to open the comment balloon and edit its contents; or right-click a comment balloon, click **Edit Comment** on the shortcut menu, then edit its contents

Show or Hide Markup

Ribbon Method

▶ Click the slide that contains a comment
▶ If the comments are not visible, click the **Review tab**, then click the **Show Markup button** in the Comments group
▶ Click the **Previous button** or **Next button** in the Comments group as needed

Move to the Previous or Next Comment

Ribbon Method

▶ Click the slide that contains a comment

▶ Click the **Review tab**, then click the **Previous button** or **Next button** in the Comments group as needed

Delete Comments

Ribbon Method

▶ Select a comment thumbnail

▶ Click the **Review tab**, click the **Delete Comment button** in the Comments group or click the **Delete Comment list arrow** in the Comments group, then click **Delete**, **Delete All Markup on the Current Slide**, or **Delete All Markup in the Presentation**

Shortcut Method

▶ Right-click the comment thumbnail, then click **Delete Comment** on the shortcut menu

APPLY PROOFING TOOLS

Use Spelling and Thesaurus Features

Ribbon Method

▶ Click any slide in the presentation

▶ For spelling, click the **Review tab**, then click the **Spelling button** in the Proofing group

▶ In the Spelling dialog box, click an option to resolve the issue, continue spell checking, then click **Close**

▶ For thesaurus, click the word for which you want to search for a synonym, click the **Review tab**, then click the **Thesaurus button** in the Proofing group

▶ In the Research pane, point to an appropriate synonym, click the **list arrow**, then click an option

Compare and Combine Presentations

Ribbon Method

▶ Open a presentation you want to use to compare to another

▶ Click the **Review tab**, then click the **Compare button** in the Compare group

▶ In the Choose File to Merge with Current Presentation dialog box, navigate to the drive and folder containing the presentation you want to compare, click the presentation, then click **Merge**

▶ Click the **Next button** or **Previous Button** in the Compare group to move to each change

OR

▶ Click a slide thumbnail in the left pane, then click a slide change or presentation change in the Revisions pane on the right
▶ Click the **Edit icon** next to the change in the slide in the center pane, then click the **Edit check box** if you want to accept the change or comment
▶ Click the **Slides tab** in the Revisions pane to view the original slide without changes
▶ Click the **Accept list arrow** or **Reject list arrow** in the Compare group to apply individual changes, apply all changes to the slide, or apply all changes to the presentation

OR

▶ Click an **Edit icon check box** to select it to apply the change
▶ Click the **End Review button** in the Compare group to apply changes

Note: PowerPoint discards unapplied changes when you click the End Review button.

POWERPOINT OBJECTIVE 7: PREPARING PRESENTATIONS FOR DELIVERY

SAVE PRESENTATIONS

Save the Presentation as a Picture Presentation

Ribbon Method

▶ Click the **File tab** to open Backstage view, then click **Save & Send**
▶ Click **Change File Type** in the File Types section of the middle pane, click **PowerPoint Picture Presentation (*.pptx)** in the Change File Type section in the right pane, then click the **Save As button** in the right pane
▶ In the Save As dialog box, navigate to the drive and folder where you want to store the presentation, then click **Save**

OR

▶ Click the **File tab** to open Backstage view, then click **Save As**
▶ In the Save As dialog box, navigate to the drive and folder where you want to store the presentation, click the **Save as type list arrow**, click **PowerPoint Picture Presentation (*.pptx)**, then click **Save**

PowerPoint

Save the Presentation as a PDF

Ribbon Method

▶ Click the **File tab** to open Backstage view, then click **Save & Send**
▶ Click **Create PDF/XPS Document** in the File Types section of the middle pane
▶ Click the **Create PDF/XPS button** in the right pane
▶ In the Publish as PDF or XPS dialog box, navigate to the drive and folder where you want to store the presentation, type a file name, select a size option button, then click **Publish**

Note: To select a slide range and other publish options, you click the Options button.

OR

▶ Click the **File tab** to open Backstage view, then click **Save As**
▶ In the Save As dialog box, click the **Save as type list arrow**, click **PDF (*.pdf)**, then click **Save**

Save the Presentation as an XPS

Ribbon Method

▶ Click the **File tab** to open Backstage view, then click **Save & Send**
▶ Click **Change File Type** in the middle pane, then click the **Save As button** in the right pane

OR

▶ Click the **File tab** to open Backstage view, then click **Save As**
▶ In the Save As dialog box, navigate to the drive and folder where you want to store the presentation, click the **Save as type list arrow**, click **XPS Document (*.xps)**, then click **Save**

Save the Presentation as an Outline

Ribbon Method

▶ Click the **File tab** to open Backstage view, then click **Save & Send**
▶ Click **Change File Type** in the middle pane, click **Save as Another File Type** in the right pane, then click the **Save As button** in the right pane

OR

▶ Click the **File tab** to open Backstage view, then click **Save As**
▶ In the Save As dialog box, navigate to the drive and folder where you want to store the presentation, click the **Save as type list arrow**, click **Outline/RTF (*.rtf)**, then click **Save**

Save the Presentation as an OpenDocument

Ribbon Method

▶ Click the **File tab** to open Backstage view, then click **Save & Send**

▶ Click **Change File Type** in the File Types section of the middle pane, click **OpenDocument Presentation (*.odp)** in the Change File Type section of the right pane, then click the **Save As button** in the right pane

▶ In the Save As dialog box, navigate to the drive and folder where you want to store the presentation, then click **Save**

OR

▶ Click the **File tab** to open Backstage view, then click **Save As**

▶ In the Save As dialog box, click the **Save as type list arrow**, click **Open Document Presentation (*.odp)**, click **Save**, then if a warning message appears, click **Yes**

Save the Presentation as a Show (.ppsx)

Ribbon Method

▶ Click the **File tab** to open Backstage view, then click **Save & Send**

▶ Click **Change File Type** in the File Types section of the middle pane, click **PowerPoint Show (*.ppsx)** in the Change File Type section of the right pane, then click the **Save As button** in the right pane

▶ In the Save As dialog box, navigate to the drive and folder where you want to store the presentation, then click **Save**

OR

▶ Click the **File tab** to open Backstage view, then click **Save As**

▶ In the Save As dialog box, navigate to the drive and folder where you want to store the presentation, click the **Save as type list arrow**, click **PowerPoint Show (*.ppsx)**, then click **Save**

PowerPoint

Save a Slide or Object as a Picture File

Ribbon Method

▶ Select the slide or object you want to save as a picture file

▶ Click the **File tab** to open Backstage view, then click **Save & Send**

▶ Click **Change File Type** in the File Types section of the middle pane, click **PNG Portable Network Graphics (*png)** or **JPEG File Interchange Format (*jpg)** in the Image File Types section of the right pane, then click the **Save As button** in the right pane

▶ In the Save As dialog box, navigate to the drive and folder where you want to store the picture file, then click **Save**

OR

▶ Click the **File tab** to open Backstage view, then click **Save As**
▶ In the Save As dialog box, navigate to the drive and folder where you want to store the picture file, click the **Save as type list arrow**, click a picture file type listed in Table PPT-8, then click **Save**

Shortcut Method

▶ Right-click the slide or object you want to save as a picture file
▶ Click **Save as Picture**
▶ Follow the steps in bullet 2 in the Save a Slide or Object as a Picture File Ribbon Method

Table PPT-8 Picture File Types

Extension	File type
GIF	GIF Graphics Interchange Format (*.gif)
JPG	JPEG File Interchange Format (*.jpg)
PNG	PNG Portable Network Graphics Format (*.png)
TIFF	TIFF Tag Image File Format (*.tif)
BMP	Device Independent Bitmap (*.bmp)
WMF	Windows Metafile (*.wmf)
EMF	Enhanced Windows Metafile (*.emf)

SHARE PRESENTATIONS

Package a Presentation for CD Delivery

Ribbon Method

▶ Click the **File tab** to open Backstage view, then click **Save & Send**
▶ Click **Package Presentation for CD** in the File Types section of the middle pane, then click the **Package for CD button** in the Package Presentation for CD section of the right pane
▶ In the Package for CD dialog box, type a name for the CD in the Name the CD text box, select the presentation you want to copy, click the **Add button**, navigate to a presentation file you want to add to the list, select the presentation, then click **Add**; then click the **Options button** to set additional specifications to meet your needs

OR

▶ Click **Copy to Folder**, name the folder and select the location in the Copy to Folder dialog box, click **OK**, then click **Close**

OR

▶ Click **Copy to CD**, then click **Yes** in the message box to package the linked files

▶ Insert a blank CD or DVD into the computer's CD or DVD burner, follow the instructions for copying the file to the CD, then click **Close**

Note: To specify whether to include linked files, password, and inspect for private information options, you click the Options button and select the settings.

Create Video

Ribbon Method

▶ Click the **File tab** to open Backstage view, then click **Save & Send**

▶ Click **Create a Video** in the File Types section of the middle pane

▶ Select a display, whether to include recorded timings and narrations, and the amount of time for each slide in the Create a Video section of the right pane, then click the **Create Video button** in the Create a Video section of the right pane

▶ In the Save As dialog box, navigate to the drive and folder where you want to store the movie, then click **Save**

Create Handouts (Send to Microsoft Word)

Ribbon Method

▶ Click the **File tab** to open Backstage view, then click **Save & Send**

▶ Click **Create Handouts** in the File Types section of the middle pane, then click the **Create Handouts button** in the Create Handouts in Microsoft Word section of the right pane

▶ In the Send to Microsoft Word dialog box, select a page layout and slide options, then click **OK**

Compress Media

Ribbon Method

▶ Click the **File tab** to open Backstage view, click the **Compress Media list arrow** in the middle pane, then click a quality

▶ Click **Close** in the Compress Media dialog box when the compression is complete

PRINT PRESENTATIONS

Adjust Print Settings

Ribbon Method

▶ Click the **File tab** to open Backstage view, then click **Print**
▶ Select options in the Settings section to meet your needs, click **Printer Properties** to set printer settings, then click the **Print button**

PROTECT PRESENTATIONS

Set a Password

Ribbon Method

▶ Click the **File tab** to open Backstage view, then click **Info** if it is not selected
▶ Click the **Protect Presentation list arrow** in the middle pane, then click **Encrypt with Password**
▶ In the Encrypt Document dialog box, type the password in the Password text box, click **OK**, retype the password in the Reenter Password text box, then click **OK**

Change a Password

Ribbon Method

▶ Open a presentation containing a password, type the password as requested, click the **File tab** to open Backstage view, then click **Info** if it is not selected
▶ Click the **Protect Presentation list arrow** in the middle pane, then click **Encrypt with Password**
▶ In the Encrypt Document dialog box, type the new password in the Password text box, click **OK**, retype the new password in the Reenter Password text box in the Confirm Password dialog box, then click **OK**

Mark a Presentation as Final

Ribbon Method

▶ Open a presentation containing a password, click the **File tab** to open Backstage view, then click **Info** if it is not selected
▶ Click the **Protect Presentation list arrow** in the middle pane, then click **Mark as Final**
▶ Click **OK** in the message box to mark the presentation as final, then click **OK** in the message box to acknowledge that the presentation has been marked as final

Note: To edit a presentation marked as final, click Edit Anyway on
the gold message bar above the slide that appears in Normal view.

POWERPOINT OBJECTIVE 8: DELIVERING PRESENTATIONS

APPLY PRESENTATION TOOLS

Add Pen and Highlighter Annotations

Ribbon Method

▶ Click the **Slide Show button** 🖳 on the status bar to switch to
Slide Show view
▶ Right-click the slide to which you want to add a pen or high-
lighter annotation, point to **Pointer Options**, then click **Pen** or
Highlighter
▶ Press and hold the **left mouse button**, then annotate the slide

Change the Ink Color

Ribbon Method

▶ Click the **Slide Show button** 🖳 on the status bar to switch to
Slide Show view
▶ Right-click the slide to which you want to add a pen or highlighter annotation, point to **Pointer Options**, point to **Ink Color**,
then click a color

Erase an Annotation

Ribbon Method

▶ Click the **Slide Show button** 🖳 on the status bar to switch to
Slide Show view
▶ Right-click the slide to which you want to add a pen or highlighter annotation, point to **Pointer Options**, then click **Eraser**
or **Erase All Ink on Slide** to erase portions or all of the ink,
respectively

Discard Annotations Upon Closing

Ribbon Method

▶ Click the **Slide Show button** 🖳 on the status bar to switch to
Slide Show view
▶ Move to the end of the slide show, then click to exit
▶ Click **Discard** in the message box to not retain the annotations

PowerPoint

Retain Annotations Upon Closing

Ribbon Method

▶ Click the **Slide Show button** 🖵 on the status bar to switch to Slide Show view
▶ Move to the end of the slide show, then click to exit
▶ Click **Keep** in the message box to retain the annotations

SET UP SLIDE SHOWS

Set Up a Slide Show

Ribbon Method

▶ Click the **Slide Show tab**, then click the **Set Up Slide Show button** in the Set Up group
▶ Specify the options that meet your needs in the Set Up Show dialog box, using Table PPT-9 as a guide
▶ Click **OK**

Table PPT-9 Set Up Show Options

Section	Option
Show type	Choose whether the show will be delivered by a speaker or browsed by an individual in a window or at a kiosk
Show options	Select whether to loop continuously; to show with or without narration or animation; and pen and laser pointer color
Show slides	Specify whether to show all or selected slides
Advance slides	Choose to proceed through slides manually or using timings
Multiple monitors	Set show to run on one or multiple monitors using Presenter view, use thumbnails to select slides, preview text, see Speaker notes in larger format, and run other programs that you don't want the audience to see during the presentation

Play Narrations

Ribbon Method

▶ Click the **Slide Show tab**, then click the **Play Narrations check box** in the Set Up group to select the box if it is not already checked

Set Up Presenter View

Ribbon Method

▶ Click the **Slide Show tab**, then click the **User Presenter View check box** in the Monitors group
▶ Click the **Show On list arrow**, then select which monitor to use as the one on which the audience will see the presentation
▶ Click the **Start button** 🌐 on the Windows taskbar
▶ Click **Control Panel**, then click **Adjust screen resolution** in the Appearance and Personalization section
▶ Click the **Multiple display list arrow**, click **Extend these displays**, then click **OK**

Use Timings

Ribbon Method

▶ Click the **Slide Show tab**, then click the **Use Timings check box** in the Set Up group
OR
▶ Click the **Set Up Slide Show button**, click the **Using timings, if present option button** in the Advance slides section to select it, then click **OK**

Show Media Controls

Ribbon Method

▶ Click the **Slide Show tab**, then click the **Show Media Controls check box** in the Set Up group

Broadcast Presentations

Ribbon Method

▶ Click the **Slide Show tab**, then click the **Broadcast Slide Show button** in the Start Slide Show group
▶ Click **Start Broadcast**, type your **Windows Live ID credentials** in the Windows Security dialog box, then click **OK**
▶ In the Broadcast Slide Show dialog box, click **Send in Email** to open a new message window containing the link to the broadcast, where you can invite people to the broadcast
▶ Add e-mail addresses, then click **Send**
OR
▶ Click the **File tab** to open Backstage view, then click **Save & Send**
▶ Click **Broadcast Slide Show** in the middle pane, then click the **Broadcast Slide Show button** in the right pane

▶ Follow the steps in bullets 2–4 in the Broadcast Presentations Ribbon Method

Create a Custom Slide Show

Ribbon Method

▶ Click the **Slide Show tab**, click the **Custom Slide Show list arrow** in the Start Slide Show group, then click **Custom Shows**
▶ In the Custom Shows dialog box, click **New**
▶ In the Define Custom Show dialog box, click the **Slide show name text box**, then type a name for the custom slide show
▶ Click each slide in the Slides in presentation section that you want in the custom show

Note: To select more than one slide, press and hold [Ctrl], then click each slide you want to add to the custom presentation.

▶ Click **Add** to add the slide(s) or select a slide in the Slides in custom show list and click **Remove** to remove the slide, then click **OK**

Note: To reorder slides in a custom presentation, select a slide, then click the Reorder Up button 🔼 or the Reorder Down button 🔽 in the Define Custom Show dialog box.

▶ Click **OK** to close the Define Custom Show dialog box
▶ Click **Close**

SET PRESENTATION TIMING

Rehearse Timings

Ribbon Method

▶ Go to the first slide in the presentation, then click the **Slide Show tab**
▶ Click the **Rehearse Timings button** in the Set Up group

Note: The slide show begins to run, and as the Recording toolbar opens and times the slide, give your audio presentation for the first slide.

▶ Click the **Next button** on the Recording toolbar
▶ Click the **Repeat button** to repeat a slide, then click **Resume recording** when you are ready to rehearse that slide again
▶ Click the **Pause button** to pause the presentation and stop the clock, then click **Resume recording** when you are ready to rehearse that slide again
▶ Click the **Close button** to stop recording, then follow the steps in bullet 3 in the Keep Timing Ribbon Method on the next page

Keep Timing

Ribbon Method

▶ Follow the steps in bullets 1–5 in the Rehearse Timings Ribbon Method
▶ Continue advancing through to the end of the presentation
▶ Click the **Close button** ☒ on the Rehearsal toolbar, then click **Yes** in the Microsoft PowerPoint message box to keep the slide timings, or click **No** to use other timings or try again

Adjust a Slide's Timing

Ribbon Method

▶ Select the slide whose timing you want to set
▶ Click the **Transitions tab**, then enter a value in the After text box or use the up and down arrows to adjust the amount of time the slide is visible

---

RECORD PRESENTATIONS

Start Recording from the Beginning of a Slide Show

Ribbon Method

▶ Click the **Slide Show tab**, then click the **Record Slide Show list arrow** in the Set Up group
▶ Click **Start Recording from Beginning of a Slide Show**
▶ Click the **Slide and animation timings check box** or the **Narrations and laser pointer check box** to either set those timings manually or to record narration and/or the laser pointer
▶ Click the **Slide Show tab**, click **Start Recording from the Current Slide of the Slide Show**
▶ Follow the steps in bullets 1–5 in the Rehearse Timings Ribbon Method
▶ Click the **Close button** ☒ on the Recording toolbar

Note: To clear timing or narration on the current slide or all slides, you click the Record Slide list arrow in the Set Up group on the Slide Show tab, point to Clear, then click an option.

Start Recording from the Current Slide of the Slide Show

Ribbon Method

▶ Click the **Slide Show tab**, then click the slide from which you want to start recording, then click the **Record Slide Show list arrow** in the Set Up group
▶ Click **Start Recording from Current Slide**

▶ Click the **Slide and animation timings check box** or the **Narrations and laser pointer check box** to set those timings manually or to record narration and/or the laser pointer

▶ Click **Start Recording**

▶ Follow the steps in bullets 1–5 in the Rehearse Timings Ribbon Method

▶ Click the **Close button** ⌧ on the Recording toolbar

Note: To clear timing or narration on the current slide or all slides, you click the Record Slide list arrow in the Set Up group on the Slide Show tab, point to Clear, then click an option.

INDEX

Exam Tips

A
Access (Microsoft), self-study products for, 7–9

C
certification
  importance of, 1–3
  requesting updated, 4
Certiport. *See also* testing centers
  exam vouchers, 2, 3, 9–10
  registering with, 3
  site login, 4, 9–10, 12
  usernames/passwords, 4, 9–10, 12
classes, taking, value of, 6
Core level exams, 5

D
dialog boxes, closing, when taking exams, 14

E
exam(s)
  choosing, 5
  clocks, 13
  instructions, 12
  preparing for, 6–9
  results, 10, 11
  re-taking, 11
  skills required to pass specific, 5
  tips, 1–4
  vouchers, 2, 3, 9–10
Excel (Microsoft), suggested self-study products for, 7–9
Expert level exams, 5

H
help, disabled, during exams, 13

L
login, to the Certiport site, 4, 9–10, 12

M
Master level exams, 5
MCAS (Microsoft Certified Application Specialist) certification, 4

Microsoft Office Specialist Certiport Center, 2. *See also* Certiport; testing centers
MOS (Microsoft Office Specialist) certification
  defined, 1–2
  process, 3–4

O
Office (Microsoft), suggested self-study products for, 7–9

P
passwords, 4, 9–10, 12
PowerPoint (Microsoft), suggested self-study products for, 8–9
pretests, taking, 3, 9
proctors, 11, 13

R
Reset button, 12

S
self-study materials, 6–7
Skip button, 12
spelling mistakes, 14

T
testing center(s). *See also* Certiport
  appointments, 10
  classes at, 6
  finding, 3, 5
  taking exams at, 4, 10–13

U
usernames, 4, 9–10, 12

W
Word (Microsoft), suggested self-study products for, 7–9

Word 2010

A
Access (Microsoft)
  databases, linking forms to, 135
  tables, used as data sources, 124
ActiveX controls (Microsoft), 133

address lists, 126
Artistic Effects, 72–73, 84
Auto Check for Errors feature, 100
AutoCorrect feature, 90–91
AutoFormat feature, 61
AutoRecover feature, 29
AutoSave feature, 113

B

backgrounds, creating, 68
Backstage view, 17, 18
bibliographies, compiling, 114–115
Bing, 22
blog(s)
   accounts, registering, 32–33
   posts, creating/publishing, 33
bookmarks, using hyperlinks as, 93–94
borders, for shapes, 79–80
building block(s)
   built-in, adding, 66, 70
   customized, creating, 108–109
Building Blocks Organizer, 66, 70
bullet(s)
   applying, 60–62
   defining pictures to be used as, 60–61
   symbol format, selecting, 60
bulleted lists, creating, 61

C

captions, adding, to clip art, 83
cell(s)
   merging, 58
   splitting, 58
character attributes, 36–42, 106–107
chart(s)
   data, modifying, 109
   creating, 107–108
   layout, modifying, 108
   saving, as templates, 108
citation(s)
   adding, 114
   marking, 117
   in Tables of Authorities, 115–116, 117
clear formatting, 37
clip art. *See also* graphics
   inserting, 82–85
   organizing, 82–83
   positioning, 84
   sizing, 84–85
Clip Organizer, 82–83
color, background, selecting, 68

column(s)
   adding, 57, 63
   deleting, 59
   for indexes, 118
   merging table cells in, 58
   moving, 58
   resizing, 58–59
   spacing, 63–64
   splitting table cells in, 58
   width, 63–64
combining documents, 112–113
command buttons, assigning macros
   to, 132–133
comment(s)
   deleting, 92
   editing, 91
   inserting/modifying, 91–92
   reviewing, 113–114
   viewing, 92
comparing documents, 112–113
compatibility mode, using, 34
Controls group, 133–134, 137
copy and paste, 41–42. *See also* cut
   and paste
cover pages, inserting, 67
cropping graphics, 74–75
cross references, 115, 120–121
cut and paste, 51, 58. *See also* copy
   and paste

D

database(s)
   engines, 135
   linking forms to, 135–136
date and time, inserting, 69–70
digital signatures, 26
.doc file extension, 33
document(s)
   applying views to, 23–26
   closing, 17–18
   combining/comparing, 112–113
   navigating, 19–20, 42–47
   opening, 17–18
   outlines, reorganizing, 25
   protection for, 26–29
   saving, 17–18, 34–35
   searching, 42–47
   sharing documents, 23–36, 102–105
   windows, navigating, 19–20
   versions, managing, 29–30
   views, using, 20
.docx file extension, 33

.dotm file extension, 135
.dotx file extension, 34
downloading templates, 36
draft versions, deleting, 30
Draw Table feature, 55–56

E

e-mail addresses, 30, 94, 121–122
encryption, 26–29
endnotes
  converting, to footnotes, 95
  creating, 94–96
  numbering, 96
envelope forms, 128–129
equations, inserting, 68
Excel (Microsoft)
  data, using, in new tables, 107
  tables, used as data sources, 124–125
exceptions, adding/removing, 90–91

F

field(s)
  adding, to forms, 137
  adding help content to, 134
  removing, from forms, 137–138
file(s)
  -names, 17
  types, 31
File tab, location of, in the Word
  window, 16
fill(s)
  gradient, 68
  pattern, 68
  for shapes, 79–80, 87
  texture, 68
Find and Replace dialog box, 19, 43–47
font(s). *See also* text
  applying, 36–42
  attributes, 106–107
  color, 39
  size, 37
  theme, 66
footers. *See* headers and footers
footnote(s)
  converting, to endnotes, 95
  creating, 94–96
  numbering, 96
form(s)
  adding fields to, 137
  creating, 126–129, 133–136
  fields, adding help content to, 134
  linking, to databases, 135–136

  locking, 136
  managing, 129–130
  manipulating, 137–139
  removing fields from, 137–138
Format Painter, 41
formatting
  default, applying, 115–116
  inserting, 82–85
  marks, displaying, 65
  using themes to apply, 65–66
formulas, applying, 107–108
Full Screen Reading view, 20

G

Go To command, 43
grammar checking, 88–90, 102
graphic(s). *See also* clip art; shapes
  adding captions to, 79
  applying effects to, 84
  applying hyperlinks to, 93
  compressing, 74, 84
  cropping, 74–75
  formatting, 71–76
  including, in documents, 71–88
  inserting text in, 78
  modifying the shape of, 74–75
  as page backgrounds, 68
  positioning, 75, 80–81
  rotating, 85
  sizing, 75–76, 81–82
gridlines, viewing, 59
groups, location of, in the Word
  window, 16

H

headers and footer(s)
  adding content to, 70, 110–111
  built-in, 70
  creating, 69
  deleting, 70
  inserting, 67
  linking sections and, 112
  margins and, 71
headings, browsing, 42
help
  accessing, 21–22
  content, adding, to form fields, 134
  options, summary of, 22
highlighting text, 39, 45
horizontal ruler, 51–53
hyperlinks
  applying, 93–94

linked to e-mail addresses, 94
used as bookmarks, 93–94
hyphenation settings, 63

I

illustrations, including, in documents,
71–88. *See also* graphics
indentation, 62–63
index(es)
creating, 118–121
cross-references for, 120–121
entries, marking, 119–120
modifying, 118–119
subentries, 120
Information Rights Management
Service, 27
Internet fax service, 31

K

keyboard shortcuts, 19
KeyTips, hiding/displaying, 21

L

label(s)
creating, 126–129
legacy, 133
languages, for indexes, 118
line spacing, 53
linking. *See also* hyperlinks
different sections, 112
forms to databases, 135–136
text boxes, 111–112
links, breaking, 112. *See also*
hyperlinks; linking
list(s)
items, demoting/promoting, 61–62
sorting items in, 62
locking forms, 136, 137

M

macro(s)
assigning, to command buttons,
132–133
-enabled templates, 135–136
managing, 129–130
options, 133–133
running, 131
recording, 133–134
security, 130
mail merge
envelope forms and, 128–129
mailing labels and, 126–127
manual, 99–100

performing, 121–122
previewing, 100–101
printing, 100–101
using other data sources, 123–125
Mail Merge Wizard, 99
mailing labels, 126–129
margins, 62–65, 71
master documents, viewing, 25
multilevel lists, creating, 61

N

navigation keyboard shortcuts, 19
Navigation pane, 42–43, 119, 120
nonbreaking spaces, inserting, 63
numbered lists, creating, 61

O

OpenType, 106
Outlook (Microsoft), 123–125

P

page(s)
blank, inserting, 65
borders, setting, 68
breaks, 64, 65
browsing, 43
cover, 67
first, attributes of, 71
layout, 48–50, 53, 62–71
numbers, 69, 98
setup, 62–65
paper size settings, 64
paragraph(s). *See also* text
aligning, 54–55
attributes, 36–42, 106–107
indentation, 47–51
spacing, 53–55
tab settings, 47, 51–53
passim (short form), 117–118
password(s), 26, 28
blog accounts and, 33
-protected forms, 136, 137
PDF (Portable Document Format),
31–32, 34
permissions, 26
photographs, applying effects to, 84.
See also clip art; graphics
pictures. *See* graphics
presentations
endnotes/footnotes for, 95
viewing, 95
printing, 20, 100–101
proofreading, 88–98

protected mode, 34
pull quotes, inserting, 66

Q

Quick Access toolbar
  custom macro buttons on, 132–133
  customizing, 17
  KeyTips and, 21
  location of, in the Word window, 16
  positioning, 17
Quick Parts, 66–68, 109–111
  gallery, 108–109
  inserting text as, 110
  saving, 109–110
Quick Styles, 40, 56–57
Quick Tables, 56

R

reference pages, creating, 114–115
References tab, 72, 79
reusable content, 62–71, 108–111
Review tab, 27, 28, 29
reviewing documents, 112–113
Ribbon
  displaying tabs on, 16–17
  hiding, 16–17
  KeyTips and, 21
  location of, in the Word window, 16
  using, 16–17
row(s)
  adding, 57
  deleting, 59
  merging table cells in, 58
  moving, 58
  resizing, 58–59
  splitting table cells in, 58
rulers, 62, 64

S

screen clippings, inserting, 76
screenshots, inserting, 76
scroll box
  location of, in the Word window, 16
  navigating Word documents with,
    19–20
searching documents, 42–47
section breaks
  inserting, 65
  removing, 65
security
  forms and, 136, 137
  macros and, 130
shadow effects, 87

shape(s). *See also* graphics
  adding text to, 78–79
  borders, 79–80
  effects, 87
  fills, 79–80, 87
  formatting, 76–82
  inserting, 76–82
  positioning, 80–81
  sizing, 81–82
  styles, setting, 79–80
sharing documents, 23–36, 102–105
SmartArt, 76–82
sorting
  list items, 62
  table content, 57
sources, managing, 115
spacing settings, 53–55
spell checking, 88–90, 102
starting Word, 15
status bar, location of, in the Word
  window, 16
Step by Step Mail Merge Wizard,
  121–122, 124, 126, 128
strikethrough attribute, 38
style(s)
  applying, 40
  character-specific, 106–107
  shape, setting, 79–80
  table, 56–57, 97–98, 117
  text box, 86–87
subdocuments, viewing, 25–26
subscript attribute, 38
superscript attribute, 38
synchronous scrolling, 24

T

tab leaders, 97, 116
tab stops
  moving, 53
  setting, 53
Table of Authorities, 115–118
Table of Contents, 96–98
tables. *See also* columns; rows
  applying formulas on, 107–108
  calculations, 107–108
  controlling page layout with, 56
  converting, to text, 59
  converting text to, 56
  creating, 55–56, 107–108
  mail merge operations and, 123–125
  manipulating, 56–59
  styles and, 56–57

templates
  applying, 35–36, 103–105
  creating, 104
  finding, on the Web, 36
  indexes and, 119
  locating, 35–36
  macro-enabled, 135–136
  managing, 105
  modifying, 103–104
  replacing placeholder text in, 36
  saving charts as, 108
text. *See also* fonts; paragraphs
  applying hyperlinks to, 93
  converting, to tables, 56
  direction, changing, 87
  effects, 40, 80, 106
  finding and replacing, 44
  highlighting, 39, 45
  inserting, 78, 110
  spacing, 53–55
text box(es)
  3-D effects for, 88
  applying, 85–88
  gallery, 86
  inserting, 67
  linking, 111–112
  manipulating, 85–88
  styles, 86–87
theme(s)
  applying, 65–66
  colors, 66
  effects, customizing, 66
  fonts, 66
3-D effects, for text boxes, 88
title bar, location of, in the Word
  window, 16
Track Changes feature, 91–92, 112–113
Trust Center, 34

U
usernames, 33

V
View buttons, location of, in the Word
  window, 16
views, applying, to documents, 23–26
Visual Basic (Microsoft), 135–136

W
watermarks, 67, 68
Web Layout view, 20, 26
window(s)
  arranging, 24

opening documents in new, 26
  switching between, 26
  viewing, side by side, 24
Windows Live ID, 30
Windows Live SkyDrive, 30
Word window, viewing, 16
WordArt, 76–82

Z
Zoom slider, location of, in the Word
  window, 16

Excel 2010

A
absolute cell references, 176–177
action macros, 208
active cell, location of, 140
Analysis ToolPak, 203
AND function, 178
array(s)
  applying, to functions, 200
  formulas, 199
Artistic Effects, 184
AutoFill feature, 156–158
AutoFilter feature, 190
automated analysis tools, 203–204
automatic workbook calculation, 199
AutoRecover feature, 151
AutoSave feature, 151

B
Backstage view, 146–151, 167
borders, for illustrations, 183
brightness settings, 184
buttons
  custom, 209
  macros and, 207–209

C
cell(s)
  active, location of, 140
  addresses, location of, 140
  aligning, 160–162
  attributes, 159
  borders, 161
  color, 161, 190, 191
  content, aligning, 160–162
  copying, 152, 156
  creating hyperlinks in, 158–159
  cutting, 155, 157
  data, creating, 151–156
  errors, common, 196–197
  formatting, 157, 160–162, 190–191

merging, 162
moving, 155–156
ranges, applying, in formulas,
    180–181
references, 176–177
selection, 156
series,157
splitting, 162
styles, 167–168
unmerged, 161–162
wrapping text in, 161–162
chart(s)
    advanced features, 202–203
    creating, 181
    sparklines and, 184–186
    templates, 203
Clipboard, 152–153, 155, 162
color
    applying, to worksheet tabs, 171
    cell, 190, 191
    saturation, 184
    scales, 191
    sparklines and, 185
    tone, 184
column(s)
    charts, 184–185
    headers, location of, 140
    headings, 162–163
    hiding/displaying, 165–166
    printing, 163–164
    series, 165–166
    titles, 162–164
    transposing, 153
command buttons, 208–209
comments, 154, 187–188
conditional
    formatting, 190–192
    logic, 177–179
contrast settings, 184
copying cells, 152. *See also* Paste
    Special option
cube functions, 201–202

D
data
    analysis, 188–190, 203–204
    invalid, locating, 197
    markers, showing/hiding, 186
    organizing, 188–190
    summary tasks, performing, 199
data bars, 191, 192
data sets, 207

date functions, 201
default settings, 150
dual axes, 202

E
e-mail, sending worksheets via, 186
encryption, 195
errors
    correcting, 198
    formulas and, 178
    tracing, 196–197
Excel window, viewing, 140
exiting Excel, 139
exponentiation operator, 176
exporting XML data, 194

F
file(s)
    manipulating, 150–151
    saving, 186–187
    types, changing, 186–187
    versions, recovering, 151
fills, 192. *See also* AutoFill feature
filter(s)
    applying, 189
    defining, 188–189
    lists, 190
    removing, 189
financial functions, 201
Find and Replace dialog box, 146
folders, manipulating, 150–151
font(s). *See also* text
    applying, 160–161
    color, 190
footers. *See* headers and footers
form controls
    inserting, 209
    setting properties for, 209
Format Painter, 162
formulas
    applying, 175–181, 196–198
    array, 199
    auditing, 196–197
    cell ranges in, 179–181
    cell references in, 176–177
    conditional logic in, 177–179
    copying, 157
    creating, 175, 177–178
    defined conditions in, 178–189
    functions in, 200–202
    invalid, locating, 197
    options, manipulating, 198–199

revising, 175
with values that match conditions, 177–178
function(s)
applying, 175–181, 196–198, 200–202
arguments, 200, 201
conditional logic and, 177–178

G

Go To dialog box, 142–143, 146
graphics. *See also* illustrations
brightness/contrast settings, 184
color/tone settings, 184
creating, 183–184
sharpening/softening settings, 183
gridlines, 148

H

header and footer(s)
configuring, 164
constructing, 147
size, changing, 167
help, accessing, 144
hot keys, using, 145–146
hyperlinks
applying/manipulating, 158–160
creating, 158–159
deleting, 159
modifying, 159
pasting, 155

I

icon(s)
previewing, 153
sets, 191, 192
IF function, 178, 191–192
IFERROR function, 178
illustrations. *See also* graphics
applying/manipulating, 181–183
inserting, 181–182
modifying, 182
rotating, 182
positioning, 182
sizing, 182
images. *See* graphics; illustrations
importing XML data, 194
iterative calculations, 198–199

K

keyboard(s)
hot keys, 145–146
KeyTips, 143–144
navigation shortcuts, 143

L

layers, filtering data into, 205
line charts, 184–185

M

macro(s)
action, 208
assigning, to command buttons, 208–209
creating, 207–209
modifying, 209
recording, 207, 208
running, 207
margins, 148, 167
merging cells, 162

N

named ranges, 179–180
navigating worksheets, 143, 145–146
Normal view, 173–174
NOT function, 178
number formats, applying, 161

O

operator(s)
precedence, 175–176
using, 175
OR function, 178
order of evaluation, 175–176

P

page(s)
breaks, 173–174
layout, 147–148, 162–164, 166–167, 173–174
orientation, 148, 166
scaling, 166–167
paper size, 148, 166
parentheses, 176
password(s)
worksheet, 194
workbook, 195
Paste Special option, 151–155
PDF (Portable Document Format), 187
Percent (%) operator, 176
permissions, 195
PivotCharts, 204–206
printing
options, applying, 147
rows, 163
titles, on odd or even pages, 164
workbooks, 146–148
worksheets, 146–148

Q

Quick Access toolbar
  creating custom macro buttons
    on, 209
  customizing, 141
  location of, 140
  manipulating, 149
  repositioning, 141

R

relative cell references, 176–177
Ribbon
  customizing, 149–150
  hiding/displaying, 140–141
  location of, 140
  using, 140–141
row(s)
  headings, 162–163
  hiding/unhiding, 165–166
  numbers, location of, 140
  printing, 163
  series, 165–166
  titles, 162–164
  transposing, 153
Rule Manager, 191
rules
  clearing, 192
  formatting, 191–192

S

saving data, 142, 186–187, 193–194
scenarios, setting up, 204
screenshots, modifying, 183
scroll bars, location of, 140
shapes, modifying, 182–183
sharing spreadsheets, 186–187
sheet tabs, location of, 140
SkyDrive, 186
Slicer, 205, 206
SmartArt, 181–183
sorting data, 190
sparklines, 184–186, 203
splitting cells, 162
starting Excel, 139
statistical functions, 200
status bar, 140
styles, for cells, 167–168
SUMIFS function, 199

T

tabs, location of, 140

templates
  chart, 203
  workbook, 141, 193–194
text functions, 201
time functions, 201
title bar, location of, 140
titles
  configuring, to print only on odd or
    event pages, 164
  creating, 162–164
  which skip the first worksheet
    page, 164
top/bottom rules, 191
Track Changes feature, 196
trendlines, 202

V

validation, 152, 154–155
versions, changing file types to
  specific, 186–187
view(s)
  buttons, location of, 140
  creating, 174
  custom, 174
  manipulating, 172–173
  splitting, 172
  workbook, 173–174

W

what-if analysis, 204, 206
window views. *See also* views
  arranging, 172–173
  manipulating, 172–173
  splitting, 172
win/loss charts, 184–185
workbook(s). *See also* worksheets
  calculations, automatic, 199
  closing, 142
  data options, 193–194
  files/folders, manipulating, 150–151
  open, running macros in, 207
  opening, 141
  printing, 146–148
  properties, 150, 193–194
  protection, 194–195
  saving, 142, 193–194
  settings, 193–194
  shared, maintaining, 195–196
  views, manipulating, 173–174
worksheet(s). *See also* workbooks;
  Worksheet window
  copying, 169–170
  creating, 168–172

data, charts based on, 181
deleting, 169
environment, managing, 145–151
formatting, 168–172
grouping, 171
inserting, 168
moving, 170
navigating, 143, 145–146
opening new windows with contents
   from, 173
page setup, 166–167
printing, 146–148
protection, 194–195
renaming, 170
repositioning, 169
selecting, 171
sharing, 186–187
tabs, display options for, 171–172
Worksheet window
   location of, 140
   navigating in, 142–143

X
.xltx file extension, 193
XML (Extensible Markup Language)
   data, importing/exporting, 194
XPS (XML Paper Specification)
   format, 187

Z
zoom controls, location of, 140

Access 2010
* (asterisk), 246
: (colon), 239
? (question mark), 246

A
ad-hoc relationships, 237
Anchor function, 233
append queries, 236
application parts, applying, 219–220
arithmetic operators, 240
asterisk (*), 246
attachment data type, 220
AutoFilter feature, 247–248
AutoNumber data type, 220, 225

B
Backstage view, using, 212
blank database icon, location of, 212
bound/unbound controls, 229, 241–242

C
calculated
   controls, 241–242
   fields, 239–240
calculations, performing, 239
Caption property, 221
charts, inserting, 242
Close button, location of, 213
Close Object button, location of, 213
code, viewing, 230
colon (:), 239
Combo Box Wizard, 242
conditional formatting, 234–246
controls
   formatting, 244
   repositioning, 244
Create button, location of, 212
crosstab queries, 237
currency data type, 220

D
data types
   basic, 220
   modifying, 223
database(s)
   access options, 218
   closing, 215
   creating, 217–218
   managing, 217–218
   names, 215
   opening, 212, 217
   saving, 215
   templates, 218
Database window, viewing, 213
date/time data type, 220
Decimal Places property, 221
Default Value property, 221
Design View, 213–214, 220–221, 248
dialog boxes, opening, 214
.docx file extension, 220

E
encryption, 218
Exit button, location of, 212
exiting Access, 211
Expression Builder, 240

F
field(s)
   adding, 231, 238
   calculated, generating, 239–240
   creating, 222–223
   deleting, 222

descriptions, 223
freezing/unfreezing, 223
hiding/unhiding, 223
inserting, 222
manipulating, 238
modifying, 222–223
properties, 221–223
rearranging, 238
removing, 238
renaming, 222
Field Size property, 221
File Name text box, location of, 212
file tab, location of, 212
files, importing data from, 227–228
filtering records, 224–225
fonts, reformatting, 233
form(s)
   arrange options, 231–33
   background graphics, 234
   blank, 219, 228
   bound controls, 229
   building, 228–231
   creating, 228
   design options, 229–231
   format options, 233–235
   headers/footers, 230
   themes, 229
   viewing code in, 230
Form Wizard, 228
Format property, 221

G
graphics
   background, 234, 242
   inserting, 242–243
   in reports, 242–243, 245
grids, aligning report outputs to, 244–245

H
headers and footers, 230, 242–243
help, accessing, 216
hyperlink(s)
   data type, 220
   inserting, 242

I
images. *See* graphics
importing data, 227–228
Indexed property, 222
Input Mask property, 221
Insert function, 231–232, 243

J
.jpg file extension, 220

K
keyboard KeyTips, 216

L
labels, in reports, 245
Layout View, 213–214, 248
logical operators, 240
logos, inserting, 242–243. *See also* graphics

M
macros, 230–231
Make Table queries, 236
margins
   forms and, 233
   reports and, 244
memo data type, 220
Merge function, 232, 243
Move Table function, 232, 244

N
Navigation bar, location of, 213
navigation forms, creating, 228–229
Navigation Pane
   closing, 213
   configuring, 219
   location of, 213
   using, 213–214
   view types in, 247–248
New Values property, 221
number data type, 220

O
objects
   changing the view of, 214
   closing, 215
   deleting, 219
   opening, 213–214
   renaming, 219
   saving, 215, 217
one-to-many relationships, 226, 237
Open button, location of, 212
Open object, location of, 213
Options button, location of, 212

P
padding options, 233
page(s)
   breaks, inserting, 242
   numbers, 242

orientation, 246
size, 246
passwords, 218
primary keys, 225, 226
Print Preview, 248
property sheets, 231

Q

queries, constructing, 235–237
question mark (?), 246
Quick Access toolbar, location of, 212
Quick Styles, 234
Quick Start area, 219

R

record(s)
appending, 227
filtering, 224–225, 246–248
sorting, 224–225, 246–248
relationships
managing, 237
setting, 225–226
report(s)
arrange options, 243–245
blank, 240
designing, 240–248
format options, 245–246
labels in, 245
outputs, aligning, to grids, 244–245
page setup options, 246
sorting records for, 246–248
views, 248
Report View, 248
Report Wizard, 241
Required property, 221
Ribbon
expanding/collapsing, 214
location of, 213
using, 214

S

select queries, 235
show options, 238
Smart Tags property, 222
sorting data, 224–225, 238, 246–248
Split function, 244
starting Access, 211

T

tab order, 243
table(s)
appending records to, 227
building, 220–222

functions, 231–232, 243–244
linked, importing data as, 227–228
source, 237
tabs
changing, 214
location of, 213
task panes, opening, 214
templates
blank form, 219
location of, 212
user, 219–220
text data type, 220
themes, applying, 229, 241
title bar, location of, 213
totals, calculating, 239

V

Validation Rule property, 221
Validation Text property, 221
view(s)
buttons, location of, 213
report, 248
types, 247–248
Visual Basic (Microsoft), 230–231

W

wildcard characters, 246

X

.xlsx file extension, 220

Y

yes/no data type, 220

Z

Zoom box, 239

PowerPoint 2010

A

advance options, 311
aligning
text, 270
text boxes, 278
animation(s)
built-in, 306–307
custom, 306–307
direction of, 308–310
sounds, 309
recording slide shows and, 324
reordering, 309–310
timing options, 307–308
Animation Painter, 309
Animation task pane, 252

annotations, 319, 320
artistic effects, 289
aspect ratios, 283, 295
audio
  compression, 296
  content, editing, 295–297
Autofit feature, 281
AutoRecover feature, 260

B

Backstage view, using, 254
border(s)
  chart, 306
  for graphics, 284–285
  table, 298–299
brightness settings, 288
bulleted
  lists, 271–272
  text, promoting/demoting, 295

C

captions, adding, 261
cascading windows, 259
CDs (compact discs), delivering
  presentations on, 316–317
chart(s)
  backgrounds, 304
  borders, 306
  data, entering, 301–302
  effects, 304
  elements, applying, 303–306
  gridlines, 303–304
  hyperlinks in, 306
  labels, 303
  layout, 302, 304
  positioning, 304
  resizing elements in, 304
  styles, 305
  types, selecting, 301
Clipboard, 265, 273, 274
color
  adjustments, 296–291
  background, 266
  fill, 266–267, 274, 291–292
  ink, 319
  line, 285
  outlines, 276–277
  saturation, 287
  theme, 293
  tone, 287
  transparent, 286, 291
column(s)
  aligning, 299

  arranging, 300
  distributing, 300
  merging, 300
  resizing, 299
  splitting, 300
  switching, 302
  text boxes, 278–279
comments, managing, 311–312
compression
  audio, 296
  graphics, 290
  when preparing presentations, 317
  video, 296
contrast settings, 288

D

Drawing Tools, 269, 274, 276–278,
  280–282

E

emphasis effects, 306
entrance effects, 306
Excel (Microsoft), 298
exit effects, 306–307
exiting PowerPoint, 249–250

F

file(s)
  compressing, 290
  -names, saving presentations with
    the same, 256
  options, configuring, 259–260
fonts, embedding, 260
Format Painter, 274

G

Glow effect, 269, 278, 284
gradients, applying, 267, 274–275
graphic(s). *See also* objects; photo
  albums
  adding captions to, 261
  aligning, 282
  applying effects to, 284, 289
  arranging, 281–286
  backgrounds, removing, 289
  black and white, 261–262
  borders, 284–285
  brightness settings, 262–263, 288
  changing, 290
  color adjustments, 286–291
  compressing, 290
  contrast settings, 263, 288–289
  converting, 292, 294
  cropping, 289–290

file types, 316
hyperlinks to, 285–286
inserting, in slides, 267
manipulating, 281–286
reordering, 262
resetting, 291
resizing, 283–284
rotating, 262
saving slides/objects as, 315–316
sharpen/soften settings, 287–288
text boxes and, 275
grid settings, 282–283
guide settings, 282–283

H
handouts, 317
headers and footers, 268–269
help, accessing, 256–257
highlighter annotations, 319
Home task pane, 252
hyperlinks
in charts, 306
to graphics, 285–286

I
images. *See* graphics
indentation, 269–270
ink color, 319

J
JPEG (Joint Photographic Experts
Group) format, 315–316. *See also*
graphics

K
keyboard
KeyTips, 253
navigation techniques, 255–256

L
line(s)
color, 285
spacing, 270–271
lists, formatting, 271–272

M
margins, 279
markup, hiding/displaying, 311–312
More Emphasis Effects option, 306
More Entrance Effects option, 306
More Exit Effects option, 306–307
More Motion Paths Effects option, 307
motion path effects, 307

N
narrations, playing, 320
numbered lists, 271–272

O
object(s). *See also* graphics
borders, 284–285
saving, as picture files, 315–316
snapping, tor grids, 282
.odp file extension, 315
OpenDocument presentations, 315
outline(s)
options, for text boxes, 276–278
saving presentations as, 314–315

P
paragraph formatting, 269–271. *See
also* text
passwords, 318
Paste Special option, 273
pattern effects, 268, 276
PDF (Portable Document Format), 314
pen annotations, 319
photo albums, 261–263. *See also*
graphics
placeholder text, 272
playback options, 297, 320
PowerPoint window
manipulating, 259
navigating in, 255–256
viewing, 250
PowerPoint Show presentations, 315
.pptx file extension, 313–316
presentation(s). *See also* slide shows;
slides
broadcasting, 321–322
closing, 255
collaborating on, 311–313
comparing/combining, 312–313
creating, 254, 261–281
delivering, 319–324
formatting, 266–269
marking, as final, 318–319
opening, 254–255
preparing, for delivery, 313–319
recording, 323–324
saving, 256, 260, 313–316
security for, 318–319
sharing, 316–317
timing, 322–324
working with multiple, 259
Presenter View, 321

print presentations, 318
proofing options, 259–260, 312–313

Q

Quick Access toolbar, configuring, 259
Quick Styles, 305

R

Reflections effect, 269, 278, 284
Ribbon
  adjusting views with, 258
  handling multiple presentations
    with, 259
  hiding, 251
  using, 250–251
row(s)
  aligning, 299
  arranging, 300
  distributing, 300
  merging, 300
  resizing, 299
  splitting, 300
  switching, 302
.rtf file extension, 314
Ruler, 269

S

save options, 256, 260, 313–314
security, 318–319, 321
servers, 264
Shadow effect, 269, 278, 284
shape(s). *See also* graphics
  adding, 292–293
  converting graphics to, 294
  default formatting, 291
  deleting, 292–293
  fill color, 291–292
  modifying, 291–292
  reordering, 293–294
  sizing, 294–295
  texture, 291–292
SharePoint Library (Microsoft), 264
SharePoint Server (Microsoft), 264
slide(s). *See also* presentations; slide
  shows
  adding, 264–265
  copying/pasting, 265
  deleting, 265
  duplicating, 265
  layouts, switching to different, 266
  libraries, 264
  non-contiguous, including, 265–266

orientation settings, 263
  pattern options, 268
  removing, 264–265
  reusing, 264–265
  saving, as picture files, 315–316
  size, adjusting, 263
  texture options, 268
  timing options, 321–324
  transitions, 310–311
slide show(s). *See also* slides
  custom, 322
  recording, 323–324
  options, 320
  setting up, 320–322
SmartArt, 272, 292–295
Soft Edges effect, 269, 278, 284
sound(s)
  for animations, 309
  for transitions, 310
spell checking, 260, 312
spreadsheets, inserting, 298
starting PowerPoint, 249–250
status bar, commands, adjusting views
  with, 258–259
style(s)
  for audio/video content, 295–296
  chart, 305
  SmartArt, 293
  table, 298

T

table(s)
  borders, 298–299
  constructing, 297–300
  effects, 298, 299
  style options, 298
Table of Contents, 257
task panes
  closing, 252–253
  displaying, 252
  using, 252–253
text
  aligning, 270
  in animations, 310
  converting graphics to, 294
  copying/pasting, 273
  direction settings, 271
  entering, 269–274
  formatting, 269–274
  indentation, 269–270
  inserting, 261
  placeholder, 272

size, 280
wrap, 279–280
text box(es)
alignment, 278
Autofit options, 281
color outlines, 276–277
columns, 278–279
default settings, 279
fill color for, 274
formatting, 274–281
gradients, 274–275
graphics in, 275
internal margins, 279
pattern effects, 276
positioning text in, 280
shape options, 278
text size settings, 280
texture effects, 275–276
word wrap in, 279–280
texture effects, 268, 275–276, 291–292
themes, 266, 293
thesaurus, 312

3-D Format effect, 269, 278, 284
3-D Rotation effect, 269, 278, 284
timing options, 321–324
Transparency slider, 268

V

versions, of PowerPoint, 264
video
compression, 296
content, editing, 295–297
saving, 317
view(s)
adjusting, 258–259
changing, 251–252
fitting slides in, 258

W

word wrap, 279–280
WordArt, 269, 291–292

X

XPS (XML Paper Specification)
format, 314